A Traveller's Guide to
Northern British Columbia

A Traveller's Guide to
Northern British Columbia

Ken Coates and Carin Holroyd

The Caitlin Press
1995

Copyright © 1995 Ken Coates and Carin Holroyd
All rights reserved. No part of this book may be reproduced in any form by any means without the written permission of the publisher, except by a reviewer, who may quote passages in a review.

Cover photo of Mount Edziza Provincial Park
by Jason Puddifoot / First Light
Index by Kathy Plett

Printed and bound in Canada

Canadian Cataloguing in Publication Data

Coates, Kenneth, 1956-
A Traveller's Guide to Northern British Columbia

   Includes index
   ISBN 0-920576-56-7

     1.British Columbia, Northern--Guidebooks. I.
     Holroyd, Carin. II. Title.
FC3845.N67A3 1995   917.11'8044   C95-910370-8
F1089.N87C62 1995

The Caitlin Press
P.O. Box 2387, Station B
Prince George, B.C. V2N 2S6
Canada

Acknowledgements

That this book exists at all is due, in large measure, to the kind assistance provided by the regional tourist associations, Chambers of Commerce, and commercial operators. They have been extremely generous in faxing information, sending pamphlets, and otherwise providing us with the material we needed to assemble the guide. We benefitted tremendously from the advice of our friends at the University of Northern British Columbia who, over the past three years, have spent a great deal of time travelling throughout the university's region. Laura, Mark and Bradley Coates also provided a much needed teenagers' perspective on the north.

We owe a special thanks to those who provided us with more extensive information. Dennis Macknak, Director of Regional Operations at UNBC, was with us at the College Heights Pub when this project was born. Sandy Macknak offered us the benefit of her travel experience — particularly in the Northwest. Nick Petryszak and Fiona Liebelt, of UNBC's Peace River-Alaska Highway office in Fort St. John, provided great advice on services in that region, and John Ball and Carolyn Willick were a tremendous help in guiding us through the Cariboo-Chilcotin and Bulkley-Nechako Valleys.

Working with Caitlin Press has been delightful. This press has already made major contributions to the culture and life of northern British Columbia and promises to do even more in the future. Carol Fairhurst and Gail Curry have provided kind, generous, and professional advice; whatever strengths of style and presentation this book might possess owe a great deal to their gentle ministrations. Cynthia Wilson, the co-owner of Caitlin Press, grabbed onto this project with great enthusiasm and has been unrelenting in her support and encouragement.

Preface

There are numerous guidebooks to British Columbia that will introduce you to the best beds and breakfasts, the most romantic spots, the most challenging hiking trails, or the classiest ski resorts. Almost all of these books, however, share one central characteristic — they virtually ignore northern British Columbia.

Although we know how much there is to celebrate and promote in the rest of the province, we want to introduce you to the northern two thirds of British Columbia. Northern British Columbia has an amazing array of attractions to offer travellers, and the people of this area, proud of their towns and region and excited about the present and the future, are keen to welcome you and to ensure that you will never forget your stay in this corner of the world. So welcome to northern British Columbia and to *A Traveller's Guide to Northern British Columbia*.

The Traveller's Guide to Northern British Columbia is a different kind of guidebook. Our intention is not to provide an exhaustive list of every hotel, attraction, restaurant, campground, or museum. Tourist associations publish excellent guides to local offerings, and travellers are well-advised to write ahead (see the list at the back of the book for addresses, telephone numbers, and fax numbers) to request this information.

What we want to do is to go one step further; we have checked out the many different options in northern British Columbia and have selected those that we consider to be the best. This doesn't mean that the places not mentioned in this book are not worth patronizing. We want visitors to know that, while northern British Columbia has the standard travellers' fare — fast-food restaurants and cafés, basic motels, chain stores, and the like — it also has a large number of exceptional, different, unique, and fascinating services and attractions. This book focuses on the latter — the very best of northern British Columbia — and not on the more routine services and stops along the way.

The definition of "the best" is, of course, subject to widely-differing interpretations. We have opted for a fairly broad meaning. This book is not about five-star accommodations and gourmet restaurants (although the north has some of each). Rather, it identifies those locations that offer excellent service, good value for money, and an introduction to the unique people and culture of northern British Columbia. We have included a number of places that might not be in standard "best of" books; we think they will help you capture the flavour of life in this part of the province. Furthermore, for some communities, where the tourist trade is not yet fully developed, we have indicated the best restaurants, accommodations, services, and attractions available in the region.

We want to encourage you to visit and then entice you to stay longer than you had perhaps initially planned. And we feel that the best way to do this is to let you in on the North's many great secrets: those little beauty spots just a tad off the beaten track, those unusual restaurants that aren't perched along the highway, and those excellent accommodations that lack the bright neon signs. We want you to experience the real northern British Columbia and to learn more about this remarkable land and its people.

This is a commercial-free book. We did not take any "freebies" from commercial operators, nor did we explain to restaurants, beds and breakfasts, or tour operators that we were in the process of assessing their operation for possible inclusion in the book — at least not until we were at the point of collecting contact information, rates, etc. The recommendations and suggestions offered on these pages are based on our experiences and preferences and on the advice received from local residents and fellow travellers.

We know that we have not been able to cover everything and everywhere in northern British Columbia, and we hope that readers will assist us with future editions of *A Traveller's Guide to Northern British Columbia*. If there is a place that you think should be included, please write and tell us. Also let us know if you have had an experience that does not mesh with a particular recommendation — restaurants, hotels, and attractions can change over time, particularly if new owners take over, and we want to keep *A Traveller's Guide to Northern British Columbia* as up-to-date as possible. Please send your comments and suggestions to the address below, or fill out the response form at the back of the book.

> *A Traveller's Guide to Northern British Columbia*
> c/o Caitlin Press
> P.O. Box 2387. Stn. B.
> Prince George, B.C.
> V2N 2S6

For the past twenty years, the northern half of British Columbia has been a by-way, a passage between the South and the North, and only occasionally a destination in its own right. We feel that this is most unfortunate, for northern British Columbia offers great variety, staggering beauty, interesting communities, and is one of Canada's most beautiful and diverse regions. So, enjoy the book, have a wonderful holiday, and let us in on your discoveries.

Table of Contents

Acknowledgements 5
Preface 6
How to Use this Guide 10
Map of the Regions of Northern British Columbia 10

1. **Northern British Columbia:** *The Great Canadian Secret* **12**
   The Land 15; A Brief History 22; The People 32; The Issues 34

2. **Navigating the North:** *Getting Here and Getting Around* **40**
   Air Travel 41; Train Travel 42; Bus 43; Car 44; Once you are Here 45; Being Prepared for the Back Roads 46; Winter Driving 47; Wildlife 48; Beds and Breakfasts 51

3. **The Cariboo-Chilcotin 55**
   Map 54; Overview 55; A Brief History 56; Getting There 59; The Great Outdoors 60; Hints for the Traveller 65; The Very Best 67; Selected Events 83

4. **Prince George:** *The Gateway to Northern British Columbia* **85**
   Map 84; Overview 85; A Brief History 86; Getting There 88; The Very Best 90; Selected Events 111

5. **The Nechako and Bulkley Valleys 113**
   Map 112; Overview 113; A Brief History 116; Hints for the Traveller 119; Exploring Aboriginal History 120; The Very Best 122; Selected Events 137

6. The Robson Valley 139
Map 138; Overview 139; A Brief History 143;
Getting There 144; The Very Best 145;
Selected Events 155

7. The North Coast 157
Map 156; Overview 157; A Brief History 158;
Getting There 163; Hints for the Traveller 165;
The Very Best 167; Selected Events 183

8. The Queen Charlotte Islands 185
Map 184; Overview 185; A Brief History 186;
Getting There 188; Hints for the Traveller 190;
The Very Best 195; Selected Events 207

9. Peace River - Alaska Highway 209
Map 208; Overview 209; A Brief History 210;
Getting There 214; Hints for the Traveller 215;
The Very Best 218; Selected Events 235

10.The Stikine and the Far Northwest 237
Map 236; Overview 237; A Brief History 238;
Getting There 241; The Stewart - Cassiar Road 244;
The Very Best 245; Selected Events 259

Appendices 260
Parks 260
Tourist and Travel Information 263
Accommodation Assistance 266
The Very Best of Northern British Columbia 267
Index 270
Response Form 287

How to Use This Guide

This guide divides northern British Columbia into the following eight regions: Cariboo - Chilcotin, Prince George, Nechako and Bulkley Valleys, Robson Valley, North Coast, Queen Charlotte Islands, Peace River - Alaska Highway and the Stikine and Far Northwest.

Prices
To assist travellers with their selections, we have included price symbols for restaurants and accommodations. These symbols cover the following price ranges (based on two people at 1994 prices):

Restaurants (not including tip)
$ .... *Under $20*
$$ .... *20 to $50*
$$$ .... *Over $50*

Accommodations
$ .... *Under $50*
$$ .... *50 to $75*
$$$ .... *Over $75*

Please note that prices may change and, in some establishments, vary by season.

★ Symbols
These symbols are found in the margins throughout the book, and represent "The Very Best of Northern British Columbia" as listed on page 267.

Radiophone Numbers
Several of the businesses listed in this guide are accessible only by radiophone. To reach a radiophone listing, dial "0," ask for the radiophone operator, and give the operator the full radiophone listing.

1
Northern British Columbia:
The Great Canadian Secret

British Columbia is Canada's vacation wonderland. While there are other contenders — Alberta has the Rockies, the Badlands, and Banff and Jasper National Parks, Ontario has Niagara Falls and the Toronto Blue Jays, Quebec offers the quixotic pleasures of Montreal and the stark beauty of the Gaspé, Prince Edward Island entices with sandy beaches and Anne of Green Gables, and Nova Scotia offers an array of coastal and historic attractions — British Columbia reigns supreme in Canada. It is an all-season paradise. Vancouver and Victoria, the twin jewels of the West Coast, offer cosmopolitan fare for the urban-inclined. There is the West Coast Trail for hikers, Whistler for skiers, the lakes of the Okanagan and Shuswap for swimmers and boaters, the "salt chuck" for sports-fishers, and countless other physical and cultural attractions.

How does one choose from among the abundant opportunities? How does a traveller decide where to spend hard-earned travel dollars and precious holiday time? British Columbia, after all, covers a much larger area than France and Germany combined, stretches 1,400 kilometres (875 miles) from north to south and 1,000 kilometres (625 miles) from east to west, ranges in topography from densely-forested coastal mountains to the most northerly extension of the Great Plains, and varies in climate from the blisteringly hot summers of the southern Okanagan to the bitterly cold winters of the Dease Lake region. British Columbia, to find refuge in that great travellers' cliché, offers something for everyone. Let's start in an important way: by introducing you to northern British Columbia. Forgive the shameless boasting, but few places on earth can match this area's diversity and pure beauty. There are many places that offer attractive and scenic features, wonderful escapes, and fascinating communities, but we are not sure how many can match this region. Come prepared to be impressed. An important point: northern British Columbia is not a single region and cannot, therefore, be described in a simple or direct fashion. It is difficult, in fact, to capture the diversity and variety of this land. It ranges from the wind-swept, rocky shores of the Queen Charlotte Islands, whose dense coastal forests often lie shrouded in ocean-blown clouds, to the open expanses of the Peace River country, where rolling plains sit at the foot of the northern reaches of the Rocky Mountains and in late summer, are carpeted in rich grain fields. The region includes to the picturesque beauty of the central coastal region, approachable by land at Bella Coola, where the waters of the Pacific meet the sharp-ridged mountains of the Coastal Range and the Alp-like splendor of the Atlin region, in the far northwest of the province, where mountain-top glaciers hang precipitously over the lake. There is also the great majesty of the Bulkley Valley, rimmed by strong mountains and carved by pulsating rivers and the rolling hills of the Cariboo-Chilcotin — cow-country — where ranches line the highways and where open mountain valleys cradle clear-blue fish-filled lakes. This, and so much more, is all part of northern British Columbia.

So, just where does northern British Columbia start and where does it end? There is no formal definition for this region — at least in the sense of a clearly-understood political or geographic line of demarcation. We are opting for a fairly broad definition — one that incorporates a great deal of British Columbia. There is a strong sense in this part of the world that there are two parts to British Columbia: Vancouver and Vancouver Island, and the rest of the province — referred to, not always kindly, as the land "beyond Hope." (Hope being a small town at the eastern end of the Lower Fraser Valley.) It is an unkind cut, but the sentiment reflects a certain provincial reality. British Columbia has a population of close to 3.5 million people. Of this number, almost half live in the Greater Vancouver area, and another 500,000 inhabit the bucolic splendour of Vancouver Island. This leaves only a few hundred thousand people for the rest of the province — with most of those in the Kamloops and Okanagan regions.

The southern boundary of our definition of northern British Columbia begins roughly at 100 Mile House (along Highway 97). The region then stretches north from this imaginary line up to the Yukon Territory's boundary. The area south of the line running through 100 Mile House is tied, by history and by the Trans-Canada Highway, to the Vancouver-Calgary corridor and has a more gentle winter climate, hotter summers, and the flora and fauna that accompany such circumstances. The area to the north, colder in winter and more isolated from the Lower Mainland-Victoria power base, conforms in greater measure to the image of a northern land. Here, one can see the crackling wonder of the Northern Lights (Aurora Borealis) in winter, feel the enervating impact of elongated summer days, experience the vast distances of a sparsely populated land, and witness the growth and tensions of land being "opened" for industrial and resource development.

This enormous region covers fully two thirds of the province. It is not really a region in the cultural or political sense. The good people of the Peace River district have relatively little contact, and little in common, with the coastal peoples of the Northwest Coast, and the residents of Prince George, who proclaim their city to be the "Capital of Northern British Columbia," routinely find their claim challenged by the citizens of Terrace and Smithers.

The patterns and influences that shaped the history of the North created a diverse set of sub-regions, each of which reflect local geography, economic circumstances, and cultural realities. Each of these smaller norths is unique and strikingly different, and each capitalizes on the promise and opportunities of their little corner of paradise. A good part of the attraction of northern British Columbia is discovering its constituent parts and learning that a vast region, all-too-quickly written off as a huge, undifferentiated, and uninteresting mass, is, in fact, one of the most diverse, interesting, and beautiful places in the country.

The Land

It is virtually impossible to briefly describe the physical characteristics of northern British Columbia; there are so many geographic areas within the region. In the interests of brevity, here is a summary of the main divisions. For more detailed descriptions or for major features, please consult the individual chapters.

Cariboo-Chilcotin

Rolling hills — classic ranching country — characterize the southernmost sections of northern British Columbia. Guarded on the west by the Coastal and Selkirk Mountains and on the east by the Monashee

▲ *The Chilcotin River winds through the untrammeled lands west of Williams Lake - tough, rugged and exciting! (David Hodges)*

and Rocky Mountains, the expansive Cariboo-Chilcotin is covered largely in pine and spruce forests (the focus for a great deal of logging activity) and sizeable open range. The area is dotted with small lakes that are well-stocked for sport fishing and well-suited for camping — particularly in the area west of Williams Lake and between 100 Mile House and Clearwater. There are several remarkable lakes in the district, including the exceptionally deep waters of Quesnel Lake and the justly famous Bowron Lakes — a wonderful chain of mountain-framed lakes ideally suited for a canoeing adventure.

Central Interior

The middle portion of northern British Columbia, lacking the striking physical features of much of the rest of the North, is generally called the Central Interior. Its dominant characteristic is the Fraser River, which runs through the region north to south. This is a land of relatively low mountains (as compared to the towering peaks to the east and west), numerous rivers, and literally hundreds of lakes. Prince George, for example, proudly advertises that there are 150 lakes within 80 kilometres (50 miles) of the city. The land is a forester's delight, for the hillsides and river valleys are covered with pine, spruce and aspen stands (with some fir and birch) — the foundation of a vibrant northern lumber and pulp and paper industry. Entering or leaving the Central Interior, one quickly realizes that this area sits like a huge bowl between the Rockies to the east and the mountains to the north and west.

Robson Valley

The eastern boundary of northern British Columbia is set by the Rocky Mountains. Along the edge of the Rockies rests the 240-kilometre-long (150-mile-long) Robson Valley. This valley, also defined by the Cariboo and Monashee Mountains, is not very wide but it supports an active farming community. Like much of the region, the Robson Valley is carved by rivers — in this case the headwaters of the famous Fraser River.

Peace River Country and the Far North

Driving north out of Prince George is a startling experience. Having pushed through several hundred kilometres of the Central Interior, you suddenly find yourself on the twisting road through the Pine Pass — in winter, one of the region's more dangerous sections of highway. The pass itself is quite spectacular, with gorgeous lakes, striking mountain views, and rapidly flowing rivers. Then, rather suddenly, you enter the Peace River Valley, first along the river and later,

▲   *Big, open skies and rolling plains are the hallmarks of the Peace River Country. (Don Pettit)*

driving out of the valley from Chetwynd, onto the prairie escarpment above the Peace River. It is as though a part of Saskatchewan has been grafted onto the fringes of the Rocky Mountains, for the rich agricultural lands of the open prairie seem strikingly out of place in the northeast corner of the province. There are wonderful scenic views throughout the district, particularly where the roads run alongside the Peace River, but the prairie has a stark beauty of its own.

The Peace River district, although close to 1,100 kilometres (688 miles) northeast of Vancouver, is still only two thirds of the way up the province. North of the Peace is a vast, almost unpopulated, far northern region which stretches from the fringe of the agricultural lands in the east, through the Dease Lake region, and to the Coastal Mountains in the west. This enormous area of mountains, rivers, and lakes, is largely tree-covered (although the trees have reduced commercial value due to low temperatures that slow tree growth) and is marked by exceptionally cold winters. While large portions of the Far North are rolling, undifferentiated hillsides, there are some striking local features, such as the treacherous waters of the Liard River and the craggy mountains of Muncho Lake Provincial Park.

Atlin and the Far Northwest

Way to the northwest, in a part of the province that locals are convinced the rest of British Columbia has forgotten, lies one of Canada's unknown jewels. It has been called Canada's Alps — and not without justification. The area is covered in the high mountains of the Coastal and St. Elias ranges. The most westerly bit, which lies south of the Yukon Territory and, through a quirk of geo-politics, west of part of the Alaskan panhandle, is connected to Kluane National Park — a World Heritage Site. This is an area of stunning beauty. The community of Atlin, bordering on Atlin Lake and resting in the shadow of several magnificent mountains, has one of the most spectacular settings anywhere in the country. The cold, clear waters of Tagish, Tutshi and Atlin Lakes provide welcome breaks in the otherwise mountainous terrain.

Bulkley Valley

Several rivers — the Nechako, the Stuart, and the Bulkley — drain a sizeable region to the west of Prince

George. This is a land of countless lakes, bountiful rivers, accessible mountain ranges, and pristine valleys. The major lakes — Fraser, Burns, Francois, Stuart and Babine — are sizeable bodies of water. The climate here is relatively benign — great for skiing and other winter sports but mild and pleasant in the summer months, when the region's internationally-known fishery attracts hundreds of people into the area. Most of the communities, save for several small mines and a handful of isolated Native villages, are found in the river valleys and along the lake shores. This area also has solid agricultural potential, and you will find a variety of farms and ranches — again in the river valleys.

Coastal Interior

Immediately to the east of the Pacific Coast lies some of the most spectacular scenery in all of British Columbia. A few large rivers — particularly the Skeena and the Nass — long ago carved out passageways through the mountains. There are, in addition, majestically long fiords, positively Norwegian in length and drama, that jut inland from the coast. These once provided a safe respite for Native settlements and, much later, for commercial fishers and loggers. This is a rugged land, spiked by high mountains and narrow passes — the latter often rendered impassable in the winter months. The combination of the mountains and the proximity to the coast generates a sizeable volume of precipitation and enough warm weather to make for fairly gentle winters and very comfortable summers. The Nass River Valley, an area that has attracted a surprisingly small number of travellers over the years, is a lovely and interesting area — made the more so by the vestiges of a volcanic eruption of some 200 years ago. (The eruption, incidentally, covered a Nisga'a village and killed several hundred people.)

Pacific Coast

The Pacific Coast is a land unto itself. Between the interior and the ocean, the precipitous Coastal Mountain range serves as an impressive barrier, broken only occasionally along its long expanse by a handful of major river valleys. The Pacific ensures a more benign climate than the interior; snow is relatively infrequent and is usually washed away before long by winter rains. But the ocean also extracts its toll. Violent winter storms send waves crashing onto the shore and can make coastal navigation and plane travel difficult, if not dangerous. There is a great beauty to this land; towering Douglas Fir and cedar trees (at least those not yet felled by the logging companies) shroud the coastline in dense rain forest mystery. The rains continue throughout the summer months, and thick banks of

Kitlope estuary, home of a large grizzly population, is south of Kitimat, on B.C.'s magnificent coast. (Ron Thiele)

fog are commonplace in the spring and fall. But when the sun breaks through, and it does with surprising regularity given the amount of annual rainfall, there are few places on earth as captivating.

Queen Charlotte Islands

Approximately 100 kilometres (63 miles) off British Columbia's northern-most coast lie the Queen Charlotte Islands. Separated from the mainland by the shallow waters of the Hecate Strait, this fascinating chain stretches some 300 kilometres (188 miles) north to south. The islands are much like the neighbouring coastline; they are covered in dense forests, buffeted by regular storms, and often blanketed in thick fog. Known as Haida Gwaii by the Haida people, the Queen Charlotte Islands are well-known for their abundant wildlife (especially hundreds of small deer), ancient totem poles, and opportunities for ocean kayaking and other wilderness adventures. A prolonged struggle over the control and use of the forests on the southern reaches of the islands resulted, in 1988, in the creation of the Gwaii Haanas National Park Reserve/Haida Heritage Site (South Moresby), which is co-managed by Parks Canada and the Haida Nation.

A Brief History

Northern British Columbia is both ancient and modern; its history begins with First Nations societies and its contemporary reality is driven by a variety of new peoples, forces, and processes. Academics continue to debate the origins and longevity of the First Nations. The current assumptions are that the original peoples migrated into the region some 8,000 - 10,000 years ago. For quite some time, scholarly arguments suggested that the people came from the north — their ancestors having crossed over from Siberia by way of the Bering Strait land bridge. More recently, scholars have argued that a second migration occurred along the Northwest Coast. The major problem with proving this theory is that global warming over the past centuries, and a subsequent higher ocean level, has resulted in the flooding of ancient settlement sites. A unique sub-branch of the discipline of archaeology — underwater archaeology — has emerged recently and its practitioners are attempting to prove or disprove this migration theory.

By the time the first Europeans ventured into the region by land and by sea, several First Nations had established viable societies in the region. The first Europeans, who characterized these cultures in harsh and unflattering terms, established stereotypes which have persisted to this day. The First Nations of northern British Columbia, a very diverse group, ranged from the comparatively sedentary, hierarchical, and culturally-rich Haida, Tsimshian and Nisga'a of the Northwest Coast to the mobile, extended family-based Beaver, Carrier, and Sekani of the interior.

These were not peoples struggling for bare survival, unsure of basic sustenance, and desperate to make it through another winter. The First Nations of the North were well-attuned to their local environment, knew the land exceptionally well, and developed sustainable social and economic systems based on locally-available resources and trade items exchanged with other groups. Theirs were also culturally rich societies — as illustrated by the Northwest Coast totem poles and long houses, diverse ceremonial and spiritual lives, and functional and appealing clothing designs.

The lives of the First Nations people changed radically with the arrival of the Europeans who came first from the sea — Captain James Cook sailed along the coast — and then overland from the east — Alexander Mackenzie made his way from the prairies to the coast. Fur traders followed the explorers in two separate thrusts: a coastal expansion and an overland expansion. The first consisted of American, British, and Russian traders who fought over the lucrative maritime trade which was, in turn, connected to a wealthy fur trade with China and the Far East. The latter was accomplished by the Northwest Company, which was anxious to outrace its continental competitor, the Hudson's Bay Company, to the untapped resources of the interior valleys. The Northwest Company-Hudson's Bay Company rivalry ended in a forced marriage between the two firms in 1821.

The fur trade brought rapid changes into the region. Because First Nations people did not have immunity to the many and varied European illnesses, introduced diseases devastated local aboriginal populations. New technology and trade goods supported such important aboriginal traditions as the potlatch and increased rivalries between First Nations. Many First Nations people found work with the European traders — particularly in the interior, where the Northwest Company-Hudson's Bay Company maintained a long and arduous trading route through Fort George and Kamloops and down into the Oregon Territory.

The fur trade dominated in Northern British Columbia until the decline in coastal resources in the late eighteenth century, the general collapse of markets for interior furs in the mid-nineteenth century, and the commencement of the British Columbia Gold Rush in the 1850s. Gold miners, who had been pushing ever westward, reached California in the 1840s and touched off the great California stampede. A few optimists headed further north, through what is now Oregon and Washington, and into British Columbia.

The discovery of paying quantities of gold on the lower Fraser River touched off the first boom; Billy Barker's "strike" in the central interior in 1862 sparked a major stampede into the Quesnel region. The establishment of Barkerville signalled the substantial beginnings of the British Columbia Gold Rush — an event which drew tens of thousands of miners into the region and spawned a wide array of social, economic, and political changes. One of the latter was the creation of the mainland colony of British Columbia, which was subsequently merged with the existing colony of Vancouver Island to form British Columbia.

Development, in the form of highway construction (by the Royal Engineers who completed the Cariboo Trail, including the treacherous passageway through the Fraser Canyon) and cattle ranching, followed the miners northward. The Cariboo Wagon Road (or Cariboo Trail) began at Lillooet (Mile 0), and ran north to Barkerville. Several settlements along the way — 100 Mile House, 108 Mile House, 150 Mile House — owe their names and part of their reason for existence, to the wagon road and the stopping house built to accommodate the early travellers. Those miners who did not strike it rich — the vast majority — either returned to the south or, the more hardy among them, extended their search for gold to more northerly latitudes. A small rush, which occurred in the Cassiar district in the 1870s, was followed by the famous Klondike Gold Rush in 1896-1898.

While the gold rush brought thousands to British Columbia, most of the subsequent development focused on the New Westminister-Victoria regions. When British Columbia joined the Dominion of Canada in

1871 — called the Spoilt Child of Confederation because of the "rich" deal it struck with central Canadian politicians — a new future loomed. The Confederation package included the promise of the construction of a railway linking the west coast province with the rest of Canada. The routing of the railway — through one of the few Rocky Mountain passes — would determine much of the province's subsequent destiny. The decision to follow a southerly route — from Calgary to Kamloops and along the Fraser River to the new city of Vancouver — ensured that the more northerly regions would remain in the economic and political wilderness for some years to come.

Dreams of additional railway-inspired booms continued to resonate throughout British Columbia. Promoters brought forward plans for new east-west and north-south rail lines. While provincial governments gave generous subsidies in an effort to ensure the completion of the all-important rail lines, most railway dreams foundered in a sea of red ink and faulty plans.

The construction of the Grand Trunk Pacific, however, offered new hope for the promoters of northern British Columbia. This route offered a new outlet to the Pacific — Prince Rupert — and was designed to cross vast, unopened territory in the British Columbia interior. Construction began in the early twentieth century. New or expanded communities grew up along the mainline — Tête Jaune Cache, initially a construction and trans-shipment site, McBride, Prince George, Smithers, and the highly touted port city of Prince Rupert. While the main centres enjoyed a short-lived speculative and construction boom, the dream of sustained prosperity soon died. The Grand Trunk, itself, ran into serious financial difficulties and was amalgamated into the government-owned Canadian National Railway system in 1921.

Northern British Columbia grew unevenly in these development years: Prince George surged forward — the largest settlement now that Barkerville had fallen on hard times; agricultural settlements took root in the Bulkley Valley; a fishing-based economy emerged in the Prince Rupert area (one of Canada's first extensively multi-cultural communities, with sizeable Native, European, and Asian populations); an embryonic farming settlement, peopled by veterans returning from World War I and farmers fleeing the ecological desperation of the Canadian Plains during the 1930s, began in the Peace River country; and an extensive ranching industry blossomed in the Cariboo-Chilcotin. North to south transportation was long and arduous; the rail lines provided the best service between communities, although marine transportation dominated along the coast.

World War II brought sweeping changes to the region, although few northern British Columbians actually saw combat. (There was a famous mutiny in Terrace involving the so-called "Zombies" — men conscripted for military service but who, until the last months of the war, were not slated for overseas service.) The war, and more particularly the need to defend the continent's northwest flank from possible Japanese invasion, resulted in the establishment of a major supply and service depot in Prince Rupert and the stationing of a small number of Canadian troops in the region. The major change in the North was initiated in February 1942 when the United States government decided to proceed with the construction of a highway to Alaska and to expand the existing network of airfields between the south and Alaska. Three potential highway routes vied for American attention: the coastal route running through Atlin; the interior route through Prince George; and the prairie route, which connected Dawson Creek and Fairbanks, Alaska.

Although logic appeared to favour the interior route, the American government opted for the prairie approach. Construction began almost immediately; a 2,400 kilometre (1,500 mile) pioneer road from Dawson Creek to Fairbanks was completed by the late fall of 1942. The construction of the Alaska Highway and related projects (the Northwest Staging Route, CANOL pipeline project, Haines Road, and numerous smaller undertakings) transformed the Peace River country and the far north of British Columbia. Although the Alaska Highway was, at war's end, still a very rough, marginally serviceable road, the region's extreme isolation had at last been broken. Communities served by the highway — Dawson Creek, Fort St. John, and Fort Nelson in British Columbia and Watson Lake and Whitehorse in the Yukon — expanded in the post-war period, although the generally poor condition of the highway put a severe cap on growth. In 1992, the region hosted a massive fiftieth anniversary celebration of the construction of the highway — an event that encouraged communities along the route to consider the impact of the war-time construction and to find ways to commemorate the construction era.

Northern British Columbia came of age, economically, in the post-war period. This was the "great" era of development; industry discovered new opportunities in long-neglected regions, and federal and provincial governments poured millions of tax dollars into the construction of regional infrastructure (roads, railways, airports, communications equipment, etc.). The Aluminum Company of Canada's (Alcan) Kemano-Kitimat project best exemplifies the spirit of the age. Alcan undertook to re-direct water from the headwaters of the Nechako River to its power station and to send electricity to a newly constructed aluminum smelter at Kitimat — a brand-spanking new company town in a scenic setting at the head of Douglas Channel. The Kitimat initiative was the largest industrial undertaking in Canadian history and a major boost to the promoters' vision of an industrial North.

There seemed to be no stopping the North in the 1950s. The expansion of the soft-wood lumber and pulp and paper industries in the first two decades after the war brought major industrial plants into Williams Lake, Quesnel, Prince George, Terrace, and Prince Rupert. The ubiquitous beehive burners, now victim to higher environmental standards, sprang up in communities throughout the region. New company towns seemed to be added to the map every year: Cassiar, the site of an major asbestos mine; the forestry towns of Mackenzie and Chetwynd; and mining communities at Gibraltar, Granisle, and Endako. Sawmills opened in town after town along the rail lines. It was an era of growth and economic development the like of which few regions in the world had ever experienced.

Governments continued to contribute to the development of the North. They constructed new roads (like the Hart Highway, which connected Prince George and the Peace River region); built a major hydroelectric project, the W.A.C. Bennett Dam, near Hudson's Hope; and expanded schools and constructed hospitals to bring northern services more in line with those offered in the rest of the province. In the 1980s, the province financed a massive infrastructure project to support the Northeast Coal initiative. This resulted in the creation of the new community of Tumbler Ridge, the construction of a rail line, and improvements to the Prince Rupert terminal. Northern British Columbia was, for the first thirty years after the war, one of the fastest-growing regions in all of Canada and a major reason for British Columbia's buoyant economy and seemingly endless prosperity.

The boom could not last; no region could sustain for long the rapid expansion and lofty ambitions of the speculators of the 1950s. Dozens of fortunes were made in these halcyon days, and communities grew faster than their most optimistic promoters dared dream. But the dream faded, slowly but surely. First Nations, who shared little in the economic opportunities of the development boom but suffered disproportionately from the dislocations, uttered strong and powerful protests. The environmental movement began to look askance at the pace and relatively uncontrolled nature of northern economic expansion. And then the markets weighed in to exercise the inevitable corrections that follow periods of unrestricted growth. Several of the mines closed, some temporarily and others permanently.

And so northern British Columbia soldiers on in the aftermath of the post-war boom. The memory of those days still stirs the hearts and pocketbooks of entrepreneurs and speculators, who foresee yet another massive growth spurt, and raises fears among environmentalists and First Nations people, who worry about the ecological, social, and cultural impact of another economic boom. The general economic situation is mixed; the forest industry is doing extremely well, fishing is at a cross-roads and faces some major and difficult changes, and the mining industry is suffering through a prolonged depression and continuing uncertainty. Tourism remains buoyant and continues to expand as northern British Columbians are increasingly realizing that one of their best natural resources is the region's comparatively pristine condition and endless recreational opportunities.

As you travel through northern British Columbia, you will see abundant signs of the region's history — particularly if you take the time to look closely and step away from the major highway corridors. The region has not always been that respectful of its past, and the number of historic sites preserved for visitors' use is fairly small. But a stop at the Port Edward Cannery Museum (near Prince Rupert), K'san Village, and the Hudson's Bay Company post at Fort St. James provides at least a glimpse into what once was the North. The rapid growth of the post-war period resulted in the hasty destruction of most of the older districts in the region's communities. Prince George's downtown area, for example, provides little evidence of the community's early years and is a testament to the unplanned expansion of the 1950s and 1960s.

Along the side roads, and at the sites of now-abandoned railway stops, you can still glimpse the historic North. Here you'll find abandoned cabins, boarded-up train stations, and old First Nations settlements. But you will also discover how recent much of northern British Columbia is. Company towns have come and gone — Cassiar, once a thriving settlement of over 1,500 people has been almost completely removed — and even a fairly new community like Kitimat seems like a permanent fixture on the regional landscape. The pulse and energy of northern British Columbia suggests that this is a land of the future — of untapped potential and economic growth. But it is also very much a creation of its past.

The ancient North lies, not so much in physical remains, but in the knowledge of the First Nations people of this region who recall, through stories passed down through generations, the experiences of their ancestors. And the historic North remains very much alive in the memories of old-timers, Native and non-Natives alike, who worked the canneries and mines, built the roads, and cut the first stands of timber. So as you seek to discover the past, look for it in historic

The People

buildings and historic sites, read about it in the memoirs of pioneers, listen for it in the stories of the elders, and feel it in the land itself.

Northern British Columbia has a diverse and interesting population, although it stands in stark contrast to much of the rest of the province. The Asian population of the region, in comparison to the Lower Mainland, is quite small. There are several pockets of East Indian people, particularly in Prince George and Quesnel, but their numbers are relatively small. (A highlight of the Christmas season in Prince George is the beautiful decorations on the Sikh Temple in town.) The Smithers area attracted a sizeable number of German settlers, although their impact on the area is less noticeable than in the past.

Despite its massive size, northern British Columbia has a very small population — only 300,000 in total (smaller than the population of Victoria, the provincial capital). Of these people, 72,000 live in Prince George and one third live in the Prince George region. There are other concentrations of population: the Peace River triangle (Dawson Creek-Fort St. John-Chetwynd), along Highway 97 (Williams Lake-Quesnel), in the Bulkley Valley (Smithers-Houston-Burns Lake), and in the Northwest (Terrace-Kitimat-Prince Rupert). This distribution of population also means that the vast expanse of the North is sparsely populated indeed; only a handful of people live within the remaining hundreds of thousands of square kilometres.

One group, the First Nations, have a major influence on the culture and lifestyle of the region. There are close to 30,000 First Nations people in northern

British Columbia — approximately 10% of the total population (the percentage is higher in the Northwest and the Far North and significantly lower in the urban centres and agricultural areas). There are a total of 16 tribal groups, with over 75 bands and dozens of predominantly First Nations communities. There are, in addition, large numbers of First Nations people, from the region and from further afield, in all of the major centres. Native Friendship Centres can be found in most northern communities.

The lives of the First Nations of northern British Columbia have undergone profound changes in the past fifty years. The very economic developments that are lauded by regional promoters carried a considerable cost for the original inhabitants who found themselves displaced from their lands and pushed to the social and economic periphery. The years have been hard, and the pain is revealed in the depressing statistics of teenage suicide, criminal convictions, community violence, high death rates, and substance abuse.

The people have not surrendered to the problems and transitions. In displacing the Department of Indian Affairs, First Nations have gained greater control over their own affairs. The Nisga'a, perhaps the best organized aboriginal group in Canada, run their own school system (including post-secondary offerings, which are handled in conjunction with the local college and the University of Northern British Columbia), have established several successful locally-run businesses, control their health care service, and have made major strides in resolving their outstanding land claim.

It is easy to succumb to the images of social and economic distress in the First Nations communities and miss the considerable evidence of cultural revival and persistence. Aboriginal art is enjoying a renaissance across the region; many communities have Native art galleries (check with the local Native Friendship Centres for more information). There are numerous First Nations cultural, social, and recreational events throughout the year — many of them open to non-Native visitors. Many communities have started their own tourist businesses; they operate hotels and restaurants or offer visitors an opportunity to travel on the land or waters with experienced Native guides.

The First Nations of northern British Columbia are not all the same. They do not share a common language, and they have very different traditions, social systems, and political structures. It is vital to understand that they deserve to be seen as separate peoples — as Haida, Nisga'a, Carrier, Sekani, Gitksan, Haisla, etc. — and not as undifferentiated "Native People." One of the great rewards of travelling in northern British Columbia is the chance to learn about, and from, the First Nations of this region. Theirs are rich, vibrant, living cultures, not museum pieces or historical relics. Do take the opportunity to learn more about the different indigenous cultures, lifestyles, languages, and art forms.

The Issues

British Columbia is a land of unusual politics — often the butt of jokes across the country — and passionate debate about public issues. Over the past five years, Northern British Columbia has become a battleground of sorts between various interest groups. As you travel across the region, talk to residents, read local newspapers, and listen to the radio stations (talk radio is a provincial pastime), you will quickly pick up on the nature and passions of the issues facing northern British Columbia. So, as something of a primer, we offer here a brief description of the major public issues.

Aboriginal Land Claims

No issue dominates regional discussions as much as aboriginal land claims. Unlike most other Native groups in Canada, the First Nations of northern British Columbia (save for those in the northeast corner of the province) have not signed treaties with the federal government. The First Nations have long argued that British/Canadian law requires a fair and just settlement of their land entitlements and have launched court challenges (including the famous Delgamuukw case, which the Gitksan-Wet'suwet'en lost) and ongoing political action. Despite what you will hear from time to time, land claims are not a new phenomenon. The Nisga'a, for example, have been trying to get the government of Canada to settle their outstanding legal obligations since the late nineteenth century — for well over 100 years.

The federal government and the province, after many decades of stalling, have now agreed to negotiate a resolution of the land claims. The rationale is not entirely altruistic or justice-driven; several analysts have argued that major resource developments are on hold pending final settlement. Negotiations are now underway, as are extensive efforts at public education, but settlements may take years to reach (similar negotiations in the Yukon Territory took 20 years), and the process is sure to generate heated discussion.

Tatshenshini Wilderness Area ★

The discovery of a major copper deposit in the Far Northwest's Windy Craggy area touched off a major debate about the appropriate balance between environmental protection and resource development. The debate went international; American Vice-President Al Gore appealed directly for the protection of the stunningly beautiful Tatshenshini wilderness area, which is becoming increasingly popular with whitewater rafters and wild animal enthusiasts. The provincial government, faced with ferocious pressure within and outside British Columbia, relented and established the "Tat" as a park. While the creation of the park resolved the immediate issue, it has not settled the ongoing debate about the relationship between wilderness preservation and resource development.

Kemano Completion Project

Alcan built the Kitimat smelter complex and stage one of the Kemano hydroelectric project in the 1950s. Under the terms of the original deal, Alcan had the right to expand its hydroelectric development at a later date. Through a long and complicated process, involving extended negotiations between the company and the provincial and federal governments, Alcan received permission in 1987 to proceed with what was labelled the Kemano Completion Project. The initiative has been the focus for intense debate ever since, with environmental groups, Native bands (particularly the Cheslatta people), and residents of the Nechako River corridor — the river most affected by the Kemano project — lining up against the company.

The provincial government established a commission in 1993 to investigate the project and to make recommendations on the future of the Kemano Completion Project. The recommendations, which sought a cautious middle ground, were released in January 1995. The provincial government, responding to a ground swell of public protest, cancelled the project. But, in not resolving the issue of compensation, the province has touched off what promises to be prolonged debate, numerous court challenges, and considerable regional uncertainty. This issue will not soon go away.

The Fate of the Fishery

Canada's East Coast has experienced a tragic decline of its ocean fishery. The situation in British Columbia is not as grim, but it may be heading in that direction. An enormous controversy over scientific surveys and approved harvests has been added to the debate over the role of the Native fishery and continuing discussions about the balance between commercial and sport fishing. The situation on the North Coast is not as bad as in the south, although there are a few struggles with American fishers working along the Alaska Panhandle, debates about the Skeena River fishery, and ongoing concern about the state of the Fraser River salmon runs (the latter is tangentially connected to the Kemano Completion Project controversy).

Forest Renewal and Forest Practices

British Columbia has been the scene of several major skirmishes between loggers and environmentalists over the years, including the hotly contested Clayoquot Sound on Vancouver Island. Similar debates, although generally without provincial or national coverage, have taken root in northern British Columbia. The issues are distressingly familiar: the trade-off between jobs and wilderness preservation, the suitability of clear-cut logging, the search for sustainable forestry practices, the future of communities, corporate profits, and reforestation. One hears a lot in the north about clear-cut logging — the practice of harvesting a large swath of timber and then replanting. Although the result can be unsightly and generates considerable opposition, forestry officials maintain that this is a reasonable and sustainable approach to soft-wood timber cutting under certain conditions.

Given that most of the towns and villages in northern British Columbia have forestry-based economies (keep an eye open for homes displaying signs saying that "this family is supported by timber dollars"), it is easy to imagine that the management of the forests is a touchy and controversial topic. The province has recently attempted a series of community-based planning processes designed to develop regional development plans that enjoy widespread support within the area. The process has been very controversial, but has produced some useful results — particularly in the Cariboo-Chilcotin. The debate over forest practices will not soon go away; the recent period of high prices for forest products has encouraged the construction of new mills and the expansion of existing facilities. Debate rages about the sustainability of the current rate of cutting and the long-term value of reforestation practices.

External Control of the Economy

Northern British Columbia's economy is substantially controlled by external companies. Some of the companies are Canadian; many are American or, increasingly, Japanese. A very substantial portion of the northern British Columbian economy is controlled by Japan, either through direct ownership or through long-term contracts for the purchase of regional products. The Tumbler Ridge coal project, for example, is tied directly to Japanese markets as is a healthy portion of the region's forest output and about 60 per cent of the sales from the Alcan smelter in Kitimat.

Most of the major Canadian companies (a notable exception is Northwood Pulp and Paper in Prince George) are controlled by southern managers. This ensures that major economic levers are held by people living outside northern British Columbia. There is actually not a great deal of discussion about this issue in northern British Columbia, but perhaps there should be. The region's "get rich quick" philosophy, inherited from the boom years of the 1950s and 1960s, remains firmly entrenched.

Survival of Small Towns

Many of the smaller towns in northern British Columbia are at risk. Company towns like Granisle and Tumbler Ridge owe their existence to the viability of a single industry. If a mine or plant closes, or the market for a particular product takes a sharp downturn, the very existence of a community can be threatened. Granisle is making a strong effort to survive the closure of the local mine, but several other communities (the best example is the former asbestos mining town of Cassiar in the northern part of the region) have simply shut down. Masset, on the Queen Charlotte Islands, was built around a military base, and continued cutbacks in national military spending have placed the future of the town at risk.

The concentration of economic activity in larger centres has, on a less notable level, harmed the surrounding smaller communities. Prince George's impressive growth of late, highlighted by the expansion of shopping facilities, has caused economic problems in such nearby centres as Vanderhoof and Quesnel. The small towns, led by committed and earnest local boosters, are struggling to hold on in the face of economic and demographic difficulties. Occasionally, these struggles erupt as major inter-community rivalries — something for which the North is known. At the other extreme, however, threats to the existence of the villages and towns have also unleashed a remarkable creativity and tenacity as local residents search for new solutions and for long-term stability.

2
Navigating the North:
Getting Here and Getting Around

Northern British Columbia is a large place; communities are separated by many kilometres, the climate varies considerably, and driving conditions are highly changeable. The region also has abundant wildlife — one of the great attractions of the north, but also a potential travel hazard. It is best to plan ahead, to leave yourself enough time to cover the vast and wonderful distances, and to make sure that you enjoy all that northern British Columbia has to offer.

Travellers are often scared off by what they hear about northern conditions — particularly relating to the Alaska Highway and the roads in the Far North. Not so long ago, southern newspapers routinely printed lengthy articles extolling the virtues of the northern regions and then warning drivers about the myriad of difficulties of travelling along unpaved, poorly served highways.

Fewer than 25 years ago, the warnings were fully justified. The federal government was rebuilding and relocating major portions of the Alaska Highway, the Stewart-Cassiar Road was rough and unpredictable, and many of the side roads in the region were unpaved and subject to difficult driving conditions. Northern travel is not yet up to southern and urban standards, but notable improvements have been made. Still, some cautionary words and advice are in order. First, however, a basic introduction to the routes and options available to travellers heading into northern British Columbia.

Getting Here

Because northern British Columbia is an amalgam of different, widely-varied sub-regions, there are many ways to get to the North and to get around in the North. Detailed directions and comments are provided in each chapter. For now, we will outline the main routes, opportunities, and problems that you will encounter.

Air travel is obviously the fastest way to get around, although you will need to rent a car if you want to see much more than a few blocks of downtown development. If you come by car, plan for a fairly lengthy drive — both to get into the North and then to get through it. Distances are considerable, and, once you have made the effort to get here, you will want to take a good look around. There is no advantage to simply racing through the region; if you do so, and seldom stray from the highway corridors, you will miss much of the "very best" of northern British Columbia.

Air Travel

Northern British Columbia is served by two large carriers (AirBC and Canadian/Canadian Regional), one small regional carrier (Central Mountain Air), and a large number of charter companies (including Waglisla Air, which provides services along the Northwest Coast). Of the two large carriers, whose flights are comparably priced, Canadian/Canadian Regional provides better service and a more traveller-centred approach. Central Mountain, based in Smithers, runs small planes on a series of routes from Terrace to

Prince George, and from Prince George to Fort St. John, Kamloops/Kelowna, and Vancouver/Victoria. They offer competitive rates and friendly service, and their low-flying planes provide charter-equivalent views of some of the spectacular interior scenery.

Train Travel

Grab it before it's too late. For the last few decades, there has been a steady decline in passenger rail service across Canada, and northern British Columbia has not been spared the budgetary axe. There are two options available. VIA Rail, which appears to be constantly threatened with closure, operates the Skeena Train from Jasper to Prince Rupert. Service is regular (one train per day in the summer months), although the departure times seem to be set by owls, not people. Prince George departures for Jasper are scheduled for 12:35 a.m. on Sunday, Tuesday, and Friday, and trains to Smithers and Prince Rupert leave at 3:00 a.m. on Sunday, Wednesday, and Friday. Rising early pays off, for the train is a leisurely, comfortable way to see the province, and the VIA Rail line runs alongside several spectacular rivers, crosses a number of high bridges, and creeps through the coastal rain forest. Fares are no longer cheap, but it is a wonderful way to travel.

Travellers leaving from Vancouver or Prince George have another option. One of the province's many under-utilized attractions is the BC Rail train which runs daily in the summer between Prince George and North Vancouver (and vice versa). The North Vancouver terminal is a bit hard to find, and 13.5 hours on the train seems like a long time, but this journey is well worth the effort — at least one-way. One would look hard and long to find a more relaxing way to travel, and the scenery is simply wonderful. The landscape changes dramatically as the train travels along the

British Columbia Rail operates regular passenger train service between Vancouver and Prince George.

coast, through the coastal rain forest, past the Whistler resort, into the Pemberton-Lilloett corridor, through the Caribou, and on to Prince George. The conductors take the time to announce spots of scenic and historic interest. The Prince George terminal is a five-minute drive out of town — in one of those industrial parks that Canadian railways insist on using. The price is attractive ($139 round trip — off-peak season, regular class). Summer rates and Cariboo Class fares (the latter including meals) are higher.

Bus

For those travelling on a budget — and wise enough to listen to the advice not to hitchhike — the bus is an option. There is regularly-scheduled bus service throughout northern British Columbia, with several buses per day on each of the major routes. Be careful about which bus you select. If you climb onto one of the milk runs, which stops in every village and hamlet along the way, the travelling time and discomfort can increase dramatically. There are usually express buses between major centres, and some of the coaches show video movies — an important diversion on the often long bus rides. Bus travel is reasonably priced (approximate prices for one-way bus tickets are as follows: Vancouver to Prince George — $85.00, Prince George to Prince Rupert — $82.00, Edmonton to Prince George — $88.00, Vancouver to Williams Lake — $65.00, Smithers to Prince Rupert — $38.00), but if you plan ahead, and if time is a factor, you will often find that discount airfares are not significantly higher.

Car

Most visitors to northern British Columbia come by one of the many roads leading into the region. There are a few major options: Highway 97, which runs north from Vancouver through Cache Creek to Dawson Creek; Highway 16 (Yellowhead Highway), which connects Edmonton, Alberta with Prince Rupert; Highways 2 and 49 in Alberta, which provide access to the southern reaches of the Alaska Highway and the Peace River country; and Highway 5, which connects Kamloops, Valemount, and Highway 16.

Inside the region, there is the famous Alaska Highway, which runs from Dawson Creek (Mile Zero, but don't say this to the folks in Fort St. John who know that actual construction began at Charlie Lake, just outside their town) to the Yukon and Fairbanks, Alaska. The Alaska Highway has been substantially rebuilt over the past 20 years and is no longer the "rough road North" of earlier legend. Further west, and running between Kitwanga (on Highway 16) and Watson Lake in the Yukon, is the Stewart-Cassiar Road — a rougher passage, but one that traverses some beautiful, undeveloped countryside. There are numerous side roads and hundreds of logging roads. The latter can be busy with logging trucks, but they also provide access to hard-to-reach campgrounds, fishing spots, and hunting grounds. Make sure you get copies of the regional Forest District maps, available at BC Tourist Information Centres, which provide extremely useful guides to the logging roads and campsites.

The heaviest traffic is on Highway 97. Discounting several longish sections which have not yet been widened to provide either four lanes or enough passing lanes to get past all the slow-moving recreational vehicles that run up and down the highway in the summer, this is a good road. Highway 16 west of Prince George can get quite busy in the peak season, but the other main highways are generally quite open. The more isolated roads, even in mid-summer, receive very little traffic.

Once You Are Here

The opportunity to move about within northern British Columbia is one of the region's greatest features. Population is sparse and scattered, and the roads and highways wind through scenery of unparalleled beauty. As you travel through the region, it is important that you be prepared and that you respect the driving conditions. Make sure that your car is in good running order, and bring along the standard supplies (a good-quality spare tire, a car jack in working order, windshield wiper fluid, and extra oil). Southerners venturing north used to get a bit carried away; they would pack three or four spare tires and enough extra supplies to last several weeks, and they would cover their windshield with bug netting (as much to stop the rocks as the bugs).

Current conditions do not justify such extreme measures. The main roads are paved and well-maintained, although most of the side roads are gravel and must be driven at slower speeds (an obvious point that is lost on many travellers). The gravel roads, however, are generally well-maintained. Take extra care during and after a heavy rainfall, for the gravel surface can get very slippery. Conversely, when it has been dry for an extended period, the side roads can get extremely dusty, and it can be difficult to drive behind other vehicles (particularly large recreational vehicles or commercial trucks). Stay well back until presented with a safe opportunity to pass, and slow down when another vehicle approaches.

Being Prepared for the Back Roads

There is an amazing network of roads, most constructed by forest companies, criss-crossing northern British Columbia. These roads are not maintained to the same standards as the provincial road and highway system, but they are generally quite drivable. The provincial government has a superb set of Forest Recreation Maps that are available at all tourist information booths. These maps will provide you with the details that you need to drive off the beaten track and to gain direct access to fabulous fishing and camping opportunities. Most travellers never learn of these maps, and, consequently, back road traffic is generally very light.

A few words of caution are in order, however. Do not try to drive at highway speeds. Back roads are not constructed for highway driving; they are working roads that are built and maintained by logging companies. Be careful when logging trucks approach; they kick up an enormous amount of gravel. Conditions can get very slippery when it rains, and small washouts are not uncommon. Services are typically at an absolute minimum, although there are a few places (like Germanson Landing, north of Fort St. James) where the logging roads lead to a small settlement. Make sure that you bring along all the supplies, including food, gasoline, and an extra spare tire, that you will need for the trip. Finally, there are smaller roads that lead off the main logging roads. Try not to venture too far onto these; they are even more isolated than the logging roads, and it could be a long walk to help.

Winter Driving

Northern winters present a different set of challenges, and a few very real dangers. Take winter driving seriously; the cost of a mistake can be extremely high. Roads get very icy, particularly in the Prince Rupert to Smithers region, and extremely cold temperatures of up to -45 C (-49 F) are not uncommon. There are a few places — Smithers to Terrace, Terrace/Kitimat, the Pine Pass area north of Prince George, and the Peace River district — that are susceptible to severe winter storms. White-out conditions, when falling or blowing snow is so thick that it is difficult if not impossible to see, are not unusual.

Be prepared and be sensible. Listen to the local radio for road reports and heed the advice. If the police and highway authorities have issued a travel advisory, do not push your luck. There are few things more terrifying than driving along an isolated stretch of highway during a snowstorm and knowing that the temperature outside the car is well below freezing. Traffic can be very light along even the main highways in mid-winter, and a slight accident can prove extremely problematic if you are not properly prepared. If you do get in trouble, stay in your vehicle. Heading off in search of help can, in sub-zero temperatures, be extremely dangerous. A final word: when driving along the highway in winter, do not pass by anyone in difficulty. Stop and offer assistance.

St. John Ambulance provides a list of items for a winter survival kit. Their advice is sound; make sure you pack this equipment before doing any northern winter driving — even if the weather forecast is favourable. The list (provided by CBC Daybreak in Prince George) is comprised of the following items: ice scrapper and brush, shovel and road salt, fuel line and windshield de-icer, blanket or sleeping bag, extra clothing, footwear and toque, candle in a deep can (to warm up the car), waterproof matches, supply of energy food (nuts and dried fruit), booster cables, flashlight, warning flares, reflective strips, tow chain, fire extinguisher, road maps, spare fuses, spare tire, and an extra set of keys located outside the passenger compartment.

Wildlife

There are several places in northern British Columbia that are particularly well-known for abundant wildlife. You often see bear, moose, and deer on the Mount Robson to Prince George trip (Highway 16), on the Hart Highway north of Prince George (Highway 97), and along the road between Quesnel and Barkerville (Highway 26). Sheep routinely come down to the Alaska highway in Muncho Lake Provincial Park, and you can see countless deer along the Queen Charlotte Island roads. (To give you a sense of numbers, on a summer 1994 trip from Mount Robson to Prince George, we saw at least 10 moose, 12 deer, three bears,

Wildlife abounds in northern B.C. Bighorn sheep can be seen along the highway in Mount Robson and Muncho Lake Provincial Parks. (Ron Thiele)

and a fox.) If you are anxious to see wildlife, the best time to travel is early in the morning or at dusk.

Wildlife viewing is a major attraction and adds to the excitement of a trip through this gorgeous land. However, and please note that this is a big however, wildlife are a major driving hazard. Moose are extremely large creatures, and automobiles and their passengers do not come out well in moose-car encounters. Each year, many such accidents in the north typically result in major damage to vehicles, death or serious injury to the animals, or, more frequently than one would like, injury to vehicle occupants. Drive very carefully at night, and watch out for animals on the road.

It is also important that you treat the wildlife with respect. They are wild animals. Bears are particularly

▶

The rare, all-white Kermode bear is a symbol for Terrace and the Northwest.
(Myron Kozak)

unpredictable, and each year, several people run afoul of an angry animal. Do not feed bears and do not attempt to get close to wild animals for a photograph (One grimaces at the recollection of a half dozen tourists getting within a few feet of an elk in Mount Robson Park in an attempt to get a close-up picture or at the sight of two men throwing rocks at a bear cub in a tree.) Stay in your car when you happen upon animals alongside the road, and do your very best not to disturb them.

Beds and Breakfasts

In our travels throughout northern British Columbia, we have stayed in dozens of hotels and motels, several resorts, and many beds and breakfasts. The beds and breakfasts are the Rodney Dangerfield of the region's tourist industry. On the south coast, and in more exotic locales like the San Juan Islands, the bed and breakfast culture has taken firm root among visitors and the tourism industry alike. Not so up north; many travellers seem willing to keep driving rather than to stop for the night at a bed and breakfast.

Beds and breakfasts are a great deal; they are often a lot cheaper than a stay in a comparable hotel or motel. Some are located in town centres and provide access to city facilities and shops; others, the majority in fact, are situated in beautiful, pristine rural settings. The folks who operate beds and breakfasts are ready and anxious for visitors. They are typically extremely well-informed about local attractions and activities and can hook you into a network of beds and breakfasts for the duration of your trip.

Just a few hints and suggestions for travellers who, willing to be a bit adventurous and anxious to discover more about the region and its people, are prepared to try out the bed and breakfast circuit:

➤ **Many beds and breakfasts do not take credit cards.** Check ahead, or carry enough cash to cover the cost of your stay.

➤ Beds and breakfasts generally have only a few rooms and are often very busy in the summertime. Make reservations ahead of time. Most operators can give you advice about beds and breakfasts along your route.

► Provincial and regional bed and breakfast associations offer reservation services. Given that it is often difficult to identify all of the beds and breakfasts in a given area, these reservation services can be extremely helpful in planning your trip and making arrangements for accommodations along the way.

► Beds and breakfasts vary widely. We have been in several operations built from the ground up as guest accommodations; others have been added onto private homes. In a few, the facilities equal or exceed those in top-quality hotels; in others, the facilities are like the guest rooms at Aunt Martha's. Some offer ensuite facilities; others ask you to share washrooms with other guests. Many have separate sitting rooms, but others have a common/living room for guests and owners. If such things matter to you, make sure you check ahead of time to avoid disappointment.

► Don't forget to factor in the "breakfast" part of the bed and breakfast when determining the comparative cost of the room. We recently paid $85 for a very nice bed and breakfast in the Cariboo district. This price covered beds for five (sleeping in three different rooms) and a wonderful breakfast for the bunch of us — a steal when you assume that a standard hotel breakfast would cost around $25-$35 for a group of five.

► Bed and breakfast operators are very used to "lookie-lous" (people who want to look around the home before they decide if they want to stay). Do not hesitate to ask if you can check out a bed and breakfast before you sign in for the evening. Proprietors welcome the visit.

► One of the great delights of staying in a bed and breakfast is the access that it provides to local knowledge. Capitalize on the opportunity. The vast majority of bed and breakfast operators know the area extremely well and are more than pleased to tell you about it.

You could easily — and comfortably — travel throughout northern British Columbia and stay in beds and breakfasts the entire time. If you are an aficionado of this form of tourist travel, then welcome to the northern variant of the new favourite. If, however, you have not yet tried the bed and breakfast route, do give it a shot. We suspect that you will be delighted with the difference — and with the unique perspectives that you will gain of the North. European travellers are much more comfortable with bed and breakfast travel than many North Americans who typically head for the highway hotels (preferably of a franchise variety). It is time for that to change.

So, drive carefully and enjoy your stay in beautiful northern British Columbia. We are convinced that, if you will slow down long enough to look around, you will realize that this is a truly remarkable piece of the world; its stunning physical setting is matched by friendly people, exciting activities, and excellent services. You will long remember your visit to northern British Columbia.

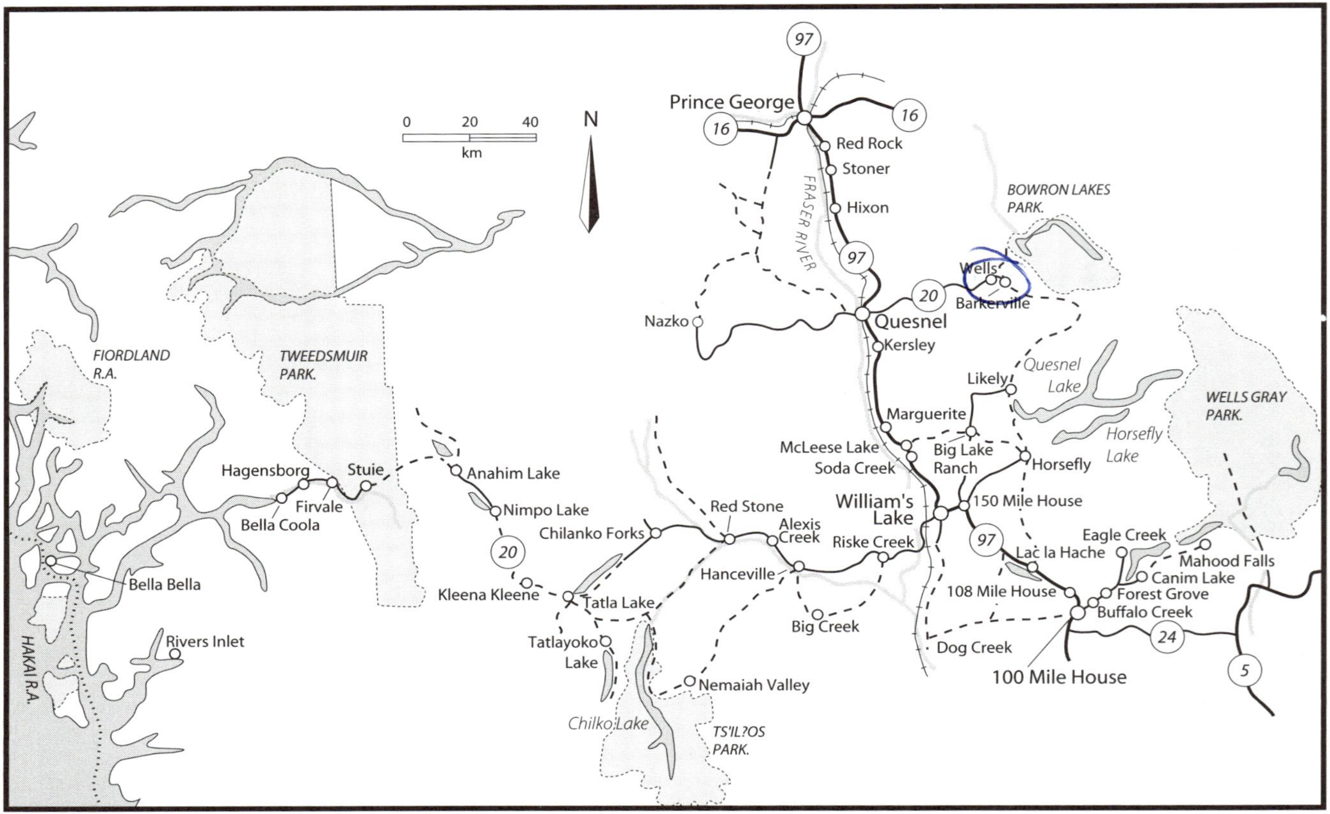
0
20
40
km
N
Prince George
97
16
16
Red Rock
Stoner
Hixon
FRASER RIVER
97
BOWRON LAKES PARK.
Wells
Barkerville
20
Quesnel
Nazko
Kersley
Quesnel Lake
Likely
WELLS GRAY PARK.
Marguerite
Horsefly Lake
McLeese Lake
Soda Creek
Big Lake Ranch
Horsefly
William's Lake
150 Mile House
97
Eagle Creek
Lac la Hache
Mahood Falls
Canim Lake
Forest Grove
108 Mile House
Buffalo Creek
Dog Creek
24
100 Mile House
5
FIORDLAND R.A.
TWEEDSMUIR PARK.
Hagensborg
Stuie
Firvale
Bella Coola
Anahim Lake
Nimpo Lake
20
Kleena Kleene
Chilanko Forks
Red Stone
Alexis Creek
Riske Creek
Tatla Lake
Hanceville
Big Creek
Tatlayoko Lake
Nemaiah Valley
Chilko Lake
TS'IL?OS PARK.
Bella Bella
Rivers Inlet
HAKAI R.A.

3
The Cariboo - Chilcotin

Alberta is supposed to be Canada's "cowboy" country, but don't tell that to the good folks of the Cariboo-Chilcotin. Several enormous ranches — including the historic Gang Ranch, which was for years one of the largest in the world — can be found here, and cowboy culture runs more than boot deep in the soil. This is the land of the Great Cariboo Trail Ride, the famous Williams Lake Stampede, guest ranches, and many operating cattle operations. So, don't attribute the cowboy hats and boots to urban cowboys; the saddlery stores in Williams Lake and elsewhere are for real!

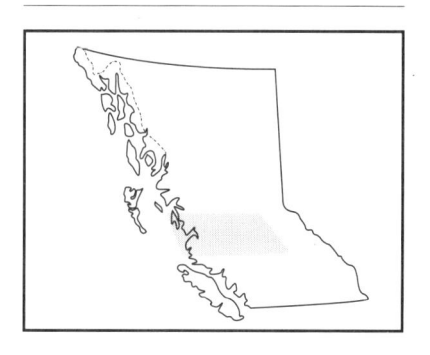

There is much more to the Cariboo-Chilcotin than cows, horses, and cowboys, although that's a rather intriguing start. This area, with its hundreds of well-stocked trout lakes, is one of the best fishing areas in all of Canada. And the spectacular scenery ranges from the dramatic coastal mountains around Bella Coola; to the jagged cut of the Fraser River; to the rolling, lake-studded hills that are the signature of this region. There is an active logging and pulp and paper industry, and the mining sector, although variable, is an important part of the economy. The Cariboo-Chilcotin also boasts the best historic attraction in British Columbia at Barkerville; vibrant communities in 100 Mile House, Williams Lake, and Quesnel; one of the best canoeing sites in Canada (the Bowron Lakes); and a seemingly endless variety of recreational opportunities.

A little bit of an orientation is in order. The Cariboo-Chilcotin stretches from 100 Mile House to Quesnel and from Highway 20 to the Pacific Ocean. The designation "Cariboo" refers to the district between Highway 97 and Highway 5. This area is liberally speckled with lakes and rivers and is a fisher's paradise. The "Chilcotin" actually refers to the plateau region between Williams Lake and Anahim Lake. This open and majestic land is home to a number of large ranches and several major lakes — Chilko Lake is one of the most beautiful in the province. Further east, lie Tweedsmuir Park and Bella Coola, which are part of the coastal and coastal mountain zones. Bella Coola is the only community on the central coast (ie. North of Vancouver Island and south of Prince Rupert) that you can reach by car.

A Brief History

The Cariboo-Chilcotin has a varied and storied past. It shares the same deep aboriginal roots as all other parts of northern British Columbia. The region first attracted European attention during the fur trade period; maritime traders were drawn to the coastal districts in the late eighteenth century and to the interior a few years later. Alexander Mackenzie's historic journey across the continent in 1793 — which took him past the Peace River and through the central interior — ended near Bella Coola. Many First Nations people, preferring traditional social and economic activities, maintained only marginal ties to the new fur trade economy.

Barkerville, centre of the great 19th century B.C. gold rush, has been resurrected as a lively, informative historical park.

The British Columbia gold rush, which ran from 1858-1865, brought about sudden and dramatic changes. The discovery of gold in the Quesnel-Barkerville area drew thousands of miners north from the gold diggings on the lower Fraser River and from further abroad. The colonial government, in constructing a road to the gold fields — the famous Cariboo Trail — opened up the Fraser River corridor with its string of roadhouses. Barkerville was transformed into a classic gold rush boomtown — creator of fortunes and misery and supporter and destroyer of dreams.

The region boomed for a few years until the gold ran out, and then the miners filtered out of the area — to gold strikes further north and to urban centres in the south. Farmers and ranchers moved into the southern reaches, initially to serve the miners and mining towns and later to service southern markets. When the gold rush ended, the region did not return to its pre-rush condition. Many of the farmers and ranchers remained when the miners left, sternwheelers continued to ply the Fraser, and the newcomer population set down the traditions that would establish the independent character of the Carboo-Chilcotin district.

The Cariboo-Chilcotin developed slowly after the gold rush, with a few mines opening (and closing), limited development of the towns, and the continued vitality of the aboriginal societies in the region. The absence of a railway — the Pacific Great Eastern, running North from Vancouver, did not reach the area until 1920, was extended to Quesnel in 1923, and was built through to Prince George in the 1950s — and the rough nature of the regional road system slowed economic expansion. The Barkerville/Wells gold fields continued to attract a limited amount of attention, albeit much less than in the heady days of the Gold Rush.

After World War II, the region quickly came to life. Sawmills and pulp and paper plants opened and provided the foundation of the current logging and lumber industry. Several new mines, particularly Gibraltar near Williams Lake, added to the region's economic stability. The post-war period also saw the rapid expansion of the tourist industry, particularly in the fishing and hunting sectors, and the construction of dozens of lodges, regional access roads, and boating facilities.

The Chilcotin district, hampered by poor roads and limited access, remained substantially isolated from the developments further east. When the local First Nations blocked gold rush-era plans to build a route to the gold fields through their lands, the short-lived but locally important Chilcotin War of 1864 began. The killing of several surveyors involved with the road construction project brought down the firm hand of British law; five of the Chilcotin people were executed. What is now Highway 20, from Williams Lake to Bella Coola, was initially built by local residents who could not convince the provincial government of the need or feasibility of a plateau to coast road. Bella Coola, at the end of Highway 20, which is a sizeable Nuxalk community, is tied to the economy and society of the West Coast.

The Cariboo-Chilcotin region now finds itself at an important cross-roads. Recently, there have been occasions when tensions between loggers, miners, environmentalists, and First Nations have bubbled over (much of this tension has accompanied the controversial CORE process of land-use management). The long-established fishing resort sector finds itself facing different pressures — from developers who wish to purchase their land holdings for resort/condominium construction. The First Nations, recovering from a difficult period of transition, which was highlighted by a multitude of brutal experiences in the government-funded residential schools, have gained a greater measure of self-government and are asserting their authority over community affairs. Tourism is very much on the rise, particularly the high-end resort sector (including fly-in fishing camps and wilderness resorts), and the provision of government services has added an important element of stability into the otherwise volatile regional economy.

Located at the southern extremity of northern British Columbia, the Cariboo-Chilcotin is readily accessible to the main population centres in the lower mainland and along the Trans-Canada Highway. 100 Mile House,

Getting There

the southern-most point in our coverage area, is only 150 kilometres (94 miles) north of Cache Creek — the junction of Highway 1 and Highway 97. The eastern access to the Cariboo-Chilcotin is by way of Highway 5, which runs north from Kamloops. The other main road, Highway 20, connects Williams Lake and Bella Coola.

You can reach the region in all the standard ways: train, bus, and airplane. BC Rail (which runs from Vancouver to Prince George) stops in, among other places, 100 Mile House, Williams Lake, and Quesnel. There is daily bus service along the main highways. There are airports in Quesnel and Williams Lake, although service is less than ideal and the carriers fly small prop planes into the communities.

The Great Outdoors

Fishing

The literally dozens of fishing resorts of the Cariboo-Chilcotin cater to every taste and price range. The expensive fly-in retreats offer anglers an opportunity to catch salmon from the salt-chuck or trout from high-country lakes. The area east of 100 Mile House and Williams Lake offers many low-key resorts — a few cabins, campsites, boat rentals, and lots of advice — for those of more modest ambition and budgets. It would be difficult to list — let alone visit — all of the fishing resorts in this district, for there are simply too many and they are too widely dispersed to cover in detail. (Write directly for information.) Please note that licenses are required and are readily available from sporting goods and other stores in the region.

If you have off-highway experience, are willing to be a little adventurous and have the right equipment — a well-serviced vehicle and a boat — get copies of the appropriate Forest Recreation Maps from the local tourist information booths. These maps will show you how to get to remote, isolated lakes that typically offer only the most rudimentary of facilities (rustic campsites, no water pumps, etc.) but have great fishing potential.

Here are a few of the major fishing areas that are easily accessible by car; there are, of course, dozens of other excellent fishing lakes — *many* with resorts and parks:

Near 100 Mile House: Green Lake, Sheridan Lake, Bridge Lake, Canim Lake, Mahood Lake
Near Williams Lake: Quesnel Lake, Horsefly Lake
Near Quesnel: Bowron Lakes
In the Chilcotin: Chilko Lake, Anahim Lake, Puntzi Lake, Nimpo Lake, Tatla Lake

For further information on fishing resorts and services, you should contact the tourist associations (addresses at the back of the book) or visit the local travel information centres. The more remote fishing camps, particularly the fly-in resorts, typically require reservations and can be extremely busy in the summer months. If you are interested in such a vacation, you should contact the camps well ahead of time. The following list includes the major remote resorts:

MacKenzie Trail Lodge (Blackwater River), *27134 NW Reeder Rd., Portland, Oregon 97231 (503/621-3416).*

Moose Lake Lodge, *Box 3310, Anahim Lake, B.C. V0L 1C0 (604/742-3535).*

McLeans River Ridge Resort (Chilko Lake), *P.O. Box 2560, Williams Lake, B.C. V2G 4P2 (604/398-7755).*

Stewart's Lodge & Camps, *Box 19, Nimpo Lake, B.C. V0L 1R0 (1-800/668-4335).*

Dean River Resort, *Nimpo Lake, B.C. V0L 1R0 (604/742-3332).*

Eagle's Nest Resort Ltd., *Box 3403, Anahim Lake, B.C. V0L 1C0 (604/742-3707).*

Pine Point Resort, *Box 139 Nimpo Lake, B.C. V0L 1R0 (604/742-3300).*

Eureka Peak Lodge and Outfitters (Gotchen Lake), *Box 1332, 100 Mile House, B.C. V0K 2E0 (604/397-2445).*

Ghost Wilderness Resort and Adventures (Quesnel Lake), *P.O. Box 4069, Williams Lake, B.C. V2G 2V2 (604/398-1087).*

Shearwater Resort (coastal) *D4-5455 Airport Rd. S., Richmond, B.C. V7B 1B5 (1-800/663-2370, 604/957-2305).*

Big Springs Sports Fishing Resorts (coastal), *4680 Cowley Crescent, Richmond, B.C. V7B 1C1 (1-800/663-4400).*

Hakai Beach Resort (coastal) *885 W. Georgia, 23rd Floor, Vancouver, B.C. V6C 3E8 (1-800/668-3474, 604/231-3721, fax: 604/231-3722).*

Guest Ranches / Wilderness Resorts

The ranching experience is one of the great attractions of the Cariboo-Chilcotin region, and a number of guest ranches are available for those anxious to try their hand at horseback riding and cattle driving. Also, the Cariboo-Chilcotin has a large number of excellent wilderness resorts. Many of these offer luxury accommodations and gourmet meals, and all provide instant access to the great outdoors. If you are planning a visit to a guest ranch or wilderness resort in the Cariboo-Chilcotin here are a few places to consider. Write or call ahead for details on rates, services, and availability.

Springhouse Trails Guest Ranch, *RR#1, Williams Lake, B.C. V2G 2P1 (604/392-4780).*

Big Bar Guest Ranch, *Box 27, Clinton, B.C. V0L 1K0 (604/459-2333).*

Elkin Creek Guest Ranch (Nemaiah Valley), *4462 Marion Rd., North Vancouver, B.C. V7K 2V2 (604/984-4666).*

Crystal Waters Guest Ranch, *Box 100, Bridge Lake, B.C., V0K 1E0 (604/593-4252).*

Cariboo Rose Guest Ranch, *P.O. Box 160, Clinton, B.C. V0K 1K0 (604/459-2255).*

Chilcotin Adventures, *P.O. Box 152, Whistler, B.C. V0N 1B0 (604/238-2274).*

Circle H Mountain Lodge, *P.O. Box 7, Jesmond, Clinton, B.C. V0K 1K0 (604/459-2565).*

River Ridge Resort and Outfitter (Chilko Lake), *P.O. Box 2560, Williams Lake, B.C. V2G 4P2 (604/398-7755).*

Vedan Ranch (near Taseko Lake), *Box 2, Big Creek, B.C. V0L 1K0 (Radiophone: Vedan Ranch, N49 55 24, on YJ Alexis Creek Channel).*

Charly's Guest Ranch (Chilko Lake), *Chilko Lake Rd., c/o Box 4788, Williams Lake, B.C. V2G 2V8 (604/394-4127).*

Chilko Lake Resort, *P.O. Box 6016, Williams lake, B.C., V2G 2V8 (1-800/667-8773).*

Half Way Ranch, *Box 34, Tatla Lake, B.C. V0L 1V0 (604/476-1100).*

Clearwater Lake Lodge and Resort, *Kleena Kleene, B.C., V0L1M0 (604/476-1150).*

Minac Lodge (Canim Lake), *Eagle Creek, B.C., V0K 1L0 (604/397-2416).*

▲ *Trail riding in the Rainbow Mountains of Tweedsmuir Provincial Park, with a magnificent view west towards the Pacific ocean.* (David Hodges)

Ruth Lake Lodge, *P.O. Box 315, Forest Grove, B.C. V0K 1M0 (604/397-2727).*

Ten-ee-ah Lodge (east of Lac la Hache), *Box 157, Lac la Hache, B.C. V0K 1T0 (604/395-7100).*

Timothy Lake Resort (east of Lac la Hache), *Box 42, Lac la Hache, V0K 1T0 (604/396-7367).*

Tatanka Guest Ranch, *Stanchfield Rd., P.O. Box 654, 150 Mile House, B.C. V0K 2G0 (604/296-4155).*

Hints for the Traveller

The Cariboo-Chilcotin is a vast, widely differentiated land that will reward the adventurous traveller. Here are a few suggestions for visitors trying to make the most of the area:

➤ The Chilcotin district is much-overlooked — especially the road from Williams Lake to Bella Coola. The rough road is no superhighway, particularly at the coastal end, but the scenery is unsurpassed and the recreational opportunities almost endless.

➤ This is one of the continent's greatest fishing areas. If you head into the lake districts east and west of Williams Lake and in the Quesnel region, you will enter world-class fishing territory. There are dozens of resorts, ranging from luxury accommodation to basic campsites, that cater to every taste and pocketbook.

➤ Take the time to talk to local experts — sporting goods stores are an excellent place to start — about where the fish are biting and how to catch them. The appropriate tackle and gear changes over the course of the summer (the hot weather drives the fish deeper into the lake). You will have much greater success if you have good advice.

★ ▶ The movie "City Slickers" has given dude ranches new life and has helped draw hundreds of urban dwellers to cattle country. The region's guest ranches have a great deal to offer, but the variety is tremendous. Give some thought to what you are after — wilderness excursions, gourmet meals, camp outs and campfires, guided trail rides, or the chance for independent horseback riding — and select the ranch accordingly.

▶ Put Barkerville in your schedule. The Government of British Columbia has done a superb job with this historic site, and the range of attractions and features makes for a very full and interesting day. British Columbia markets itself as a natural attraction and as a land of tomorrow, but the province has a vibrant and interesting past. Barkerville offers an excellent opportunity to explore British Columbia's history.

▶ Drive carefully when you are off the main highways. There are hundreds of kilometres of gravel roads in this district, and they will lead you to many fascinating places. But gravel roads present a different driving challenge than the main routes. Loose gravel, often narrow roads, and regular twists and turns will slow you down considerably. Do go slowly, and take care — if only to protect your windshield from flying rocks.

▶ The Cariboo-Chilcotin first emerged as a major tourist destination in the 1960s, when the area attracted hundreds of travellers each summer to lakeside resorts at Lac la Hache, McLeese Lake, and elsewhere. Many of the traveller's facilities in the area date from this era, but the process of rebuilding is underway — as revealed by the beds and breakfasts opening up in the area and by major investments in resorts like Best Western 108 Mile Resort and The Hills Health and Guest Ranch.

➤ Fishing resorts are not just for fishers. These isolated, remote spots are beautiful, quiet, and secluded. They are excellent places to relax, hike, watch birds, and to get away from the noise and bustle of the city. Most lakes have excellent campsites (public or private) and there are many very good lodges in the region.

➤ The Cariboo-Chilcotin district has a vibrant artistic community. While there are only a few city stores selling local products, you will find numerous small shops — many operated out of artists' homes.

The Very Best of the Cariboo-Chilcotin

100 Mile House

During the gold rush days of the 1860s, the Cariboo Wagon Road started at Lillooet (Mile 0) and stretched all the way north to the gold fields of Barkerville. There were a number of places to stop along the way and the one-hundred-mile mark happened to be one of them. Before the gold rush, this community was known as Bridge Creek House, and it catered to fur traders and settlers in the area. Today, 100 Mile House is a bustling community of 1,900 people that serves the surrounding region and cater to the numerous visitors who come to ski, horseback ride, golf, or mountain bike.

PLACES TO EAT
Red Coach Inn: *($$$)* For a fine dining experience, your best bet is the Red Coach Inn dining room or the dining rooms at the **108 Mile Resort** *($$$)* or **The Hills**

($$$) (see the descriptions under Places to Stay). The Red Coach Inn is located at *170 North Cariboo Highway, c/o Box 760, 100 Mile House, V0K 2E0 (604/395-2266).*

The Tastebuds Restaurant: *($)* Taste Buds serves a variety of delicious burgers and other snacks like chicken fingers, fries, and salads. The food is inexpensive and very tasty. The non-smoking section is quite small and the place gets a little smoky. *257 S. Highway 97 (604/395-4123).*

Cariboo Diner: *($)* The Cariboo Diner's specialties are perogies and fish and chips, but it also serves hamburgers, chicken fingers, salads and sandwiches. The food is of good quality and is sold at reasonable prices. It is extremely popular with the locals and can get quite crowded and smoky. *441 S Highway 97 (604/395-2020).*

★ **Schloss Café:** *($)* This cozy café is a good place to stop for a light meal or for a European dessert and specialty coffee. *225 S. Birch Ave. (604/395-2257).*

Other Possibilities: Also worth checking out are the **Friends** ($$) restaurant in the Lakewood Inn on the Cariboo Highway *(604/395-4005),* which is highly recommended by locals as one of the best deals and best meals in town, and **Greta's Deli and Coffee House** ($) at 260 Birch, which serves cappuccinos and light snacks *(604/395-2131).*

PLACES TO STAY
The Red Coach Inn: *($$)* This hotel, 100 Mile House's best, has an excellent dining room. The hotel is near a golf course and cross country ski trails *(1-800/663-8482).*

Beds and Breadfasts: There are a number of beds and breakfasts near 100 Mile House, including the **Wolf Den** *($$, Box 215, Forest Grove, B.C. V0K 1M0, 604/ 397-2108)* and **Nana's Bed & Breakfast** *($$, eight kilometres (five miles) north of 100 Mile House on Highway 97, 604/791-5699).*

THINGS TO DO

Shopping: Rosewood Books, located in the Owen Square, is a good place to stop and browse. There are a number of books by local authors and there is a good selection of books on horses. *460 S. Birch (604/395-5252).* **Sweet and Classy,** gift and candy specialists located in the Cariboo Mall, stocks a number of gift items, Belgium chocolates, fudge, and ice cream and sells espresso and cappuccino. **Hemmingway's,** at *150 S. Birch*, is a kitchen specialty and gift shop. **Jondeval's** and **Barb's Airbrush Artistry,** both in the Pinkley Complex at *150 Horse Lake Rd.*, are good places to visit.

OUTDOOR RECREATION

As is the case in most of northern British Columbia, the best things to do in the 100 Mile House area are outside. Golfing, fishing, hiking, skiing, horseback riding, mountain biking, and swimming are all minutes from downtown 100 Mile House. Check in at the 100 Mile House Tourist Information Centre for up-to-date information. Note the world's largest pair of cross-country skis!

The Great Cariboo Ride: If you *really* want the cowboy experience and are prepared to make a commitment to the effort, 100 Mile House has something very special for you. The Great Cariboo Ride, organized and run by a local non-profit society, is an annual, nine-day trail ride through the Cariboo-Chilcotin. The ride covers a large area that runs along the Fraser

★

River, across the Gang Ranch, and into the back country. The Great Cariboo Ride accommodates all levels of riding skill; it provides an easy introduction for the novice and a challenging experience for the more advanced rider. This is a truly unique opportunity. *The Great Cariboo Ride, P.O. Box 1025, 100 Mile House, B.C. V0K 2E0 (604/395-4156).*

108 Mile House

A few kilometres north of 100 Mile House along Highway 97 is the small community of 108 Mile House. There is not much to see from the highway, but this little settlement has several excellent resorts, some first-rate beds and breakfasts, and recreational opportunities galore.

PLACES TO STAY

108 Mile House is home to the Best Western 108 Mile Resort and the Hills Guest Ranch. Both of these resorts are wonderful places to spend a few days. The scenery in this area is lovely, and kilometres of skiing and biking trails wind all over the neighbouring hills.

★

Best Western 108 Mile Resort: *($$$)* 108 Mile Resort is a year-round retreat that offers golf and hiking in the summer and excellent cross-country skiing in the winter. Gunner's Cycle and Cross-Country Ski Sales and Rentals (underneath the 108 Resort restaurant) rents mountain bikes and cross-country ski equipment. 108 Mile Resort has a small outdoor swimming pool, tennis courts, horseback riding, an indoor hot tub and sauna, and, right in front of the resort, an 18 hole golf course. The resort is well-marked from Highway 97; watch for the billboards. *Telqua Dr., Box 2, 108 Mile Ranch, B.C. V0K 2Z0 (1-800/667-5233).*

The Hills Health and Guest Ranch: *($$$)* The Hills Health and Guest Ranch offers horseback riding, hay rides, guided hikes, tennis, and a variety of health spa activities, including aerobic and pool classes, saunas, and massages. The Hills is located along Highway 97 near the main entrance to 108 Mile House. There is a prominent sign near the road. *c/o 108 Ranch, C26, 100 Mile House, V0K 2E0 (604/791-5225).*

Beds and Breadfasts: If you would prefer to stay in an excellent bed and breakfast, try **The Log House** *($$, C347, 108 Mile Ranch, B.C. V0K 2Z0, 1-800/610-1002, 604/791-5353).* Dale and Joan Bummer are

Great snow conditions and rolling terrain make the Cariboo an exceptional area for cross-country skiing and other winter recreational sports.
(108 Mile Resort)

welcoming hosts who enjoy sharing their beautiful log home with their guests. Follow the directional signs from the 108 Mile Heritage Site. Other nice beds and breakfasts in this area are **Arcona House** *($$, Chilcotin Crescent, V-18, 108 Mile Ranch, B.C. V0K 2Z0, 604/ 791-6555)* and the **Schmid-Meil Oldys and Schmid-Meil Sisters Bed & Breakfast** *($$, 59 Telqua Dr., 108 Mile Ranch, B.C. V0K 2Z0, 604/791-5644)*.

THINGS TO DO
108 Mile House Heritage Site: This heritage site shows visitors one of the famous Mile Houses on the Cariboo Wagon Road as well as six other historic buildings. One of these buildings is a log Clydesdale barn that was built to house over 200 Clydesdales and is the largest log building in Canada.

150 Mile House

A few minutes drive south of Williams Lake is the pleasant, quiet community of 150 Mile House. As you drive through, take a look at the old one room schoolhouse that sits beside the new elementary school.

PLACES TO STAY
Beds and Breakfasts: There are a few beds and breakfasts in 150 Mile House, including **The Williams Lake Log House** *($$, Box 956, 150 Mile House, B.C. V0K 2G0, 604/296-3663)* and **Trish and Ted's Bed & Breakfast,** *($$)* which is located at *#14 Ridgeway Place (Box 986, 150 Mile, B.C. V0K 2G0, 604/296-4485)*.

Williams Lake

Williams Lake, with a population of 18,000, is the largest community in the south-central interior of the province. It has been the focal point and service centre of the Cariboo and Chilcotin ranches since the turn of the century. Today, the predominant industry is forestry, including logging, wood manufacturing, and direct support industries. Mining exploration and development also generate a great deal of economic activity. This is an area of big open spaces and wide-eyed Cariboo adventures. Horseback riding, fishing, hiking, cross-country skiing, and other outdoor activities all take place here.

PLACES TO EAT
Rockwell's Cappuccino: *($)* If you arrive in Williams Lake searching for a café latte or an espresso, Rockwell's is the place to go. Along with specialty coffees, Rockwell's serves soups, sandwiches, bagels (baked on the premises), cookies, and other desserts. *72C S. 2nd Ave. (604/392-3633).*

Tastee Freeze: *($)* Williams Lake's Tastee Freeze is located right on the highway and is a favourite with people travelling through town. It is a counter-style restaurant and offers a range of breakfast and lunch foods. The food is good, inexpensive, and quickly served. Families and kids' sports teams, in particular, patronize this Tastee Freeze, as kids like the food and you can fill them up in a relatively healthy way without breaking the bank. *1059 Cariboo Highway (604/392-7333).*

Trattoria Pasta Shoppe: *($$)* Trattoria is a warm and ★ cozy self-service pasta restaurant (you place your order at the counter, and the food is brought to your table). It serves all kinds of delicious pasta dishes from linguini with chicken, mushrooms and sundried tomatoes to penne primavera with sausage to tortellini gorgonzola. All pasta is made to order and served with a slice of fresh french baguette. Trattoria also serves a variety of excellent homemade desserts and muffins. *23A South 1st Ave. (604/398-7170).*

★ **Richard's Bistro:** *($$)* The food here is very good. Pastas, soups, sandwiches, and other specialties are served, and great care is obviously taken with each dish. The bread is homemade, the soups are made from scratch, and the pasta dish we tried was excellent. Quality and taste of this degree compelled us to order dessert — a piece of the most wonderfully creamy cheesecake. Don't miss Richard's Bistro. *54 North Mackenzie (604/398-5105).*

Laughing Loon Neighborhood Pub: *($$)* The Laughing Loon Neighborhood pub is extremely popular with locals and visitors. It is located just off the highway on the south side of Williams Lake, and many people travelling through make a point of stopping here. The décor is interesting, and delicious snacks, salads, and entrees are served. Due to licensing restrictions, children are not permitted. *1730 S. Broadway (604/398-5666).*

Double J Café: *($)* If you feel like Tex-Mex food, try the Double J Café, Tex-Mex Grill and Cantina on South McGuire near Yorkton Street, underneath Miki's Cabaret. The building is not impressive from the outside, but the food is good. *105B S. MacKenzie (604/392-5441).*

PLACES TO STAY

If you are doing more than passing through, this is a good time to stay at one of the guest ranches or lodges listed earlier or at a bed and breakfast.

Hotels/Motels: Williams Lake has a number of easy to find hotels and motels. Two of the better ones are the **Fraser Inn Hotel** *($$, 285 Donald Rd., Williams Lake, V2G 4K4, 1-800/452-6789, 604/398-7055)* and the **Overlander Motor Inn** *($$, 1118 Lakeview Cres.,*

Williams Lake, V2G 1A3, 604/392-3321), which has a good restaurant.

Soda Creek Acres Bed, Bales & Breakfast: *($)* Accommodating people and horses, this bed and breakfast, which sits on 75 acres of land, has horses, chickens, a dog, a cat, and a rabbit and is an ideal place to stay if you are travelling with children. The bed and breakfast area has a private entrance and two bedrooms, a washroom, and a sitting area. Breakfast consists of delicious sourdough pancakes, bacon, orange juice, and coffee. The hosts here are Bernice and Robert Johansen, and they have lots of information to share about the area. The countryside around Soda Creek Acres is lovely, and about two kilometres (one mile) away lies the tiny town site of Soda Creek itself — complete with log jail and old community hall. Soda Creek Acres is located 30 minutes north of Williams Lake, about four kilometres (three miles) off Highway 97 along the Soda Creek Townsite Road. A small sign on the west side of Highway 97 marks the turn-off to Soda Creek Acres. *RR4 S15 C7, Williams Lake, B.C. V2G 4M8 (604/297-6418)*.

Rowat's Waterside Bed & Breakfast: *($$)* Located near Scout Island and within walking distance of the Stampede Grounds, this bed and breakfast is very convenient if you happen to be visiting during the Williams Lake Stampede. Marg and Jack Rowat offer a variety of rooms with private bathrooms, a fireside lounge, and their "Cariboo Cowboy Breakfast." *1397 Borland Rd., Williams Lake, B.C. V2G 1M3 (604/392-7395)*.

Rustler's Roost Guest Ranch: *($$)* About an hour's drive northeast of Williams Lake just off of Highway 97 lies the Rustler's Roost Guest Ranch. This working horse and cattle ranch is located in the beautiful Beaver

Valley. Rustler's Roost has a ranch house with three guest rooms, a main house with a dining room and lounge, horseback riding, hiking trails, stream fishing, swimming in the lakes on the property, and horseshoe pits. In early May, guests are welcome to join in the cattle drive to the summer range, and around the first week of October it is possible to participate in a cattle round up. Visitors can also purchase a day package or a western chuck wagon barbecue dinner that is served from the back of an authentic western chuck wagon. *Box 189, Horsefly, B.C. V0L 1L0 (604/243-2244).*

THINGS TO DO

Station House Gallery Shop: The Station House Gallery Shop is housed in the BC Rail Station and sells books, pottery, jewellery, and locally produced art. Beside the gift store, there is also a small gallery featuring larger and more expensive works, such as paintings and sculptures. *1 N. Mackenzie Ave.*

Reflections Gallery North: This small gallery features paintings by local artists. Stop in and browse. *98 N. 2nd Ave.*

Native Arts and Crafts Shop: The Native Arts and Crafts Shop sells good quality local Native crafts, such as moccasins, jewellery, gloves, and souvenirs. *99 S. Third Ave.*

Cariboo Saddlery: This store will make it clear you are in ranching country. With cowboy boots, saddles and harnesses for sale, this is a fun shop to peek into. *183 Oliver St.*

Scout Island Nature Centre: Located at the west end of the lake, this nature centre has a series of exhibits on wildlife, birds, waterfowl, and fish. There are also a number of nature trails that explore the wetland marsh ecosystem. Bring the family for an enjoyable and educational outing. *Scout Island Road.*

Museum of the Cariboo-Chilcotin: This museum's collection of historic photographs and pioneer artifacts provides good background information on Cariboo pioneer life from the Gold Rush days until the 1920s. *113 - N. Fourth Ave. (604/392-7404).*

Woods and Mill Tours: If you are interested in learning more about British Columbia's interior forests, various woods and mill tours are available. The tours sometimes feature lunch at logging camps and instruction on various methods of harvesting and silviculture. Contact the Cariboo Lumber Manufacturer's Association for more information *(604/392-7778).*

Williams Lake Stampede: On the July 1st long weekend, one of the most exciting events in the Cariboo, the Williams Lake Stampede, takes place in Williams Lake. Barrel-racing, calf-roping, steer-wrestling, wild horse riding, bull-riding, and other events on the Canadian Professional Rodeo Association circuit are highlighted. In addition, there is a pancake breakfast, a parade, logging truck races, chariot races, pony chuck wagon races, and all kinds of live entertainment. ★

Bella Coola

The coastal town of Bella Coola is well off the standard tourist route. The small number of services and facilities is no indication, however, of the attractiveness of the area. The drive from Williams Lake, though a bit rough in spots, is spectacular and well worth the journey. Do take care on the twisty spots toward the coastal end of the trip!

PLACES TO EAT
Try the **Homesteader Restaurant** *($, 604/799-5379)*.

PLACES TO STAY
Places to stay in the Bella Coola area include the **Tweedsmuir Lodge** *($$$, Bella Coola, B.C. V0T 1C0, 604/982-2402)*, the **Bay Motor Hotel** *($$)* in Hagensborg *(c/o Box 216, Bella Coola, B.C. V0T 1C0, 604/982-2212)*, the **Bella Coola Motel** *($$)* at Burke Ave. and Clayton St. *(c/o Box 188, Bella Coola, B.C. V0T 1C0, 604/799-5323)*, and the **Cedar Inn** *($$)* on MacKenzie St. *(c/o Box 774, Bella Coola, B.C. V0T 1C0 (604/799-5316, fax: 604/799-5610)*.

Quesnel

During the gold rush, Quesnellemouth (Quesnel) was an important place for many miners. Steamboats ran from Soda Creek on the Fraser River to Quesnel — the entrance to the gold fields. Today Quesnel, or "Goldpan City" as it has nicknamed itself, is a bustling community of about 8,200 people on the banks of the Fraser River.

PLACES TO EAT

★ **Vaughan House:** *($$$)* Vaughan House offers fine dining in a restored older home. Elegant surroundings and pleasant service enhance the already excellent food. Vaughan House serves delicious appetizers, seafood dishes, schnitzels and other entrées. The restaurant also prides itself on serving a number of heart-smart dishes which are identified on the menu with a heart symbol. Vaughan House has a good selection of wines and desserts. *714 Front St. (604/992-6852)*.

Begbie's Lounge and Restaurant: *($$$)* Named after the first Chief Justice of British Columbia, William Begbie, Begbie's lounge is filled with photos and other memorabilia from the gold rush days. The lounge serves drinks and snacks, but for a more substantial meal head next door to the restaurant. Begbie's restaurant serves soups, salads, pasta, burgers, and a variety of international entrees. With its attractive décor and good service, Begbie's is popular with both visitors and local residents. *500 Reid St. — on the first floor of the Tower Inn (604/992-2201).*

Granville's Coffee House: *($)* It is easy to see why ★ Granville's is such a busy and popular place. A counter-service style restaurant, Granville's serves a number of breakfast items, "loaded" deli sandwiches, soups, lasagna, macaroni, a wide range of beverages (including cappuccinos and yogurt shakes), and many extremely yummy desserts. Worth a visit. *383 Reid St. — near St. Laurent (604/992-3667).*

Hokey-Pokey Kitchen: *($)* The Hokey-Pokey Kitchen is housed in an interesting log building that is located on the main route through town. Big and delicious sandwiches, pastas, soups, and salads are served. Good quality food at reasonable prices. *102 Carson (604/992-2700).*

Ulysses Restaurant: *($$)* For souvlaki, spanokopita or any other tasty Greek dishes, check out Ulysses. *122 Barlow St. (604/992-6606).*

Captain Frank's Seafood: *($)* For fish and chips, try Captain Frank's Seafood, which is located in the Dragon Mountain Plaza off the highway at the south end of Quesnel. *462 Juniper (604/747-3223).*

Gary's Restaurant: *($)* Known for having good breakfasts, Gary's is located in the Maple Park Shopping Mall. *201-2222 Maple (604/747-2742).*

Cariboo Burger Palace: *($)* This restaurant which advertises the best burgers for 2,000 miles met with the approval of our teenage critics. Located next to the highway by the Maple Park Shopping Mall at the south end of Quesnel. *2249 Maple (604/747-1272).*

PLACES TO STAY
The Tower Inn (discussed below) is the nicest place to stay in Quesnel, but there are a number of other hotels and motels along the highway, both north and south of the city, and in the downtown area.

The Tower Inn: *($$)* The inn has a large number of executive rooms and suites at reasonable prices. Begbie's Lounge and Restaurant is also located on the first floor of the hotel. *500 Reid St. (1-800/663-2009, fax : 604/992-5201).*

THINGS TO DO
Cariboo Hotel: The Cariboo Hotel usually has live music on the weekends. *254 Front St. (604/992-2333).*

Recreational Facilities: The town has excellent recreational facilities, including a swimming pool and skating rink. There are batting cages and a mini-golf course beside Ceal Tingley Memorial Park.

Highway 26 East

East of Quesnel on Highway 26 are a number of attractions. Stop at the Travel InfoCentre at the junction of Highways 97 and 26 and pick up a guide to the area. The pamphlet entitled "Historic Driving Tour - Quesnel to Barkerville" describes the history of many places along the drive.

PLACES TO STAY

The Wells: *($$)* This bed and breakfast offers good, clean, and inexpensive accommodations. *Pooley St., Box 39, Wells, B.C. V0K 2R0 (604/994-3427, fax: 604/994-3494).*

Becker's Lodge: *($$ - $$$)* Becker's Lodge, located on Bowron Lake, has campsites, log cabins, chalets, and a lodge with a lakeview restaurant. *c/o Box 129, Wells, B.C. V0K 2R0 (604/992-8864).*

Bowron Lake Lodge and Resorts: *($$)* This resort also has cabins, a campground, and a lodge with a dining room. The Bowron Lake Lodge rents mountain bikes as well as canoes and boats. *c/o 672 Walkem St., Quesnel, B.C. V2J 2J7 (604/992-2733).*

THINGS TO DO

Cottonwood House: About 25 kilometres (16 miles) from the junction of Highways 97 and 26 is Cottonwood House. It first operated as a roadhouse — a stopping place for early travellers — in 1865. It is one of the oldest buildings in British Columbia and one of the few Cariboo roadhouses still standing. From May until Labour Day, there is a living history program at Cottonwood; interpreters, in period costumes, give tours of the house and can be seen working on the property.

Wells: Wells is a small and interesting community composed of loggers, miners, and artists. The community's population (300) swells every summer, but it decreases substantially in the winter when heavy winter snows can leave the highway blocked and the community isolated for a number of days. A number of buildings from the early 1900s are still dotted around the town which makes for fun exploring. **Island Mountain Arts** offers a number of summer art courses on pottery, paper-making, and weaving. People from all over come to attend these classes. Wells, B.C. V0K 2R0 (604/994-3466)

★

Barkerville: In its heyday, Barkerville was the largest city west of Chicago and north of San Francisco. Billy Barker's discovery of gold on Williams Creek in 1862 attracted a rush of fortune seekers from all over the world. Between 1862 and 1870, over 100,000 people travelled the Cariboo Wagon Road to descend on the gold fields and the boomtown called Barkerville. Today's Barkerville, a provincial historic site, has over 125 heritage buildings, period merchants, stagecoach rides, the Theatre Royal, and a large number of displays, shows, and tours. Actors in period costume stroll the streets and engage in discussions about issues and events of the gold rush days. There are a couple of good restaurants on site as well as a bakery and a root beer salon. Great fun for the whole family. The Barkerville town site is open year-round but the shows and restaurants open mid-May and close around mid-September. Admission is valid for two days. The rates are $5.50 for adults, $3.25 for youths and seniors, and $1 for children. There is also a family rate of $10.75. P.O. Box 19, Barkerville, B.C. V0K 1B0 (604/994-3332).

★ **OUTDOOR RECREATION**

Bowron Lake Provincial Park: After you pass Wells and before you reach Barkerville, there is a sign pointing the way to Bowron Lake Provincial Park. This is a beautiful area of the province, and, as the lakes form a circle, canoeists can begin and end their trips in the same place. Canoeing the Bowron Lakes, a 116 kilometre (73 mile) journey, has become very popular with British Columbians and visitors alike, and one must now reserve ahead of time to ensure yourself a place. If you are just passing through the area, however, you can easily rent a canoe for a day from one of the two lodges in the area. Even a day's paddling will give you a sense of the beauty and majesty of the area.

Hixon

A small community about 60 kilometres (38 miles) south of Prince George, Hixon is primarily supported by the forest industry. A few places worth mentioning here include **Dorothy's Antiques,** a wonderful shop full of all kinds of treasures *(604/998-4477)*, fresh homemade bread at the **Paradise Motel** *(604/998-4685)*, and the **Fireplace Inn,** *($$)* a small restaurant which is extremely popular with the local population.

Selected Events in the Cariboo - Chilcotin

Cariboo Marathon	100 Mile House	February
Children's Festival	Williams Lake	June
Williams Lake Stampede	Williams Lake	July 1st weekend
Billy Barker Days	Quesnel	July
Horsefly Rodeo	Horsefly	July
Great Cariboo Ride	100 Mile House	July/August
Nemiah Valley Rodeo	Nemiah Valley	August
Lac la Hache Country Music Festival	Lac la Hache	August
Horsefly Fall Fair	Horsefly	August
Bella Coola Fall Fair	Bella Coola	September
Cariboo Fall Fair	Williams Lake	September
Old-Fashioned Christmas	Barkerville	December

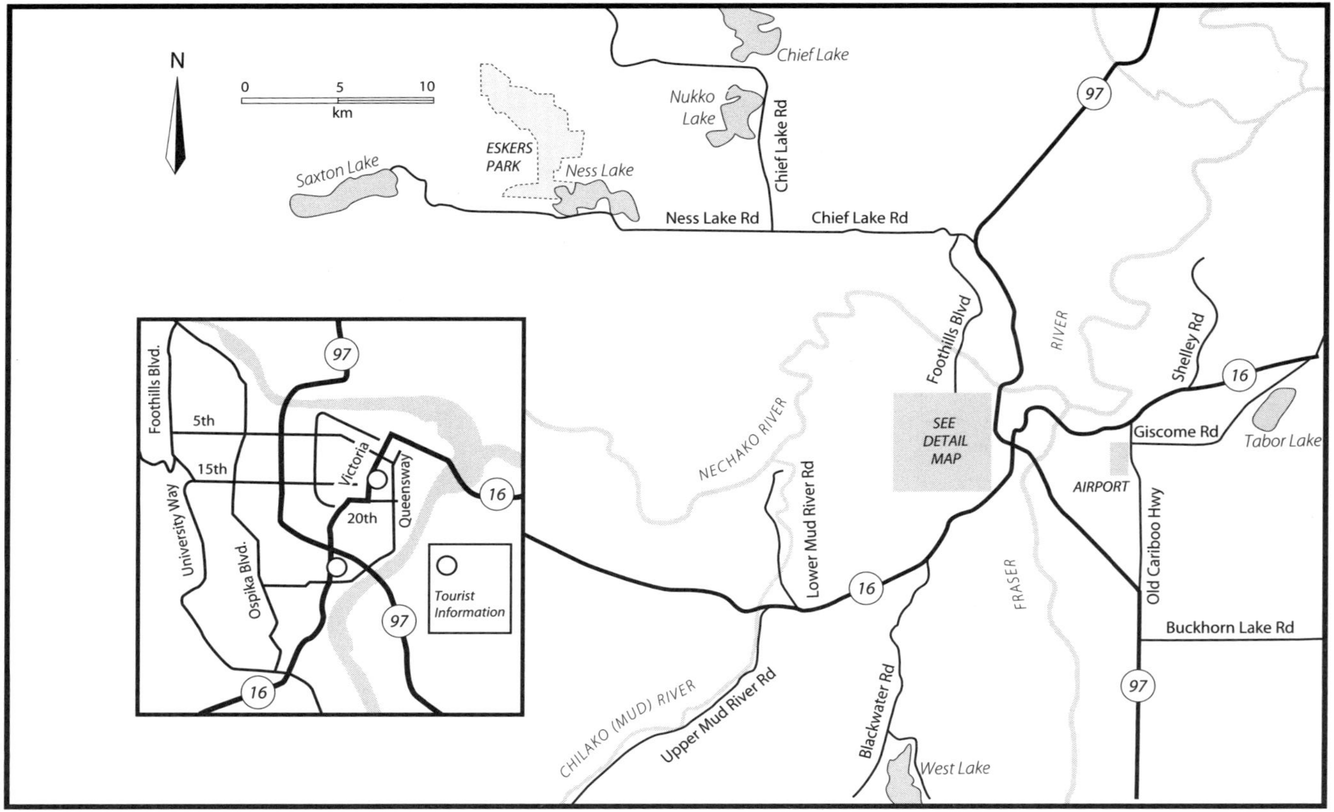
N
0
5
10
km
Saxton Lake
ESKERS PARK
Ness Lake
Nukko Lake
Chief Lake
Chief Lake Rd
Ness Lake Rd
Chief Lake Rd
97
Foothills Blvd
RIVER
Shelley Rd
16
Giscome Rd
Tabor Lake
SEE DETAIL MAP
AIRPORT
Old Cariboo Hwy
NECHAKO RIVER
Lower Mud River Rd
16
FRASER
Buckhorn Lake Rd
97
CHILAKO (MUD) RIVER
Upper Mud River Rd
Blackwater Rd
West Lake
Foothills Blvd.
5th
15th
University Way
Ospika Blvd.
97
Victoria
Queensway
20th
16
97
16
Tourist Information

4
Prince George:
The Gateway to Northern British Columbia

Visitors arriving at Prince George's airport are greeted by a large sign proclaiming that this central interior city is "The Capital of Northern British Columbia." It's a title that Prince George wears proudly and well deserves. One of the province's fastest growing and most rapidly changing municipalities, Prince George is anxious to shuck its image as a smelly pulp town and is determined to take its place among the leading communities in western Canada.

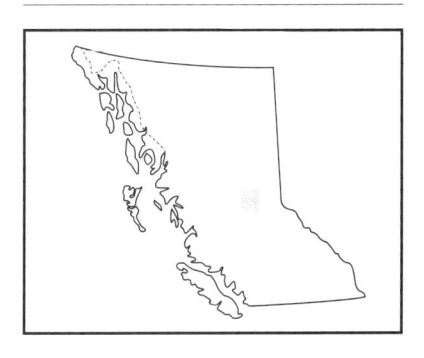

Prince George is, as its earnest and enthusiastic Mayor John Backhouse repeatedly declares, "a city on the move." The past decade has seen some dramatic changes in Prince George — unlike changes that have hit any other part of the province. For starters, there is a brand new university; the University of Northern British Columbia opened its doors in September 1994. More than just an important new educational venture, the University of Northern British Columbia is Prince George's finest architectural feature. There is also a new civic centre, some major new shopping complexes, and several new subdivisions. Currently under construction in Prince George are a much overdue law court building, which may contribute to revitalizing the downtown core, a multiplex arena (to host the city's new Western Hockey League franchise "stolen" from Victoria), and a new swimming pool complex.

A lot of the old Prince George can still be seen. The pulp mills — Canadian Forest Products and Northwood — sit near the junction of the Nechako and Fraser Rivers, and on still days the pungent aroma of the mills wafts over the downtown area (called "the bowl" locally). We hasten to add that the investment of many millions of dollars has cleaned up the mills dramatically, and those who remember the Prince George of the 1960s and 1970s will be truly surprised by the improvement.

The downtown core is in desperate need of a face-lift, but repeated attempts at revitalization have stumbled on financial hurdles. And there is an industrial and transient cast to the town that is particularly evident to those who rush through along the main highways and do not take the time to look around. Do stop, for Prince George has a great deal to offer visitors, and its quality of life, level of services, sporting activities, and friendliness are much appreciated by local residents.

A Brief History

The junction of the Fraser and Nechako Rivers has long been home to the people of the Lheit-Lit'en First Nation. The Fraser Gorge/Canyon was, and is, an important fishing spot, and several parts of the Prince George town site were used by Native people for generations. The Hudson's Bay Company established the Fort George trading post here in 1807, and the area played an important role in the development of interior trade. The region was not greatly affected by the British Columbia gold rush boom of the 1860s.

The coming of steel — in this case, the construction of the Grand Trunk Pacific Railway line in the early years of the twentieth century — brought new prominence to Prince George. Fueled as much by speculators' dreams as economic reality, the city grew dramatically and then settled into the more realistic role of an important division station on the railway.

The expansion of the interior logging industry in the northern interior, which commenced in the 1950s, sparked an enormous boom throughout the region. As the major supply centre for the North, Prince George was the primary beneficiary of the economic growth. It was this period that earned Prince George its reputation as a hard-drinking, rowdy, boisterous kind of place — an image that remains fixed in many British Columbian minds (which is not helped by southern newspapers that find the imagery quite compelling). The arrival of the pulp mills in the 1960s brought even greater growth and gave the city both a solid industrial base and enhanced stability.

Prince George has experienced a series of ups and downs. The economy fluctuated quite dramatically through the 1970s, and then experienced a serious depression in the early 1980s. The economic gloom did not lift until the early 1990s, when the coming of UNBC and the continued growth of the town as a regional administrative centre convinced local residents that their community did, indeed, have a vibrant future.

Prince George has grown dramatically over the past five years; the city's population has reached 72,000, and more than 100,000 people live in the area. Because of its role as a regional service centre — drawing shoppers and visitors from throughout northern British Columbia, Prince George actually has the amenities of a much larger city. Don't be surprised, therefore, when you hear locals speak with pride about their symphony, the active performing arts community, and the many government and professional services available in town.

Getting There

Prince George, approximately 700 kilometres (438 miles) north of Vancouver on Highway 97, is smack in the centre of the province. The city is actually in the middle of an "x," for it is also almost 700 kilometres to Prince Rupert on the west coast and to Edmonton and Calgary in Alberta. Highways 97 and 16 meet in Prince George, so access is easy. It can be a long drive, and the last bits — from Quesnel, from McBride, and from Vanderhoof — are not the most scenic in the province. Don't despair, for there is lots to do in Prince George.

As is the norm in the North, the highway approaches to Prince George, designed more for commercial traffic than for the tourist trade, are through the more unattractive parts of town. Proceeding north from Vancouver, Highway 97 passes through the BCR Industrial Park and then, by way of a by-pass, swings west of the downtown and heads north along an eight kilometre (five mile) industrial and warehouse strip. Travellers heading into town from Jasper on Highway 16 pass the airport and the new medium security jail and then catch a scenic view of the pulp mills before plunging into the industrial area near the CN railyards. The approach from Vanderhoof is somewhat more attractive; drivers sweep past the College Heights residential and shopping district (and the entrance to UNBC), the COSTCO store, and the golf course on their way into town.

The Prince George by-pass (it was the western boundary of the city until the 1970s — which gives a quick indication of how much the town has grown in the last 25 years) begins just north of the junction of Highways 16 and 97 and is typical of almost any city in North America. Here you will find all the old standards: a big mall (Pine Centre), several strip malls (the Spruceland Mall is a cut or two above the norm and is worth a look), chain stores galore (including a large Canadian Tire outlet), numerous fast-food restaurants and the ubiquitous highway motels and hotels designed for those seeking nothing more than a shower, a quick hit of junk television, and a comfortable bed. It's all pretty standard, and if it's what you want, you will find what you're looking for here. But this highway strip is no more representative of Prince George than any highway strip is of any city.

Prince George is also well-served by commercial airlines. Canadian and AirBC provide several flights per day from Vancouver. Canadian also flies north to Fort St. John, and AirBC has a connector flight to Dawson Creek, Grande Prairie, Edmonton, and Calgary. There is a local airline, struggling to stay aloft (financially, that is) called Central Mountain Air. They use small planes — flying cigar boxes to some — but offer good service to Kamloops, Kelowna, Fort St. John, Smithers, and Terrace. The Central Mountain folks are very friendly, and the scenery on their flights (the Smithers-Terrace route, on a clear day, is without parallel in the country) is simply spectacular.

If you want more local information, stop by the Prince George Tourist Information Centre, located downtown at the corner of 15th and Victoria. The well-stocked information kiosk has numerous pamphlets, and the well-trained staff can help you navigate your way around the city. Prince George is not a particularly easy town in which to move around in; the combination of the two rivers, a complex street system, and considerable urban sprawl all contribute to making navigation a challenge.

The Very Best of Prince George

Places to Eat

Prince George is not famous for its restaurants, but local conditions are improving rapidly. New-style restaurants — adding to the steak and family restaurants that already dot the town — have opened lately, and one hopes that they will do well.

DINING

★ **The Taj:** *($$)* Here's one worth a visit. The Taj is a first-class East Indian restaurant that provides good food in generous portions and at excellent prices. You will find a wide selection of appetizers, curries, chicken and seafood dishes, and house specials. A particular favourite — and perhaps the best food deal in the city — is the Vegetarian Platter For Two, which includes nan, samosas, an eggplant dish, mixed vegetables, rice and a few other delights. The restaurant is only open in the evening, but you can order from its menu in Kokamos during the day. (The two restaurants are attached and share both a kitchen and an owner.) *455 Quebec St. (604/561-0803).*

★ **Da Moreno:** *($$$)* Da Moreno prides itself on being Prince George's finest restaurant — an opinion that is widely shared in the community. The food is first-rate Italian and the service is attentive and courteous. Plan for a proper and sophisticated meal — and a bill to match. The pastas are all excellent. Other favourites include the warm artichoke salad, the antipasto platter, the mushroom polenta, and the enticing offerings on the desert tray. *1493 3rd Ave. (604/564-7922).*

The Log House Restaurant and Recreational Vehicle Park: *($$$)* Now this is one of those "only in Prince George" kind of places: a fine restaurant, delightfully decorated inside, on beautiful Tabor Lake. It's a few kilometres out of town, and the directions are not particularly easy to follow, but the persistent shall be rewarded. The Log House is filled with dozens of stuffed animals (we call them trophies up here in the North) and numerous historical artifacts from the Prince George area. The wide selection of appetizers and entrees are all tastily presented. Each table is served fresh bread, a cauldron of wonderful homemade soup, and a small serving of palate-cleansing sorbet. This is the kind of place one saves for a "special" evening — a real winner. And don't worry about the RV Park; although it is on the same grounds, you won't even see it from the restaurant. *11075 Hedlund (604/963-9515).*

★

Other Art Cafe: *($$)* Other Art Cafe is one of Prince George's landmarks. The first place in town to offer yuppie delights — cappuccinos and lattes, vegetarian dishes, and folk music — Other Art quickly attracted transplanted urbanites, summer tree-planters, the university crowd, and the "outdoors" set. Each month, the establishment dedicates its walls to a different local artist, and each weekend, and on occasional weekdays, the small stage is graced by local and touring entertainers. Performances range from blues, jazz, and folk musicians, to poetry readings and theatre sports. Special events, usually with an open mike, commemorate Earth Day, International Women's Day, and other such events. Other Art and Cappuccino serves salads, soups, sandwiches, and a few special lunch and dinner entrées. Desserts are great! The Sunday Brunch — a

★

four course treat for $9.95 — is a delicious option and is often accompanied by background music provided by members of the Prince George Symphony Orchestra. (Note that this restaurant was, at the time of publication, in financial difficulty and may soon close. It is a sign of Other Art's importance to Prince George that a community-based "Save Other Art" initiative was launched in an effort to keep it in operation.) *1148-7th Ave. (604/561-1553).*

★ **Rosel's:** *($$$)* The classiest place in Prince George, Rosel's is comfortably ensconced in a refurbished old house near the downtown core. From the friendly welcome to schnitzels and sweet desserts, Rosel's makes you feel at home. Our favourite is a summer lunch on the verandah — a special Prince George treat. Note that Rosel is a great fixture in the local art and culture scene and knows the city extremely well. Don't be afraid to ask! *1624-7th Ave. (604/562-4972).*

Meteora Taverna: *($$)* One of the two good Greek restaurants in town, Meteora is a small, popular lunch spot serving delicious souvlaki, calamari, Greek salads, dolmades, and the like. Entrées are accompanied by heaping portions of potatoes, rice, and Greek salad. Pictures of Meteora (the place after which the restaurant was named) adorn the walls, and a copy of Michelangelo's "David" stands at the front of the restaurant. (The more modest or the easily distracted should sit with their backs to him!) *1238-5th Ave. (604/564-3005).*

★ **Winston's Dining Room:** *($$$)* Located in the Coast Inn of the North, Winston's is an elegant restaurant offering first-rate entrees and superb desserts. *770 Brunswick Street (604/563-0121)*

Shogun: *($$)* The only Japanese restaurant in northern British Columbia, Shogun is also located in the Coast Inn of the North. The Shogun is a teppan-yaki style restaurant where a chef cooks your food on a grill in front of you. Diners choose from a combination of chicken, beef, prawns, and scallops. The selection, combined with a variety of vegetables, is cooked in a flashy and entertaining exhibition. Along with the teppan-yaki entrées, the Shogun serves sunomono salads, tempura, miso soup, and a sampling of other Japanese items. *770 Brunswick St. (604/563-0121).*

Earl's Place: *($$)* Earl's Place is a popular western Canadian up-market restaurant chain that caters to the university and college crowd and to anyone else who might be interested in fine burgers, ribs, pasta dishes, and great yoghurt shakes. It's one of Prince George's hottest spots and is often quite busy. If you want some easy-going dining, and a little bit of the young adult atmosphere, then stop by. And try the Chicken Hunan; it's the best choice on the menu. *1440 E. Central, (604/562-1527).* ★

Chinese Food: British Columbia is famous for its Chinese food restaurants, but this is not a northern British Columbia specialty. There are many Chinese restaurants in Prince George; most offer the standard fare and cater to non-connoisseurs. The **China Sail** *($$, corner of 5th Ave. and Tabor Blvd., 604/564-2828)* is the most popular and offers a comfortable, open setting. Their Honey Garlic Pork is excellent. The **Green Village Restaurant** *($$, 2348 Westwood, 604/563-9997) is also good.* For our other favourites, try the special fried rice at the **Canton Inn** *($$, 5204 Domano Blvd., 604/964-7300)* in College Heights and the War Wun Ton at **Casey's Steak Pit** downtown *($$, 193 Quebec St., 604/563-0084).*

FAST FOOD/SNACKS

Carmel's: *($)* Situated at the junction of two major highways, Prince George is a prime truckers' town. There is a certain amount of truth to the old adage that the truckers know where the best food in town is to be found. (Best in this context means value for money, large quantities, friendly service, and noisy chatter. It also has something to do with the size of the parking lot — have you ever seen a logging truck try to go through a McDonald's drive-through?) Carmel's, located on Highway 97 near the Fraser River bridge, is one of the best truck stops in the North. The atmosphere is richly northern, and the food is good. *1538 Highway 97, (604/562-5612).*

Micjac Café: *($)* If you want a small touch of French Canada — or want to meet some of the local French Canadians — stop in for a chat or a coffee with Jacques Pelletier, owner of the Micjac (named for Jacques and his wife Michelle). We were introduced to this out-of-the-way breakfast and lunch spot by French Canadian friends who assured us that the French Canadian delicacy poutine was far more delightful than the list of ingredients (fries, gravy, and cheese curd) suggests. They were right — and a few minutes with Jacques only adds to the atmosphere and enjoyment. You'll have to search a little to find the café; it is east of Queensway in a semi-industrial area. The Micjac Café also serves sandwiches, burgers, salads, and breakfast items. *825 Second Ave. — off Scotia St. (604/562-3183).*

A&A Burger Bar: *($)* This obscure drive-in fits in the category of something a little different. It is located north of town along Highway 97 — and just after the Hart Highway Elementary School. The Burger Bar looks like a set out of America Graffiti — a small wooden block that completely lacks neon signs and the splash and sparkle of modern fast-food restaurants. All you will get are great burgers, excellent fries, good milkshakes, and friendly service — all at a very good price. Keep your eye out for this one, for it is worth the stop. *3803 Hart Highway (604/962-2063).*

Amigo's Taco Shop: *($)* Located downtown and across the street from Northern Hardware, Amigo's is a favourite lunch spot. The menu in this clean and simply-decorated restaurant is on the wall above the counter. Amigo's serves burritos, tacos, taco salads, mexifries, and other delicious Mexican treats. Highly recommended is the soft chicken taco with honey mustard sauce. The service is quick and friendly and the food is tasty. *229 Brunswick (604/562-8226).*

The Bagel Street Café: *($)* This bagel shop, Prince George's first and to this point only, is one of the abundant signs that Prince George has come of age. The brightly coloured downtown storefront, located next door to Da Moreno's, captured the locals' attention overnight. You may find a line-up — and with good reason. The bagels are fresh, the coffee excellent, and the service friendly and quick. The menu list includes bagel sandwiches, several varieties of cream cheese, bagel pizzas, cappuccino, and a wide variety of healthy juices. They keep a large stock of newspapers on hand for those who want to catch up on current events while chomping on their bagels. *1495 3rd Ave., (604/563-0071).*

★

Muffin Break: *($)* The Muffin Break, at the corner of 15th and Johnson Street, near the bypass, is a popular spot for local clubs to meet and socialize. Before they head off on an hour-long jog, a group of runners meet here every Saturday morning at 8:00 a.m. for a muffin, juice, or coffee. Feel free to join in. Muffins, cinnamon buns, soup, coffee, and salads are available at reasonable prices. *1455 Johnson St. (604/561-0767).*

Grabba-Jabba / Java Mugga Mocha: *($$)* Grabba-Jabba is another of the "yuppie" chain restaurants whose opening signals the continued transformation of Prince George. It's in a bit of an odd location — in a strip mall along the by-pass — and the prices are a tad high, but if you are looking for a good sampling of salads, rich desserts, and cappuccinos and lattes, Grabba-Jabba is worth a quick visit. *104-892 Central E., (604/562-0092).* If you are downtown and looking for similar fare, check out **Java Mugga Mocha**, at *304 George St. near the Holiday Inn (604/562-3338).*

PUBS

College Heights Pub: *($$)* The College Heights Pub will always have a fond place in our hearts; it was here that the idea for this book originated. Several of us gathered at this College Heights fixture — it's a bit hard to find — for lunch. The food was, as always, cheerfully served, quick, in copious quantities, and very fine. It is the perfect place for a hearty eater who desires a pint of local brew with a meal. The daily lunch specials are great value (particularly the Friday steak and salad deal), the perogies are very good, and the plate of nachos is enough to choke a moose. *5787 Albert Place (604/964-4500).*

Alpine Pub: *($$)* Local pubs have become quite a tradition in Prince George. The Alpine Pub is located in the Hart Highlands subdivision north of the city and may be a bit difficult to find. The atmosphere is very genial and easy-going, the beer is cold and cheerfully served, and, like a few of the other pubs in town, the food is surprisingly good. The schnitzels are particularly appetizing. *6145 S. Kelly Rd. — in Hart High-*

lands (604/962-5333). Downtown, try out the **BX Neighbourhood Pub** *($$, 433 Carney, 604/561-2900).*

Places to Stay

Prince George is not a resort town. As a consequence, its hotels and motels lack the allure of Jasper, Banff, or Whistler and tend, instead, toward accommodations for the commercial traveller or the over-night visitor. There is lots of standard fare, particularly along the bypass, although rooms can be hard to find mid-summer.

The Bed and Breakfast industry is setting down roots in Prince George. The more than 20 beds and breakfasts in the city vary widely in price and facilities. A brochure is available from the Prince George Tourist Information Centre, and the **Prince George Bed and Breakfast Association** can also be contacted for a copy of their pamphlet, further details, or reservations *(604/561-2337, fax: 604/562-6699).*

Coast Inn of the North: *($$$)* If you are looking for something a little special, try the Coast Inn of the North — the largest hotel in town, with good restaurants, nicely appointed rooms (many have recently been re-done), and good service. *777 Brunswick St., Prince George, B.C. V2L 2C2 (604/563-0121).*

Holiday Inn: *($$$)* The Holiday Inn is also nice, although it is in a less attractive part of town and has a smaller range of options. The first-rate Sports Bar is a good place to follow major sporting events, and the Coronet Twin Theatre is actually attached to the hotel. *444 George St., Prince George, B.C. V2L 1R6 (604/563-0055).*

Esther's: *($$)* This family hotel, located along the bypass, may be just what the family needs after a long drive. Like a large terrarium, it is filled with tropical plants and several indoor swimming pools. The children will be drawn to the indoor water slides (at an extra charge — even for hotel guests), and the entire family can enjoy a Sunday buffet brunch. The rooms are not spectacular, but the idea here is that you'll spend your time doing other things. *1151 Commercial Dr., Prince George, B.C. V2M 6W6 (604/562-4131).*

★   **Cambridge Bed & Breakfast:** *($$)* One of the attractions of beds and breakfasts is the opportunity to meet good, local people, and two of the best — anywhere — are Herb and Marilyn Hess. Their Cambridge Bed and Breakfast, offers nice rooms, superb food, and exceptionally friendly hosts. *5228 Cambridge Rd., Prince George, B.C. V2N 2B5 (604/964-2623).*

Bedford Place: *($$)* This is a "top-of-the-line" bed and breakfast. *135 Patricia Blvd., Prince George B.C., V2L 3T6 (604/562-4557).*

Westhaven Cottage by the Lake: *($$)* West of Prince George, Westhaven Cottage by the Lake, operated by Ray and Maureen Griffin, is located at West Lake. *23357 Fyfe Rd., S34, C38, SS3, Prince George, B.C. V2N 2S7 (604/964-0180).*

Winston's Bed & Breakfast: *($$)* If you want a more central, downtown location, try Winston's Bed and Breakfast. *655 Summit St., Prince George, B.C. V2M 3W9 (604/562-8269).*

College and University Residences: Not everyone has the money for upscale hotels and beds and breakfasts. And cheap rooms can be hard to find in Prince George — particularly in the summer months when the annual migration of tree planters hits town (you'll known them by their decrepit cars, unshaven faces, and evident joy at being out of the bush). The planters head for the camps for several weeks at a time, and you can imagine their delight, and their demeanour, when they get a weekend break in the big city. There are two new places for those looking for a cheap but nice place to stay in the summer. Check out the residence at the **College of New Caledonia** *($, 3330-22nd Ave., 604/ 562-2131)* and the **University of Northern British Columbia** *($, 3333 University Way, 604/960-5555)*. UNBC's facilities and location are more attractive, but less private (four single rooms to a unit); CNC's accommodations are cheaper and closer to downtown — near the bypass and within easy walking distance of a dozen fast-food restaurants *(604/561-5849)*.

Things to Do

As the largest city in the north, Prince George has a great deal to offer locals and visitors alike.

SHOPPING
Prince George, a regional commercial centre that is finally beginning to catch up with the North's demand for greater selection and better prices, boasts a number of unique and interesting shops. There are, of course, the standard department and chain stores; you'll find them easily enough by heading for the downtown area, the Pine Centre Mall, the Spruceland Mall or the Parkwood Mall. We'll stick with the more unique and interesting place

Outdoor Equipment
Northern Hardware: This store, a Prince George legend, is famous for its selection and for the outstanding quality of its service. It offers an amazing variety of hardware items, things for the home and garden, and

sporting goods. Almost everyone in town has a story about a desperate search for a missing piece for some appliance or an out-of-stock piece of equipment that ended only when they had the good sense to check out Northern Hardware. In the basement of the store are boxes and drawers full of dust-covered parts and pieces, and the exceptionally helpful staff are always more than willing to go searching for you. *1386-3rd Ave.*

Island Alpine: If you are looking for outdoor clothing and equipment, Island Alpine is the best choice in town. This small shop stocks a variety of hiking boots, camping gear, sunglasses, jackets, and other items for the outdoor crowd. Island Alpine also sponsors travel and adventure slide shows and films from time to time. See if anything is on while you are visiting. *316 Victoria St.*

ISL Enterprises: Another surprisingly good outdoor shop, located off the north end of the Nechako River bridge on Highway 16, is ISL Enterprises. This combined outdoor equipment, drafting, and computer store — a rather eclectic combination — specializes in gear for tree planters and hikers. *610 Richardson Rd.*

Northern Trout Fitters: This is the best fly-fishing place in Prince George. *181B Quebec St.*

Northland Sports Shop: Northland Sports Shop offers great advice and a very wide selection of sports equipment. *8087 Hart Highway.*

Howie's Marine: Located along the Nechako River next to the Pacific Northwest Brewing Company, this store sells canoes, boats and supplies. *623 Preston.*

Ultrasport: This is the best spot in town for running, cycling, and Nordic skiing equipment. The staff is very knowledgeable and their selection is first-rate. *1237 4th Ave.*

Winterland Sports: This store sells and rents downhill and Nordic ski equipment and clothing. *1191 - 1st Ave.*

Specialty Foods/Bakeries

Jet Lin Noodle: The shelves in this Asian grocery store are well-stocked with an eclectic mixture of Chinese and Japanese groceries, dishes and knickknacks. It is a fun store to wander through, particularly for those who have travelled or lived in Asia. You can even find several kinds of dim sum and freshly-made Chinese noodles! *185 Dominion.*

Ave Maria: Ave Maria is in a completely different vein. This store sells health food and religious books and gifts. (This kind of mingling of offerings is commonplace in the North.) Ave Maria is also one of the few places in town where you can find milk in glass bottles and free range eggs. *1638 - 20th Ave.*

The Pastry Chef: This bakery, which has three outlets in Prince George, offers a full range of bakery goods and treats. Their cookies are particularly good. *Pine Centre Mall, 380 George St., and 222-100 Tabor Blvd.*

The Deli House: This is the best delicatessen in town and is located across the street from the commanding Ukrainian Orthodox Church. *3578 Massey.*

Books/Information

Bookstores: Not so long ago, Prince George used to be something of a reader's wasteland; a few small shops sold the standard set of best-sellers. Now, Prince

George has two first-rate bookstores, both of which sponsor readings and special events. **Mosquito Books**, located at *1209-5th Ave.*, is the older and smaller of the two stores. The staff is superbly helpful and are truly interested in books and Canadian culture. Mosquito Books is a great supporter of local book-launchings — the number of which has increased dramatically since the arrival of UNBC. Great place! **Books on Fourth**, located less than two blocks from Mosquito Books *(1229-4th Ave.)*, has a larger selection and is also a wonderful bookstore.

Gundy's: If your taste in reading runs to magazines, check out Gundy's. Because this store distributes magazines throughout northern British Columbia, it has a huge selection, covering every imaginable taste (and some you can't imagine!). They also carry a good collection of local and regional books and one of the larger assortments of mass market fiction (what a friend affectionately refers to as "mind candy"). *1210-3rd Ave.* If you are near the by-pass, check out **Spruceland News.** *651 Central W.*

Internet Café: This is a recent addition to the city. The proprietor of this café has networked eight computers into the Internet and for $5 an hour, customers can surf the Internet or play one of the computer games. If you are new to the Internet, you are allowed free time until you know what you are doing, and staff are available to give you a hand. The Internet Café also has a coffee and beverage bar, and it sells a variety of Self-Help Crafts of the World items. *4th Ave. and Brunswick St. (604/563-4583).*

Arts and Crafts

Arterie: You can purchase local artwork at the Arterie — a volunteer-run artists' cooperative. The offerings vary from year to year and season to season, but there is often first-rate artwork on display. *1160 - 3rd Ave.*

Prince George Native Friendship Centre: The Native Friendship Centre has a small art gallery and art shop attached to its premises. Native art is experiencing a major rebirth in northern British Columbia, and there is very good artwork by relatively unknown artists on display at this store. *144 George St.*

Manor House Gallery: The Manor House Gallery can be found in the North Nechako subdivision (they also run a bed and breakfast). This wonderful home has been converted into a show-piece for local, regional and provincial art and is well worth a visit. *8384 Toombs (604/562-9255).*

Prince George Hobby Centre: If you are looking for artistic or hobby supplies, stop by the Prince George Hobby Centre in the Spruceland Mall. The store is always busy, the staff is extremely helpful, and the shelves are stocked with the most bewildering bits and pieces (plus an occasional model or two). *681 Central .*

ATTRACTIONS AND ACTIVITIES
Casual visitors to Prince George, particularly those who hole up downtown and don't venture around the place a bit, often wonder what local residents do for excitement. The answer is a bit complex, for there is actually a great deal to do in Prince George and the surrounding area — much of it outdoors. For visitors and residents alike, there is actually quite a bit going on in town.

Arts and Culture
Studio 2880: Theatre Northwest and Prince George Theatre Workshop stage a variety of excellent plays each year, and the Prince George Concert Association

sponsors numerous special musical performances. Studio 2880 sells tickets to these and other local cultural events (and for upcoming events in Vancouver), provides facilities for artistic groups, and is a wonderful place to make contact with local artists. *2880 - 15th Ave. (604/562-2880).*

Park Drive-In Theatre: This theatre (located on Chief Lake Road right next to the drag-strip, which makes for some interesting pre-movie sound effects) is a bit far out of town and offers the standard movies (several months after they play in town). Most important, the snack bar is well-stocked and the radio reception is very good. *9660 Raceway Rd. — off Chief Lake Rd. (604/967-4342).*

Prince George Art Gallery: The art gallery is in the process of constructing a new facility near the civic centre. In the meantime, the gallery is located in the Studio 2880 complex. *2880 - 15th Ave. (604/562-2880).*

Prince George Public Library: Prince George's first-rate library, located in the civic centre complex, has a reputation for excellent public service and a fine collection of books and other reading materials. *887 Dominion (604/563-9251). (Nechako branch is located at 7343 S. Kelly Rd.)*

Fraser Fort George Museum: Located in the Fort George Park, this museum provides a very good introduction to the natural and human history of the region. It is fairly small and will not take a big chunk out of your day. *333-20th Ave. (604/562-1612).*

Prince George Railway Museum: Railway buffs will be intrigued with the Prince George Railway Museum, which highlights several well-restored pieces of rail stock and has some informative displays on the impact of the railway on northern British Columbia. *850 River Rd (604/563-7351).*

Huble Farm: About 30 kilometres (19 miles) north of town is Huble Farm. This friendly and very accessible turn of the century operation, run by animators in period costume, has a number of interesting activities for children. For more information, contact the Regional District of Fraser-Fort George at *604/563-9225.*

Indoor Activities
Sprucelands Family Fun Centre: Arcades have a bad name, and often deservedly so. They tend to be teen hang-outs — the kind of places that parents want their children to avoid. Prince George's Sprucelands Family Fun Centre, behind the Spruceland Mall, is the complete opposite. It is big, well-run, clean, bright, friendly, and safe. They have dozens of arcade games and a full-size indoor miniature golf course. The place is set up for young children and families, and is quite inexpensive. *694 Ahbau (604/563-8180).*

Bubba Balloos: If you are travelling with young children, a new and wonderful attraction is Bubba Balloos — a well-controlled, bright, and very enjoyable indoor jungle gym. The place is extremely well-supervised and has a small food counter and gift shop, arcade, and oodles of fun for youngsters. *556 North Nechako Rd. (604/563-7529).*

Chalky's Billiards: The process of recapturing the old games and venues for common use is becoming a Prince George tradition. A new entry into the field is Chalky's Billiards, which is located across the street from the Holiday Inn. Chalky's has strict rules — no drinking, no drugs, no loitering, and no swearing —

that they enforce to ensure patrons have a good, clean, hassle-free time. Their effort is worth supporting, and it is nice to be able to play pool in such a setting. *511 George St. (604/564-1283).*

Bowling: There are three bowling alleys in town. The two five-pin alleys are **Nechako Bowling Lanes** *(1665-3rd Ave., 604/564-7315)* and **5th Avenue Bowladrome** *(1241-5th Ave., 604/997-4430).* **Strike Zone,** at *2366 Westwood Dr. (604/563-2695),* is a brand-new, state-of-the-art, computer-scoring, ten-pin bowling alley.

Bingo: Bingo is something else altogether. The game has caught on big-time in the North and is worth going to see — if only to catch something of the flavour of northern life. There are two large commercial bingo halls in town: **Goodtime Bingo** *(490 Vancouver, 604/561-0444)* and **Bonanza Bingo** *(1395-6th Ave., 604/564-7070).* Both are located in converted supermarkets. The setting is familiar — lots of cigarette smoke, bored callers, and slow-moving card sellers — but the ambiance is surprisingly active and friendly. It is quite delightful to watch the skilled bingo players handle 25 to 30 cards and, at the same time, keep up an uninterrupted conversation with neighbours. It is cheap entertainment — a few dollars will buy you a set of cards for the night.

Sports

Recreational Facilities: Prince George is famous throughout the province for its dedication to sports. The city produces champions and championship teams in many sports, from diving to skating and from minor football to high school volleyball. Not surprisingly, therefore, Prince George has excellent sports facilities (including the local YMCA on Massey Drive), dozens of leagues and teams, and a tremendous local following for sports activities. You can check out the track

The University of Northern British Columbia, opened in August 1994, sits on Cranbrook Hill overlooking Prince George. (Rob Melynchuk)

and field and spectator sports (soccer tournaments, football, and the like) at **Massey Stadium** *(across the street from the YMCA on Massey)*. Nearby, you'll find a set of baseball diamonds (the city has dozens of them) where, on most summer evenings, you'll come across a full slate of games. Junior soccer takes place on the **Rotary Park fields**, *at Ospika and 15th*. The **Prince George Golf and Country Club** — visitors welcome — is the best course in the city *(2515 Recreation Place, 604/563-0357)*. The club also has the city's curling rink and a good set of squash and racquetball courts. If you want something a little less crowded and less expensive, try out the **Aspen Grove Golf Course** south of town *(4555 Leno, 604/963-9650)*. The **Four Seasons Leisure Pool** *(700 Dominion St., 604/561-7636)* has length swimming, a diving tank, a wading pool, and a water slide.

Other Places of Interest

University of Northern British Columbia: Settled on top of Cranbrook Hill, the university is worth a visit. This is Canada's newest university and the first one built from the ground up in over 25 years. It is an architectural delight. Visitors often comment on the beautiful and practical structures, which were specially designed with northern winters in mind. All of the buildings are connected so that one can go from one to the other without going outside. This is not such a big deal in the summer, when people typically stroll across the roof, but it is greatly appreciated mid-winter, when temperatures can plunge to -30C (-22 F) or lower. Visit the library — truly the intellectual and spiritual heart of the campus — and then stop in the Northwood Winter Garden or in the cafeteria for something to eat and drink. Check out the conference centre and the sports facilities (small gym, squash courts, whirlpool, and jacuzzi) before you leave. *3333 University Way (604/960-5555).*

Pulp Mill Tours: Northern British Columbia's pulp mills get a lot of abuse, particularly from newcomers who turn their noses up at what locals call "the smell of money." Why not see for yourself? **Northwood** *(on the Fraser Flats, 604/962-9611)* and **Canadian Forest Products** *(2011 Pulpmill Rd., 604/563-0161)* both offer summertime guided tours of their facilities. The pulp mills — Prince George apparently produces more pulp and paper than any other community in the world — are marvels of modern technology and science and are well worth a visit. It is also good to see the other side of the on-going debate over the future of forestry in the province.

OUTDOOR RECREATION

The Prince George area is an outdoor-lover's Mecca. There are over 100 lakes within a fifty mile radius of the city. Some of these (West Lake, Ness Lake) are great for swimming and most offer good to excellent fishing. The tremendous number and variety of trails in the district range from peaceful walks in meadows or along river banks to challenging rock-climbing sites. (Stop at Mosquito Books and purchase a copy of the Caledonia Rambler's *Guide to Hiking Trails Around Prince George*.)

Skiing: In winter, the city offers easy access (two and one-half hours or less drive) to several superb ski hills, including **Purden** and **Tabor** to the east, **Powder King** to the north, and **Murray Ridge** near Fort St. James to the west. In town, there's the **Hart Highland Ski Centre** — a small, volunteer-run community facility that is a superb place for children. Follow the signs along the Hart Highway north of town. The **Otway Cross-Country Ski Centre**, one of the best in the province and the home base for the Provincial Cross-Country Skiing Development Team, is located about fifteen minutes out of town. This great ski area has numerous trails covering a varied terrain. Otway, which charges $5 for drop-in skiers, has a 1.5 kilometre (one mile) lit trail open in the evenings. Follow Otway Rd., off Foothills Bvld.

City Parks: Connaught Hill Park, located in the middle of the city, provides a panoramic view of the downtown core and the junction of the Fraser and Nechako Rivers. **Fort George Park**, situated along the Fraser River, has a bandstand (the Prince George Symphony's outdoor concerts are a great treat), a playground, and a model train ride. It is in a beautiful location and, in mid-summer when the flowers are in bloom, is a delightful picnic site. A picnic and stroll in the park combines well with a visit to the Fort George Museum. Access to the park is by way of 17th or 20th off Queensway. The approach to **Cottonwood Park** is

▲ *Prince George's Fort George Park, overlooking the Fraser River, includes picnic grounds, a museum and a steam-train ride. (Earl Brown)*

enough to deter all but the most determined, for it crosses the train tracks and passes through a large industrial area. But do persist, for the trails, which run along the banks of the Nechako, are very attractive, surprisingly secluded, and enjoyable. You can get to Cottonwood park off 1st Avenue. **Forests for the World**, a demonstration forest, located on Cranbrook Hill, provides a great hiking and jogging opportunity within a few minutes of downtown. Access is off Foothills Blvd., between 5th and 15th Ave. **Moore's Meadows**, one of the best walking parks in the city, is located off Foothills Blvd. north of 1st Ave.

Regional Parks: Wilkins Park, a great picnic site, is just north of the city near Miworth. **West Lake** is a little further away (west on Highway 16 and then south on

Blackwater Road), but offers great swimming and water sports. A bit down the road is the beginning of a hiking trail that will take you down to the Fraser River and, if you are persistent, to Fort George Canyon. About 25 kilometres (16 miles) out of town near Ness Lake, **Eskers Provincial Park** provides first-rate hiking trails, several excellent picnic spots, and a simply beautiful setting. It is well worth the drive.

Selected Events in the Prince George Area

The Prince George Citizen Iceman	*January*
Canadian Northern Children's Festival	*May*
Canada Day Celebrations	*July 1*
Prince George Air Show	*July*
Salmon Valley Country Music Festival	*July*
Prince George Exhibition	*August*
Sandblast *(skiing down sand hills)*	*August*
International Food Festival	*August*

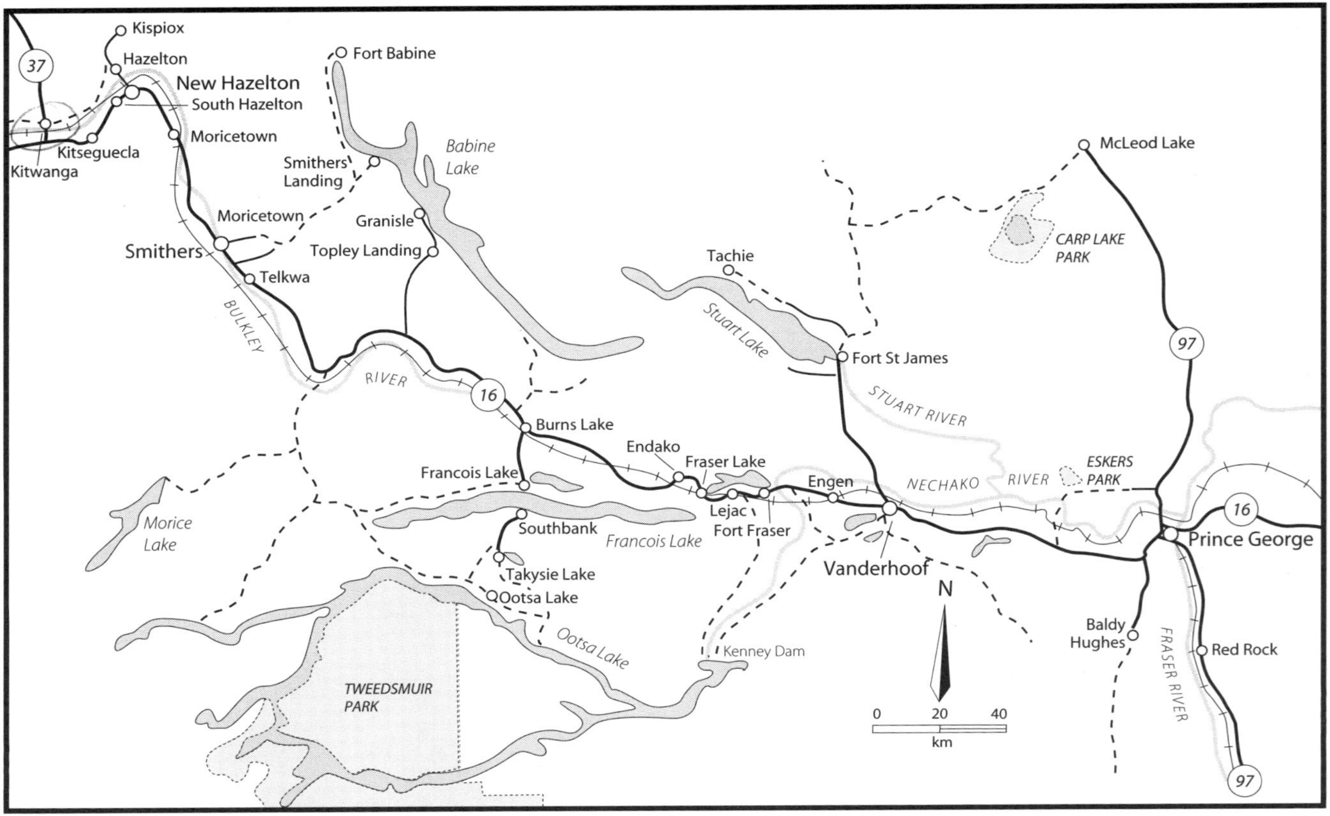

37
Kispiox
Hazelton
New Hazelton
South Hazelton
Moricetown
Kitseguecla
Kitwanga
Fort Babine
Babine Lake
Smithers Landing
Moricetown
Granisle
Topley Landing
Smithers
Telkwa
BULKLEY
RIVER
16
Burns Lake
Endako
Fraser Lake
Francois Lake
Lejac
Fort Fraser
Southbank
Francois Lake
Takysie Lake
Ootsa Lake
Ootsa Lake
Morice Lake
TWEEDSMUIR PARK
Kenney Dam
Tachie
Stuart Lake
Fort St James
STUART RIVER
Engen
Vanderhoof
NECHAKO
RIVER
ESKERS PARK
McLeod Lake
CARP LAKE PARK
97
16
Prince George
Baldy Hughes
FRASER RIVER
Red Rock
97
N
0
20
40
km

5

The Nechako and Bulkley Valleys

If there is one area in British Columbia that cannot be fully appreciated from the main highway, this is it. The area west of Prince George along Highway 16, stretching from the city boundaries to Kitwanga, is not one of instant, obvious charms. There are some beauty spots; the scenery around Smithers is among the very best in all of northern British Columbia. But, just a short distance off the main road, the real attractions of this corridor are found in towns like Granisle; the resorts of Babine, Stuart, Fraser, François, and other lakes; and exceptional campgrounds and scenic sites.

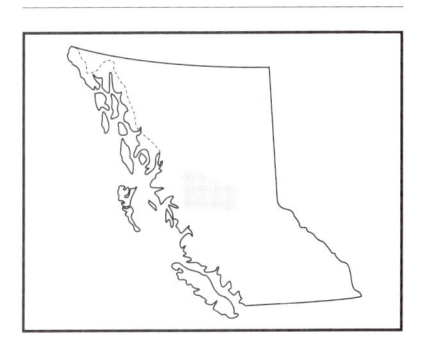

It is always depressing to watch tourists, by the hundreds, race through this part of northern British Columbia. They set pavement on fire to catch the ferry in Prince Rupert, to reach the Stewart-Cassiar road for the drive up to the Yukon and Alaska, or to head south from Prince George for southern and urban centres. The Vanderhoof-Bulkley Valley region epitomizes this area — a land visitors view almost exclusively from highway-bound vehicles. From this perspective, the area appears to offer little to those interested in staying longer. What a mistaken point of view! For the

Vanderhoof-Bulkley Valley region is home to some of Canada's best sports fishing, remarkable natural attractions, fascinating historic sites, interesting communities, and hundreds of recreational opportunities.

Why do people rush so quickly along Highway 16? The answer lies, in part, in the history of the area. This corridor owes its economic and social development to several major initiatives: the construction of the Grand Trunk Pacific Railway in the early twentieth century (now part of Canadian National Railways); the improvement of the highway system in the 1950s and 1960s; and, most significantly, the incredible resource boom of the post-war era. The latter initiative resulted in the opening of several large mines and the rapid expansion of forest operations in the district. This expansion occurred in an era before land-use planners. Initially, because towns emerged around the railway lines, commercial and industrial establishments were situated at the centre of town life. Then, in the post-war boom, highway strips were developed through the middle of most settlements, resulting in a rather unattractive visage, and major industrial plants received pride of place in regional development.

So, as you drive along Highway 16, you will pass through a series of towns — Vanderhoof, Burns Lake, Fraser Lake, Houston, Smithers, and the Hazeltons — that seem very much alike. Facing the highway will be the standard hotels, fast-food restaurants, gas stations, basic traveller's services, lumber yards, and a few remaining bee-hive burners. You will see — at least initially — little of historical and cultural interest, and, hoping that the next community will be a little more attractive, you will likely feel compelled to continue on your way. If there was a northern variant to that old adage "Don't judge a book by its cover," it would be this region

There is another side to these communities and to the region in which they are situated. Smithers is the best example; the magnificent Hudson Bay Mountain looms like a sentinel over the town. The physical setting of Smithers is so dramatic that you, like many travellers, will be drawn into the dynamic, attractive, and forward-looking community. Vanderhoof, similarly, presents a rather standard, even unattractive, image along the main drag — no reason to stop unless you are hungry for fast-food or need to top up your tank. But

The majestic Seven Sisters Mountains overlook the communities of Hazelton and New Hazelton.
(Myron Kozak)

off the highway, you find a 1950s kind of town, which is set along the Nechako River. While it's a shame that Vanderhoof, like most northern communities, has not capitalized on its beautiful location, the river provides a welcome contrast within the settlement. New Hazelton is a standard northern highway town. But only a short distance away, the original old river community of Hazelton, with many of its old buildings, provides a taste of life in by-gone days. And so it goes in Burns Lake (which is actually defined more by the lake to the south than the highway that cuts the town in half), Fraser Lake, and elsewhere.

The Vanderhoof-Bulkley Valley district is one of the most interesting areas in British Columbia for outdoor enthusiasts — particularly canoeists, sports fishers, boaters, and campers. Just a short trip off Highway 16 lie some of the most beautiful lakes in the province. These lakes abound with resorts, fishing camps, and rustic campgrounds. What's more, the area also contains first-rate attractions — from white water rafting to national historic sites, excellent accommodations, and several fine restaurants that are often in the most unexpected locations.

So, slow down a little, plan for a few days along Highway 16, and be prepared to be surprised. If you do nothing else, spend an extra night in Smithers — one of the great delights of northern British Columbia — where you will discover something totally unexpected about the quality, richness, and vitality of community life in this part of the world.

A Brief History

While northern British Columbia has a well-deserved reputation as the youngest, newest part of the province, it has a rich and ancient history. The First Nations have very deep historic roots in this area; the history of the newcomers pales in comparison to the thousands of years of First Nations occupation.

The roots of newcomer history in this region lie in the fur trade era. Simon Fraser, explorer of the river that now bears his name and one of the first Europeans to reach British Columbia, established a trading post at Fort St. James, on Stuart Lake. The trading post remained in operation until the early twentieth century. The Hudson's Bay Company, which merged with its rival the North West Company to dominate the northern fur trade, expanded operations in the region and eventually reached Hazelton, where a small post was opened. There was a small gold strike in the Omineca district north of Fort St. James in 1869-1871 (some miners still work the creeks in this district), and you can reach the Manson Creek and Germanson Landing areas by way of area logging roads. The miners had a much tougher route; they had to travel upriver to Hazelton, overland to Babine Lake, and on to the Omineca.

The coming of the railway sparked the next phase in the development of the Vanderhoof-Bulkley Valley region. Vanderhoof, like most of the communities along Highway 16, owes its origins as a settlement to the construction of the Grand Trunk Pacific. The railway attracted ranchers into the rich Nechako River valley. As the railway pushed westward, other settlements sprang up — Fraser Lake, Burns Lake, Telkwa, and Smithers — all dependent on the trains for their existence. The latter two communities tussled over the status as the railway division point, and Smither's victory ensured the town a more prosperous future. Smithers had the added benefit of having several mines on nearby Hudson Bay Mountain.

Through the 1920s and 1930s, the region lay in a quiescent state. Fur trading, railway operations, ranching and farming, and small, localized industry provided income to local residents. The outbreak of World War II brought major changes: the upgrading of regional trails and tracks into what eventually became the Yellowhead Highway (Highway 16) and renewed government interest in the northern half of the province. The post-war era saw the rapid expansion of the lumber industry and, as a direct consequence, the expansion of existing towns and the creation of new ones (like Houston, east of Smithers).

This period also saw the arrival of new resource frontiers. The construction of the Kenney Dam by Alcan diverted water from the Nechako River for the use of the Kitimat Works aluminum plant. Several mines, most notably the mine at Endako (near Fraser Lake) and at Granisle, were established. Granisle, a classic company town that faced total collapse when the mine closed a few years ago, has rebounded by repackaging itself as a retirement/recreational community. Houses and town lots are being offered at rock-bottom prices in an attempt to keep the settlement alive. To date, the effort appears to be working.

Northern British Columbia is on Canada's resource frontier, and the Nechako-Bulkley Valleys are among the richest of the areas in the province. It follows, then, that the settlements reflect the history of resource development — furs, fishing, agriculture, mining, hydroelectric development and forestry. And, over the past twenty years, tourism has emerged as one of the cornerstones of the regional economy. So, although this is still a rugged, largely undeveloped, and wide-open territory, there is a great deal to see and do.

Hints for the Traveller

And so, we invite you to spend some time in the diverse and fascinating Nechako and Bulkley River Valleys. The following hints will help you to capitalize on your time in the region:

➤ If you are at all interested in the outdoors and fishing, spend some time exploring the Stuart, Ootsa, Fraser, Babine, Takla, and François lakes. There are very good resorts on all of the lakes, and proprietors have excellent advice on how to make the most of your visit.

➤ Granisle, the former company town that is re-creating itself as a retirement/tourist centre, is worth visiting. If the mayor gets hold of you, you might well end up staying!

➤ If you have time, take in Ootsa Lake and Tweedsmuir Park by taking the circle route (not a paved road) from Burns Lake to Houston. The scenery is spectacular, and the people are very friendly. There are several excellent resorts in this area, and the fishing is superb.

➤ Don't just drive through Hazelton. Leave the main road, visit old-town Hazelton, and stop at the K'san National Historic Site. And do take the time to learn something about the First Nations in this area. The aboriginal peoples (the Gitksan-Wet'suwet'en) have been at the forefront of contemporary challenges over land rights and self-government. You will better understand why if you give yourself the time to absorb the beauty of both their culture and traditional lands.

➤ Plan to spend extra time in Smithers. This town is one of the absolute delights of northern British Columbia. The restaurants are first-rate, there is excellent shopping (particularly for items relevant to the area, such as sporting goods, books, and clothing), and the place has a special vitality that is seldom seen in small-town Canada. All of this, topped off with a spectacular location at the foot of Hudson Bay Mountain, makes Smithers an absolute gem. Even the A&W is not your average fast-food restaurant; it is well-deserving of all of the corporate and community awards it has posted on its walls.

▶ If you are not looking to rough it, but want a nice campsite by a lake with lots of things for the kids to do, there are plenty of campgrounds in this area. Tourist traffic is comparatively light during the summer, and the warm weather and long days (you are several hundred kilometres north of Vancouver and hence get more than one hour extra daylight during the summer) make for excellent camping. While there are lots of places to choose from, we recommend Tyee Lake (turn-off near Telkwa), Red Bluff on Babine Lake, and Paarens Beach/Sowchea near Fort St. James.

Exploring Aboriginal History

There are several sites in this district where the history of the northern First Nations can be explored in detail. The Kitwanga Fort National Historic Site and the settlements of Gitwangak, Kitwancool, Kitseguecla, and Kispiox all have buildings, totem poles, or historic markers which document the rich, vibrant aboriginal history of the Gitksan people. Cedarvale, west of the turn-off to Highway 37, is an old Anglican mission settlement — now all but abandoned. Moricetown is another interesting aboriginal site. Located between Smithers and New Hazelton, this prominent First Nations fishing site was named after the famed northern missionary Father A.G. Morice. The Native fishers

K'san National Park showcases the rich and vibrant cultures of the First Nations of the Hazelton area. (Myron Kozak)

here gaff salmon that head upstream in the summer; it is well worth seeing.

The best location, and one of the most intriguing in northern British Columbia, is the K'san National Historic Site at Hazelton. K'san is a reconstructed aboriginal village that consists of several long houses, a small museum/display area, and a retail store. Cultural presentations are scheduled during the tourist season. The combination of the cultural vitality of the place and its exquisite location make K'san an important stop. Similarly, Fort St. James (north of Vanderhoof on Highway 27) is home to the Fort St. James National Historic Site. Another Parks Canada attraction, this historic site, a reconstructed Hudson's Bay Company trading post (rebuilt to c. 1890), offers excellent insights into aboriginal and non-aboriginal life during the nineteenth century fur-trading era.

The Very Best of the Nechako-Bulkley Valleys

Like much of northern British Columbia, the land, rivers, and lakes of the Nechako-Bulkley Valleys are the main attractions. But the people, cultures, and communities of these valleys have a great deal to offer as well. Besides, if you are going to take our advice and move slowly through this district, you will need some places to stop, eat, and sleep. We've thrown in a few special attractions for you to consider as well. Travelling from east to west, we have divided the region into five sections: Vanderhoof/Fort St. James, Fort Fraser/ Fraser Lake/Endako, Burns Lake/Houston, Telkwa/ Smithers, and the Hazeltons.

Vanderhoof - Fort St. James

Vanderhoof, with a population of 4,000 people (12,000 including the surrounding area) is a small farming and logging community nestled along the Nechako River. Because of its proximity to Prince George, the shopping and services are perhaps more limited than you might expect in a town of this size. Vanderhoof is a very good jumping-off point to some of the many resorts and lodges in the lakes district.

Fort St. James, a small town of 2,000 people just north of Vanderhoof, gets relatively little attention. Built on the shores of beautiful Stuart Lake, this fascinating community offers access to excellent parks, swimming, and fishing. Buoyed by an active logging industry, Fort St. James is a busy place, and with the Fort St.

James National Historic Site in the middle of town, the settlement is also beginning to develop as a tourist centre. The emphasis, however, remains on serving the many hunters and fishers who travel into this region every year.

PLACES TO EAT
Tachick Lodge and Saddle Bar Lounge: *($$$)* This ★ lovely gourmet restaurant serves a variety of steak, schnitzel, pasta and seafood entrees. All are served with a large variety of delicious vegetables and potatoes. The food is mouth-watering; every morsel is cooked to perfection. There is a particularly interesting element to the décor: the bar stools are saddles. Open from April to December on Friday, Saturday, and Sunday evenings. *Located 22 kilometres (14 miles) down the Kenney Lake Road south of Vanderhoof (604/567-4929).*

O.K. Café: *($)* The O.K. Café is in a remodelled general store — one of several Vanderhoof buildings that are being restored as a heritage park. Excellent lunches are served by waiters and waitresses dressed in period costume. Open in the summer only. *On Highway 16 in Vanderhoof (604/567-2594).*

North Country Inn: *($$)* Specializing in German/Canadian food, this downtown Vanderhoof restaurant is well-regarded locally for its friendly service and generous portions. *2625 Burrard (604/567-3048).*

Sandy's Cappuccino: *($)* For a quick snack in Fort St. ★ James, try Sandy's Cappuccino, which serves light meals and fine coffees *(604/996-8228).*

Whiskey Jack Restaurant: *($$)* The food at this restaurant, which is located just north of Fort. St. James, is good, the service is excellent, and the off-the-beaten track location adds to the appeal. Located on North Road — take the highway north toward Germanson Landing *(604/996-8828)*.

PLACES TO STAY
Tachick Lodge: *($)* This quiet, rural resort, complete with the previously-mentioned gourmet dining room, offers inexpensive and rustic lakeside accommodations. *Located south of Vanderhoof on the Kenney Dam Road, Box 1112, Vanderhoof, B.C. V0J 3A0 (604/567-4929).*

Stuart Lodge: *($$)* If you would rather be on a large lake (and close to town facilities), try the Stuart Lodge near Fort St. James. The setting is spectacular, outdoor activities are at your doorstep, and the facilities are very comfortable. *Stones Bay Rd., Box 838, Fort St. James, B.C. V0J 1P0 (604/996-7917).*

Amblewood Bay Bed & Breakfast: *($$)* There are not many beds and breakfasts in this area, but one choice is the Ablewood Bay Bed and Breakfast in Fort St. James. *Kring Rd., Box 1493, Fort St. James, B.C. V0J 1P0 (604/996-7922).*

Campgrounds: The many campgrounds in the Vanderhoof-Fort St. James district range from excellent government campgrounds to rustic forestry sites. Two of the most popular in the region are **Paarens Beach Provincial Park** and **Sowchea Bay Provincial Park**. Both are near Fort St. James and offer excellent swimming, easy access to town, and first-rate fishing.

Fishing and Hunting Lodges: The many fishing and hunting lodges in this area vary widely in price and facilities. Several places worth considering are **Douglas Lodge** *($$, Stones Bay Rd., Box 1030, Fort St. James, B.C. V0J 1P0, 604/996-7080, fax: 604/996-*

7079), **Nechako Lodge** *($$)* on Knewstubb Lake — 100 kilometres (63 miles) south of Vanderhoof on the Kenny Dam Road *(c/o Box 2413, Vanderhoof, B.C. V0J 3A0, 604/690-7740)*, and **Nakalat Lodge** *($$)* on the North Arm of Stuart Lake *(P.O. Box 549, Fort St. James, B.C. V0J 1P0, 604/565-0455)*.

THINGS TO DO

In and around the communities, there several unusual sites, attractions, and opportunities. If you are a golfer, try the **Stuart Lake Golf Course** in Fort St. James.

Yinka Dene Language Institute: This institute was established to preserve the Carrier languages, and staff are actively involved in developing curriculum materials and in training language teachers. You can visit the Language Institute in the *College of New Caledonia Building, 3231 Hospital Rd. (604/567-9236)*.

Reade Antiques and Fine Collectibles: This Vanderhoof store offers visitors a chance to sample the flavour of the old North. *3520 Ericson.*

Fort St. James National Historic Site: The finest attraction in the area, this reconstructed Hudson's Bay Company trading post offers restored buildings, historical interpretations, and a glimpse of northern life from a century ago. *Box 1145, Fort St. James, B.C. V0J 1P0 (604/996-7191).*

OUTDOOR RECREATION

Like much of this region, the Vanderhoof/Fort St. James district is known primarily for its outdoor activities, particularly fishing and hunting. While in Fort St. James, don't forget the many charms of Stuart Lake (including excellent swimming and great fishing), the nice summer-time hike to the top of **Mount Pope**, and, in winter, the **Murray Ridge Ski Hill**.

Rich Hobson Frontier Cattle Drive Society: Although the ranching industry is much smaller than in the Cariboo-Chilcotin, there is some activity in the region. Contact this society if you are interested in the cattle driving experience. *2685 Church St., Box 2552, Vanderhoof, B.C., V0J 3A0 (604/567-4664).*

Fort Fraser - Fraser Lake - Endako

Fort Fraser and Fraser Lake, with populations of 600 and 1400 respectively, and Endako, a small highway settlement, are located approximately 160 kilometres (100 miles) west of Prince George on Highway 16. The two major employers in the area are Fraser Lake Sawmills and Endako Mines. Logging, lumber manufacturing, ranching, and tourism are the major industries. This area is, and has long been, home to the Carrier Indian people. Trumpeter Swans use the area between Stellako River and Fraser Lake as a nesting area. The bridge west of Fraser Lake provides a great spot to watch these magnificent birds.

PLACES TO EAT

★ **Stellako Lodge and Resort:** *($$$)* The small, wonderful restaurant at Stellako Lodge and Resort offers diners delicious food and friendly service. The menu is limited, but since each item sounds so good, it is still difficult to decide! *Located about 10 kilometres (six miles) south of Highway 16 on the east end of François Lake, near Fraser Lake (604/699-6695).*

Wagon Wheel Inn: *($)* This small establishment on the highway between Vanderhoof and Fraser Lake serves yummy hamburgers *(604/576-5422).*

PLACES TO STAY

Resorts and Lodges: Like in the Cariboo-Chilcotin, resorts and lodges vary from impressive resorts like the

Stellako Lodge to very basic lodges providing unserviced cabins and rustic facilities. Your choice will depend on your pocketbook and on your particular outdoor interest. If you are interested in fishing or in an off-the-highway retreat, the **Stellako Lodge and Resort** *($$)* is a lovely spot with excellent fly fishing nearby *(Box 400, Fraser Lake, B.C. V0J 1S0, 604/699-6695)*. Other suggestions are the **Birch Bay Resort** *(Box 484, Fraser Lake, B.C. V0J 1S0, Radiophone: N698462 Vanderhoof YP)* and the **Francois Lake Resort** *(Box 389, Fraser Lake, B.C. V0J 1S0, 604/699-6551)*.

THINGS TO DO
Forget-Me-Knots Antiques: As well as some wonderful antiques, this Endako store carries locally-produced crafts and is a local gathering spot for coffee and conversation. *On Highway 16 in Endako.*

Molyhills Golf Course: MolyHills Golf Course on François Lake Road and near Fraser Lake is a nice golf course *(604/699-7761)*.

Burns Lake - Houston

Burns Lake, which has a population of approximately 2,300 people, is the main service centre for the entire Lakes District — which encompasses more than 300 fishing lakes and about 10,000 people. Forestry (Babine Forest Products and Decker Lake Forest Products), ranching, and tourism are the main industries of this area. The major farm products are hay and beef.

Houston, an active, new industrial town that is based on the region's strong lumbering industry, has a population of 4,000. The town's most distinctive feature, the world's largest fly fishing rod, is located by the Tourist InfoCentre on Highway 16. Houston is a good base for camping and outdoor activities in the Babine Lake Region.

Granisle, about 50 kilometres (31 miles) north of Highway 16 between Burns Lake and Houston, a once-vibrant mining community, fell on hard times when the mine closed and now has a population of 600 people. The residents who remained after the closure have been promoting their town as a recreational and retirement community. The effort has been working, and you'll find few Canadian communities with this much civic spirit.

PLACES TO EAT
Mulvaney's Pub: *($$)* This little pub serves generous portions of terrific food. Offerings include burgers, sandwiches, soups, and salads. *Located on Highway 16 across from the mall on the east side of Burns Lake (604/692-3078).*

Alberto's Pizza: *($)* This restaurant offers good pizza, pizza subs, salads, fries, and burgers. *Located on Highway 16 in downtown Burn's Lake (604/692-7707).*

PLACES TO STAY
House Erica Bed & Breakfast. *($$)* This bed and breakfast, located between Fraser Lake and Burns Lake, offers clean rooms, a sauna and fitness gym, and a delicious European-style breakfast. A creek runs through the property and there are great opportunities to walk and explore nearby. *Box 1264, Burns Lake, B.C. V0J 1E0 (604/699-8507).*

Grande Isles Resort: *($$)* A major part of the town's effort to transform itself into a recreational centre, this is the best place to stay in Granisle. *Hagen St., Box 130, Granisle, B.C. V0J 1W0 (1-800/661-6577).*

Other Resorts and Lodges: The many other resorts and lodges in this area include the following:

Campbell's Babine Lodge at Topley Landing via Highway 108. *Box 9, SS1, Topley Landing, B.C. V0J 1W0 (604/697-2310).*

Stoker's Wilderness Guest Ranch, *Brown Rd., RR #2, Burns Lake, B.C. V0J 1E0 (604/695-6640).*

Beaver Point Resort on Tchesinkut Lake, 16 kilometres south of Burns Lake. *Box 587, Burns Lake, B.C. V0J 1E0 (604/698-6519).*

THINGS TO DO
Shopping: There is a nice fudge shop in Houston; look for it on the south side of the highway.

The Endako Hotel: Located on Highway 16, this hotel is a fascinating, throw-back kind of place. Stop in for a drink! *(604/699-8006).*

Carnoustie Golf and Country Club: This golf course is located 16 kilometres (10 miles) west of Burns Lake off Highway 16 at Deck Lake *(604/698-7677).*

OUTDOOR RECREATION
Tweedsmuir Provincial Park: One of the most fascinating hiking and camping areas in all of British Columbia, this provincial park can be reached via Burns Lake. ★

Once rivals, Smithers and Telkwa, with populations of 5,000 and close to 1,000 people respectively are known for their artistic activity, community spirit, cultural events, and commitment to the environment. The

Telkwa - Smithers

district promotes itself, with good reason, as a four season wonderland. Ski Smithers, on Hudson Bay Mountain, offers wonderful winter skiing; there are many lakes and rivers with excellent fishing; and hunting is first-rate. The Bulkley Valley setting is spectacular, and the people in this area are proud of their communities.

PLACES TO EAT

★ **The Little Onion:** *($$)* Located along Smither's main street, the Little Onion offers travelers a fine dining experience. Dishes are carefully crafted, and special attention is given to spices and cheeses. Daily specials supplement an already interesting menu. The focaccia bread — which comes with your meal — is superb. *1089 Main St. (604/847-6121).*

★ **Java's:** *($$)* The cappuccino revolution continues and flourishes in this fine Smithers institution. Java's also has muffins, salads, and extra-special deserts. They occasionally bring in musicians to provide evening entertainment. *3735 Alfred Ave. (604/847-5505).*

Anabelle's Garden: *($$)* This Filipino restaurant, located in Smithers, offers a variety of fish, steak, and Chinese dishes. Their specialty, Laga Laga, is a Filipino fondue featuring various fishes, seafood, and meats (your choice). *1-3830 2nd Ave. (604/847-4703).*

A&W Family Restaurant Smithers: *($)* We have steadfastly avoided fast-food restaurants in this guidebook, but we have to make one exception. The Smithers A & W, located along Highway 16, is superb. The interior décor is surprisingly warm and friendly and not fast-food sterile. The place is first-rate, clean, and comfortable. The restaurant has all sorts of awards tacked up on the walls, and it is easy to see why. *4086 5th Ave. (604/847-3700).*

Fourth Street Deli: *($$)* One of Telkwa's highlights, this sprightly little lunch and dinner spot features excellent meals and a warm atmosphere. *4th St. (604/846-9268).*

Picco Bello Trattoria: *($)* Located a few doors down from the Fourth Street Deli in Telkwa, this pizzeria serves tasty pizza and other dishes. *1630 4th St. (604/846-9866).*

PLACES TO STAY

Hudson's Bay Lodge: *($$)* A large complex on the east end of town, the Hudson's Bay Lodge is one of the most popular spots in Smithers. The lodge is especially set up for the many skiers who descend on the place in the winter and offers good year-round accommodations. *3251 E. Highway 16, Smithers, B.C. V0J 2N0 (604/847-4581; fax: 604/847-4878).*

Lakeside Gallery and Bed & Breakfast: *($$)* This bed and breakfast is scenically located a few kilometres west of Smithers on Lake Kathlyn *(two kilometres/1.2 miles west of the Smithers airport on the Hetherington Rd.). Smithers, B.C. V0J 2N0 (604/847-9174).*

The Stork Nest Inn: *($$)* The Stork Nest Inn in Smithers is a new European-style motel which offers free country-style breakfasts. *1485 Main St. Smithers, B.C. V0J 2N0 (604/847-3831).*

Driftwood Lodge: *($$$)* One of the most attractive rural accommodations in this area, Driftwood Lodge is located twelve kilometres (eight miles) outside of Smithers on the Babine Lake Road. This bed and breakfast offers hiking trails, a hot tub, and great views of the valley. *RR #2, S53, C11, Smithers, B.C. V0J 2N0 (604/847-5016).*

Tukki Lake Lodge: *($$)* For more rustic accommodations with excellent outdoor activities, you might try the Tukii Lake Lodge, which is located on Babine Lake at Smithers Landing. *Box 3693, Smithers, B.C. V0J 2N0 (604/847-8122).*

Douglas Motel: *($$)* In Telkwa, the place to stay is the Douglas Motel — a quiet and cosy spot just off the highway and facing the Bulkley River. *P.O. Box 291, Telkwa, B.C. V0J 2X0 (604/846-5679).*

Campgrounds: Campsites are available at various locations in and around Smithers: a private campground east of town along the highway, a municipal campground along the river, and **Driftwood Provincial Park**, which is located a few kilometres outside of town.

THINGS TO DO

Bookstores: Check out the two bookstores in Smithers: **Mountain Eagle Books** at *1237 Main St.* and **Interior Stationery** at *1156 Main St.*

Juniper Berry Pottery Studio: This Smithers store offers locally-produced crafts. *1215 Main St.*

Horsfield's Leather: This special store is located in Telkwa's old Hong Chong's Laundry and Bath House building (c. 1920) in downtown Telkwa. Don Horsfield is a superb craftsperson, whose specialty leather products include fishing rod cases, reel cases, saddles, gun cases, and handbags. Such rare old-world talent is worth a long look.

Nature's Pantry: Nature's Pantry, a health food store, is located at *3827 Broadway Ave.* in Smithers.

Ragamuffin Deli: This Smithers delicatessen offers friendly service and inexpensive food. *1065 Main St.*

Bakeries: Paul's Bakery *(3840 Broadway Ave.)* and Schimmel's Fine Pastries *(1172 Main Street)*, both located in Smithers, are good places to stock up on fresh bread and pastries.

Museums and Galleries: The **Bulkley Valley Museum** and the **Smithers Art Gallery** are both located in the middle of Smithers (off Highway 16). *1425 Main (604/847-5322).* **Adam's Igloo,** a taxidermy museum, features the wildlife of northern British Columbia and provides an excellent introduction to the diverse and fascinating fauna of the area. Located west of Smithers on Highway 16 *(604/847-3188).*

Smithers Folk Festival: This delightful annual festival offers visitors first-class entertainment, local talent, and a small-town feeling. It takes place on a weekend in mid-June at the Bulkley Valley exhibition grounds.

Historical Buildings: Telkwa is worth a visit on its own. Once a rival to Smithers for regional prominence, this turn-of-the-century town faded but refused to die. Many of the old buildings have survived and have commemorative plaques; it makes for an interesting and informative walking tour.

OUTDOOR RECREATION
Smithers sits in the middle of a wilderness paradise. The town is nestled at the foot of **Hudson Bay Mountain** — home of the **Ski Smithers** facility. Conditions are usually excellent, and the town does not have the extremely cold winter temperatures that often bedevil skiers in other areas of the North. There are numerous fishing resorts and lakes in the district and endless opportunities for hiking (ask for directions to **Hudson**

★

Bay Glacier and Twin Falls, both recommended), canoeing, and wilderness camping.

★ **Suskwa White Water Rafting:** If you want something unique, consider a white water rafting trip. Suskwa White Water Rafting offers an excellent set of options: a one day float down the Suskwa for those wanting a short but exhilarating trip and longer trips along the Babine River for the more adventurous. The guides are extremely helpful and safety-conscious, and the settings are spectacular. *Box 3262, Smithers. B.C. V0J 2N0 (604/847-2885).*

Moricetown

Located between Smithers and Hazelton, Moricetown, with a population of 700 people, sits in a picture-book setting. The town's greatest feature is the Moricetown canyon. Moricetown is an historic aboriginal fishing place, and local Natives, using spears and nets to catch salmon, work the river each summer. Non-aboriginal fishers are not permitted to fish in or near the canyon. There is an excellent lookout just off the highway that provides a great view of the fishing activities.

The Hazeltons

The Hazelton area, with a population of 1,300 people, is both a surprise and a delight. As you come along the highway, you will think this is simply another highway service town, complete with roadside hotels, a few cafés, and a couple of gas stations. You'll have to look more closely, for there are actually three towns: New Hazelton (along the highway), South Hazelton (west of New Hazelton and off the main road), and Old Hazelton (north of the highway).

PLACES TO EAT

Hummingbird Café: *($$)* This restaurant is the best place to eat in the Hazeltons; it has good food and a million-dollar view. Because it on the road toward Old Hazelton, most highway travellers don't even know what they've missed. The menu includes a wide variety of salads, soups, sandwiches, and special entrées. *2710 Highway 62 (604/842-5628).*

Hazelton's Deli: *($)* This New Hazelton restaurant specializes in pizza and frozen yoghurt and also sells pasta and sandwiches. *4361 10th Ave. (604/842-5622).*

PLACES TO STAY

28 Inn: *($)* The newest place in town, the 28 Inn offers good, clean rooms at reasonable prices. Ask for a room in the new building, not in the annex across the street. *4545 Yellowhead Highway, c/o Box 358, New Hazelton, B.C. V0J 2J0 (604/842-6006).*

Resorts: There are several small resorts in the Kispiox Valley, a particularly excellent fishing spot, that are only a short drive north of Hazelton. One place worth considering is the **Sportsman Kispiox Lodge** *($$, RR #1, Box 1, Site M, Hazelton, B.C. V0J 1Y0, 604/842-6455)*, which offers rooms, home cooked meals, fishing guides and advice, rafting and canoeing, and lots of local lore and information. Also worthy of note is **Kispiox Steelhead Camp** *($$, R.R. #1, Hazelton, B.C. V0J 1Y0, 604/842-5435).*

THINGS TO DO

R.A.S. Fine Arts: If you are interested in contemporary aboriginal art, R.A.S. Fine Arts is located in a log building along Highway 16 in New Hazelton. The store highlights the work of Ron Sebastian, a well-regarded local carver and artist. *3379 Fielding.*

Kermode Trading Post: This brightly-coloured store, located on the road to Old Hazelton, sells local arts and crafts. *Highway 62, Two Mile.*

★ **K'san Village:** The K'san Village is a reconstructed First Nations settlement and a National Historic Site that includes a museum/display area, a well-stocked craft store, totem poles, long houses, an artists' studio, and cultural presentations (including potlatches). K'san is a true delight and should not be missed, for it provides an excellent glimpse into traditional aboriginal life and culture. Hazelton is one of the country's best places to view totem poles; you could not find a much more spectacular setting to see these wonderful works of aboriginal art. *Highway 62, Hazelton (604/ 842-5544).*

Old Hazelton: On the way to Old Hazelton, you cross over a single-lane bridge that is a sight to behold; the setting — over a steep gorge — is breath-taking. Old Hazelton provides another surprise. A survivor of the riverboat days (there is even an old riverboat at the foot of one of the town's main streets), Old Hazelton is quaint and interesting.

OUTDOOR RECREATION

The Nechako and Bulkley Valleys, together with the surrounding lakes districts, are of particular interest to outdoor enthusiasts. Fishing, hiking, camping, boating, and hunting opportunities abound. But travellers should remember that the same resorts, lakeside cabins, and rustic camps built primarily for fishers and hunters make excellent retreats for those wishing to get away from the hustle and bustle of the city and from the more active pace of the highway communities. The settings — from Stuart to François Lake, and from Granisle to Tweedsmuir Park — are sensational, and there are plenty of accommodation options available.

Selected Events in the Nechako and Bulkley Valleys

Pleasant Valley Days	Houston	May
Burns Lake Rodeo	Burns Lake	June
Smithers Rodeo	Smithers	June
Kispiox Rodeo	Kispiox	June
Smithers Folk Festival	Smithers	June
Mid-Summer Festival	Smithers	June
Bluegrass & Country Music Festival	Burns Lake	July
Moose Mountain Days	Fraser Lake	July 1st weekend
Lakes District Fall Fair	Francois Lake	August
Pioneer Days	Hazelton	August
Al Baxter Memorial Rodeo	Fort St. James	August
Rich Hobson Cattle Drive	Vanderhoof	August
Bulkley Valley Exhibition	Smithers	August
Telkwa Barbecue	Telkwa	September
Skeena Valley Fall Fair	Terrace	September

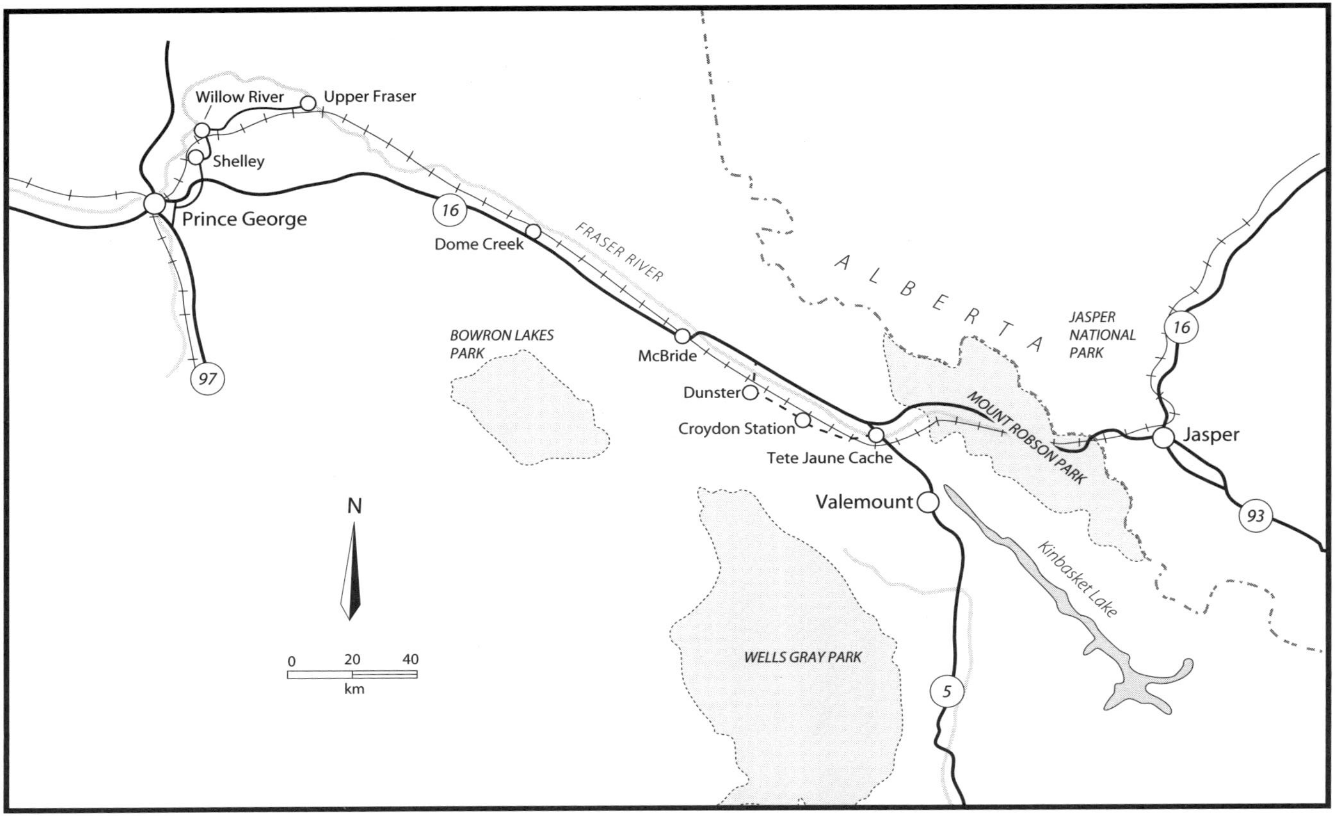
Willow River
Upper Fraser
Shelley
Prince George
16
97
Dome Creek
FRASER RIVER
BOWRON LAKES PARK
McBride
Dunster
Croydon Station
Tete Jaune Cache
Valemount
A L B E R T A
JASPER NATIONAL PARK
16
Jasper
MOUNT ROBSON PARK
93
Kinbasket Lake
WELLS GRAY PARK
5
N
0
20
40
km

6

The Robson Valley

Northern British Columbia, a land of untapped beauty and opportunity, has within it one area that, rather remarkably, has largely escaped the attention of travellers. The Robson Valley — a large expanse in the east-central interior — consists of three main points: McBride, Valemount, and Mount Robson Provincial Park. This area's physical grandeur and dazzling array of recreational opportunities should entice travellers by the thousands. To date, however, the Robson Valley remains relatively undeveloped and substantially unknown. It is one of British Columbia's great remaining mysteries and most wonderful discoveries.

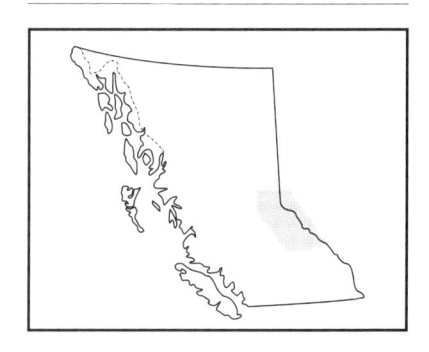

Three mountain ranges converge at Valemount-McBride. To the east lie the Rocky Mountains of Banff and Jasper National Park fame. On the eastern fringe rises the mighty, majestic, and dazzling Mount Robson — the highest mountain in the Rockies and one of the most stunning land forms in all of Canada. On a clear day, the mountain seems to take over the sky and to dwarf all that lies in its shadow. But the mountain is even more fascinating on cloudy or stormy days; because Mount Robson is large enough to create its

▲ *Rafters enjoy a clear view of Mount Robson, the highest peak in the Canadian Rockies. (Cheryl Livingstone - Leman)*

own weather patterns, it can be aswirl in storm clouds and blustery winds.

The southern boundary of the Robson Valley is formed by the northern end of the Monashee Mountains — the final extension of a range that reaches south to the British Columbia-Washington border. And, finally, along the western flank of the valley rest the distinctive Cariboo Mountains — somewhat lower in elevation than the Rockies, but no less dramatic or interesting.

The broad Robson Valley, part of the Rocky Mountain Trench, runs between the Rocky and Cariboo Mountain ranges. McBride and Valemount sit in the middle of a sizeable valley that measures about five kilometres (three miles) east to west and 240 kilometres (150 miles) north to south. The approach to

Mount Robson, in contrast, is by way of a much narrower passage which follows the headwaters of the mighty and historic Fraser River. The combination of striking, high mountains and a vast valley plain has created a recreational paradise. The valley and surrounding mountainsides offer high-quality skiing, snowmobiling, hunting, fishing, camping, hiking, river boating, wildlife viewing, mountaineering, and wilderness adventure.

The secret to the Robson Valley's relative anonymity — rest assured that local tourist operators and associations are doing their very best to publicize and promote the many attractions in the region — lies in the greater fame of the surrounding areas. Jasper is only an hour drive from Valemount and an hour and a half from McBride. Wells Gray Provincial Park is a scant two hour drive to the south. And the justly-famed Banff-Jasper Parkway, a wide, well-serviced highway that cuts through the middle of the Rocky Mountains, entices travellers away from the Valemount-Kamloops corridor.

This combination of location and travel habits has had a notable impact on the Robson Valley's tourist offerings. The valley serves primarily as a passage way for travellers heading from Edmonton and Jasper to Kamloops, Prince George, and Vancouver. As a result, the local tourist industry has concentrated on offering casual visitors low-price hotels, tourist cafés, short-stay campgrounds, and gas stations. There are no great destination resorts in the area, but there are preliminary plans afoot for a Whistler- or Banff-style development. Travellers should enjoy this state of affairs while it lasts, for it offers them a chance to avoid the crowds, get to know the locals, experience the wilderness on a more personal level, and be in the vanguard of the discovery of a new tourist region.

There are only a few villages in the Robson Valley and few signs of major development in the near future. Logging is the primary industry, although tourism is catching up rapidly. Located at the base of Canoe Mountain, Valemount with a permanent population of around 4,025 and an area population of 12,000, is the largest centre. McBride, about 100 kilometres (63 miles) away, has a population of about 620 people. Tete Jeune Cache, at the junction of Highways 16 and 5, and the Mount Robson area each has only a handful of residents.

Services in Valemount and McBride are targeted at local residents rather than visitors and are relatively basic. Locals travel to Jasper for their movies and to Prince George or Kamloops for major shopping trips. Valemount is the more active of the communities. When we camped in town in August, we were astonished by the level of activity. Through the evening and early morning, our campsite (too near to the highway, we discovered) was inundated by the noise of cars, trucks (lots of trucks), several trains, a low-flying airplane, and, to top things off, a helicopter. McBride, whose economy is based on logging, farming, and ranching, is more relaxed and low-key; there is much less bustle and activity on the streets.

The Robson Valley adds up to more than the sum of its largest centres. Small hamlets — Dunster, Crescent Spur, Dome Creek, Tete Jeune Cache, and Mount Robson — are also a focus for community activities and events. You will find more activities going on here than you might expect — from local access television to a vibrant artistic community and from political activities to environmental movements.

A Brief History

The first non-Natives to explore the Robson Valley were associated with the early western fur trade. The trade made only a few inroads and did not produce any substantial trading posts. Miners, drawn north by the discovery of gold in the British Columbia interior, likewise scoured the area, but to little avail.

The first major development occurred in the early years of this century, when construction of the Grand Trunk Pacific (eventually the Canadian National Railway) brought hundreds of workers into the region. Tête Jaune Cache, a major shipping and supply centre, grew to a population of several thousand, but the population collapsed after the construction boom ended. A handful of settlers came in the wake of the railway, but not enough to create large communities or to attract a great deal of external attention. The town site of McBride, established in 1913, was named after then-premier Sir Richard McBride (anachronistically-known as "The People's Dick").

1913 also saw the creation of Mount Robson Provincial Park, the second provincial park in British Columbia. This large park (almost 220,000 hectares - 550,000 acres), which includes a number of high alpine meadows and lakes, is dominated by the majestic Mount Robson 3,954 metres high (almost 13,000 feet high). Many years would pass before the wisdom of the British Columbia government in establishing the park would become evident, but visitors to Mount Robson have good reason to be thankful for their foresight.

After World War II, a rapidly expanding lumber industry brought more people into the valley, particularly to McBride and Valemount, who provided greater stability to the local economy. More recently, the region has become a focal point for wilderness-related activities; it is one of the continent's more important heli-skiing centres, a major snowmobiling site, and a highly-prized area for camping, mountaineering, hiking, wilderness photography, fishing, and hunting.

Getting There

The Yellowhead Highway (Highway 16 in British Columbia) provides access to the Robson Valley from Jasper and points east. It is an easy and beautiful drive over from Jasper; the road is well-maintained, and traffic is relatively light (particularly when compared to the busy Banff-Jasper Parkway).

Highway 16 also connects the region to Prince George which is a long 300 kilometres (188 miles) away; there are very few services in the intervening area, and the beauty of the countryside is scarred by some ill-advised clear-cut logging right along the highway. The length and nature of the drive has served as a major (and unfortunate) deterrent for residents from the Prince George area, only a small number of whom have discovered the many opportunities that lie a few hours to the east.

Southern access is provided by Highway 5, which joins the Robson Valley with Kamloops and points south. (Kamloops is located at the northern end of the Coquihalla Highway, which provides expressway access to the lower mainland and the Okanagan.) The drive to Kamloops is relatively long — four hours and close to 400 kilometres (250 miles) — but the scenery is diverse and there are numerous interesting side attractions along the way (including the scenic Wells Gray Provincial Park).

There is, of course, bus service from the east, west, and south. Bus travellers should contact Greyhound for information on routes, fares, and times. In terms of air service, there are, at present, no regularly-scheduled flights into the Robson Valley — another sure deterrent for the modern time-pressed traveller — although there are landing strips in the main communities.

The Very Best of the Robson Valley

McBride

The community of McBride, with a population of approximately 620 people, is located on the Yellowhead Highway about 225 kilometres (140 miles) east of Prince George. Both agriculture and forestry play dominant roles in McBride. The community provides services to numerous beef, sheep, dairy, hog, and field crop producers. It is home to one major forestry company and several smaller ones. While the community is not particularly striking at first glance, the surrounding scenery is spectacular, and the people are friendly. There is good cross-country skiing and snowmobiling in the winter and hiking, fishing, mountain biking, bird-watching, and golfing in the summer.

PLACES TO EAT

Powerhouse Pub: *($$)* Located on the western outskirts of town beside a ball diamond, the Powerhouse Pub is the best place to eat in McBride. It is clean and friendly and the burgers, sandwiches, soups, snacks, and salads are all delicious. If you are travelling with children, there is an outside seating area, complete with a fooz-ball game, where minors can be served. Watching the locals play baseball while you eat supper is an additional bit of fun. *600 First Ave. (604/569-2504).*

Valley Bread Basket Bakery and Deli: *($)* Once you drive under the "Welcome to McBride" sign, this small bakery is located along Main Street on your left-hand side. Yummy breads, rolls, and goodies await you here.

PLACES TO STAY

★ **Wildeman Lodge Bed & Breakfast:** *($$)* McBride has a number of easily-found motels, but our strong recommendation is the Wildeman Lodge Bed and Breakfast. The Wildeman Lodge, a spacious cedar home beside a winding mountain stream, is set on a 108 acre property. The house is beautifully decorated, and the six guest rooms are warm and inviting. Five of these rooms share washrooms across the hall. The sixth room, at a slightly higher rate, has an ensuite washroom. Dinners, lunches, or packed lunches can all be ordered if you wish. Your hosts, Paul and Tammy Wildeman, are friendly and interesting and work hard to make your stay enjoyable. Ask them for advice on what to see and do in the area. The Wildeman Lodge is located about six kilometres (four miles) outside of McBride. From Highway 16, turn onto McBride's Main Street and continue driving until you come to Eddy Road (2nd Ave.). Turn left and travel five kilometres (three miles), cross over the railway line, dip down to Hankins Creek, and turn into the lodge opposite the old wooden railway trestle. *3545 Eddy Rd., c/o Box 124, McBride, B.C. V0J 2E0 (604/569-2529).*

Campgrounds: For those of you who are interested in camping, there really isn't anything close to McBride. The closest places are **Purden Lake Provincial Park**, 60 kilometres (38 miles) east of Prince George, or the campgrounds listed in the Mount Robson and Valemount sections of this chapter.

Dunster

Dunster is a tiny community located east of McBride and about five kilometres (three miles) off Highway 16. If you have the time, it is worth taking a little detour and exploring the back roads of this area. The **Dunster Elementary School**, with its tiny hockey rink, and **Hill's General Store** both warrant a look. Dunster hosts a farmer's market in August and September and is rumoured to host an ice cream festival sometime in the summer. About 13 kilometres (eight miles) along the Dunster-Croydon-Tête Jaune Cache back road is

◄

Glaciers and wildflowers await those who choose to hike into the alpine areas.
(Ron Thiele)

★ The **Terracana Ranch and Resort** *($$$)* is open from May 15 to September 30. The resort, just off Highway 16 and about 50 kilometres (30 miles) east of McBride, is situated right by the Fraser River and has spectacular views of the Rocky and Cariboo mountains. Guests stay in modern and spacious one- and two-bedroom log chalets and are able to participate in a variety of activities, including canoeing, jet boating, horseback riding, and mountain biking. The resort has its own restaurant, the **Alpenrose**, which serves Swiss and continental cuisine. *Highway 16 West, Small River, Box 909, Valemount, B.C. V0E 2Z0 (604/968-4304).*

Tête Jaune Cache

Continuing along the highway east from Prince George, the next little community is Tête Jaune Cache. Tête Jaune Cache was a bustling town of up to 3,500 men during the construction days of the Grand Trunk Pacific railway, and remnants of this time can be seen all over the area. In the summer, historical tours, originating from both Mount Robson and Valemount, include this area.

PLACES TO EAT

Tête Jaune Cache Country Restaurant: *($)* This little restaurant, formerly called Jimmy's, is located just off Highway 16 (behind the Tete Jaune Lodge). From the outside, the building is not particularly impressive, but inside there is a small restaurant that specializes in Greek food. The food is good, and the night we ate there, local musicians came by and entertained the patrons. Definitely a fun spot to check out. *Blackman Rd., Highway 16 (604/566-4338).*

PLACES TO STAY

Tête Jaune Lodge: *($)* This motel is situated right off the highway. *Highway 16, Box 879, Valemount, B.C. V0E 2Z0 (604/566-9815).*

Rainbow Retreat Bed & Breakfast: *($$)* The highlight of this area, and actually one of the highlights of northern British Columbia is the Rainbow Retreat Bed and Breakfast. This wonderful spot is worth going out of your way for and should definitely not be missed if you are travelling by. Rainbow Retreat is a bed and breakfast, but it is also a gourmet restaurant. ★

When we called to reserve our room for the evening, Keith Burchnall, one of the owners and chefs, asked us if we would like to have supper and, if so, what would we like. Taken a bit aback, we asked what our choices were. "Vietnamese, French, Greek ... whatever you would like" was the reply. We selected Thai food (our favourite and unavailable in the north, or so we had thought) and spent the drive out dreaming about the prospect.

The evening and the meal surpassed our wildest expectations. Rainbow Retreat is a lovely and welcoming log home with a fireplace and a piano in the living area (played by our host throughout the evening). Stained glass and other artwork decorate the walls. We were welcomed inside, shown to our cozy room upstairs, and then welcomed back to the living room for a drink before dinner. As we warmed up before the fire, Helen Burchnall presented us with our menu for the evening. (We had opted for the $20 meal but a $30 five course meal is also an option.)

Our meal consisted of beef noodle soup, meikrob (deep fried noodles with special shrimp dressing), chicken satay with basmati rice, and mixed vegetables with shredded cabbage. Six kinds of condiments, including a delicious pineapple chutney, were also served. For dessert there was homemade jack fruit, lime, pandan, and coconut milk ice cream and warm lemon bars. Everything was indescribably delicious!

For both of us, dinner, breakfast, and our room came to a total of $97 — the best value anywhere! Rainbow Retreat is licensed but does not take credit cards. It is located up the hill on the north side of the highway across from the Tête Jaune Lodge. (In winter, you will have to leave your car at the bottom of the hill and Keith will come to drive you up.) *P.O. Box 138, Valemount, B.C. V0E 2Z0 (604/566-9747).*

Campgrounds: Robson Shadows *(c/o Box 157, Valemount, B.C. V0E 2Z0 604/566-4821)* is about 8km west of Mount Robson. There are two campgrounds in the park: the provincial campground, and Emperor Ridge *(Hwy 16, Mount Robson B.C. V0E 2Z0 604/566/4714)*.

THINGS TO DO

★ **Mount Robson Provincial Park:** Mount Robson, the highest peak in the Canadian Rockies, towers 3,954 metres (13,180 feet) over the western entrance to Mount Robson Provincial Park. It is indeed an awesome sight. The Mount Robson Visitors Centre, located at the Mount Robson viewpoint just off the highway, is open from May until September and provides details about attractions within Mount Robson Provincial Park. In the centre downstairs there are displays on natural and human history and audio-visual presentations about the park.

Mount Terry Fox: Mount Terry Fox is named after the Canadian young man who lost a leg to bone cancer and then undertook a run across Canada to raise funds for

Park Naturalists help visitors interpret the history, geology, plant and animal life found in the area. (Cheryl Livingstone-Leman)

cancer research. His spirit captured the hearts of people around the world and, when a recurrence of cancer forced him to end his run, millions grieved. Terry Fox died on June 28, 1981. Every September, the Terry Fox Run is held to raise money for cancer research. There are two viewpoints from which to view the mountain. One is located on Highway 16 near Mount Robson. The other is on Highway 5 just north of Valemount. Both sites are maintained as rest areas and have picnic sites.

OUTDOOR RECREATION
Hiking: Trails at **Mount Robson Provincial Park** range in length from six kilometres (four miles) to 70 kilometres (44 miles). Please ensure that you have the right

equipment and experience for the hike you are attempting, and check in with park staff before setting out. For a terrific day hike, go to Kinney lake on the Berg Trail (3 hours return). The **Mount Terry Fox Trail** is a long climb to the top of Mount Terry Fox. It requires at least four hours each way, and there is no water until a small alpine lake is reached. Views from the top of the mountain are excellent. The hike begins on Stone Road, which is opposite the Highway 5 Terry Fox rest area. Turn onto Stone Road and then turn left, cross the railway tracks, bear left, and watch for signs to the Mount Terry Fox trail parking lot.

Valemount

Valemount is surrounded by three mountain ranges: the Cariboo Mountains to the west, the Monashee range to the south, and the majestic Rockies to the east. The village itself is nestled at the foot of Canoe Mountain, and Swift Creek marks its northern boundary. On the banks of the creek is **George Hicks Park** — one of the best places for watching spawning Chinook salmon. Valemount is an active, vibrant community whose citizens and visitors enjoy life in the outdoors. Skiing (particularly heli-skiing), canoeing, hiking, snowmobiling, hunting, and mountaineering are some of the activities enjoyed in the Valemount area. The forest industry is the main employer but tourism is becoming increasingly important.

PLACES TO EAT

The Great Escape: *($$)* A favourite of the Valemount locals, this restaurant serves steak, chicken, pasta, burgers, salads, ribs, and specialty dishes. They also advertise that private gourmet dinners can be arranged. *5th Ave. (604/566-4565).*

Loose Moose Pub: *($$)* This new and very clean pub has good service and tasty food. *1405 5th Ave. (604/566-BEER).*

PLACES TO STAY
There are a large number of hotels, motels and beds and breakfasts around Valemount.

Sarak Motor Inn: *($$)* This inn has large rooms and, of particular importance if you are travelling with children, an indoor pool, sauna, and whirlpool. *Box 339, Valemount, B.C. V0E 2Z0 (604/566-4445, fax: 604/566-9722).*

Alpine Motel: *($$)* This motel has a pool and sauna. *Box 228, Valemount, B.C. V0E 2Z0 (604/566-4471, fax: 604/566-4767).*

Mount Robson Guest Ranch: *($$)* The Mount Robson Guest Ranch rents cabins and campsites and has a dining room. *Box 17, Valemount, B.C. V0E 2Z0 (604/566-4370, fax: 604/566-4170).*

Peggy's Place: *($$)* Four kilometres (three miles) west of the Mount Robson Visitor Information Centre and then north on Swift Current Creek Road. No credit cards or cheques accepted. *Box 703, Valemount, B.C. V0E 2Z0 (604/566-9842).*

Crooked Creek Bed & Breakfast: *($$)* This bed and breakfast, located in a quiet mountain setting along Crooked Creek Road, is just minutes from Valemount. *Box 18, Valemount, B.C. V0E 2Z0 (604/566-9196).*

Brady's Bed & Breakfast: *($$)* This bed and breakfast is also near Valemount. Take the Blackman Road to the Buffalo Road. The bed and breakfast is approximately one kilometre (0.6 miles) up the Buffalo Road. *Box 519, Valemount, B.C. V0E 2Z0 (604/566-9906).*

Summit River Lodge and Campsites: *($$)* Located 23 kilometres (14 miles) south of Valemount on Highway 5, Summit River offers five bedrooms and 23 campsites. *Box 517, Valemount, B.C. V0E 2Z0 (604/565-0396).*

Campgrounds: There are two campgrounds in the Valemount area: **Yellowhead Campsite and Trailer Park** *(Highway 5, c/o General Delivery, Valemount, B.C. V0E 2Z0, 604/566-4227)* and **Valemount Campground** *(P.O. Box 217, Valemount, B.C. V0E 2Z0, 604/566-4312).*

THINGS TO DO
Valley Brew Mountain Goodies: This interesting little shop sells local pottery, cappuccino, fine chocolates, and some handmade clothing. Drop by and visit with the friendly owner. *1444 5th Ave.* (Pottery by another local artist is sold at the Valley Sentinel offices, further up 5th Ave.)

★ **OUTDOOR RECREATION & HELI-SKIING**
Canadian Mountain Holidays: This company runs a number of guided hiking and walking trips for all interests and abilities. The trips involve helicopter rides into remote areas of the British Columbia/Alberta mountains and are on the expensive side, but they certainly look exciting. Canadian Mountain Holidays also runs seven day heli-ski trips. *Canadian Mountain Holidays Heli-Skiing, 217 Bear St., Banff, Alberta, T0L 0C0 (1-800/661-0252).*

Mount Robson Adventure Holidays: Based at the Mount Robson Adventure Centre (Mount Robson viewpoint), this company runs nature-viewing float trips down the scenic Fraser River, a Mount Robson nature tour by van, an easy guided canoe trip, a guided hike, and a guided backpacking trip in Mount Robson Provincial Park. *Box 687, Valemount, B.C. V0E 2Z0 (604/566-4386, fax: 604/566-4351).*

Robson Helimagic Inc.: Robson Helimagic runs three, five, and seven day heli-skiing packages. *Box 18, Valemount, B.C. V0E 2Z0 (604/566-4401, fax: 604/4333).*

Selected Events in the Robson Valley

Yellowhead Loppet (X-country)	McBride	February
Robson Valley Fall Fair	Valemount	August
Swift Creek Salmon Run	Valemount	Aug./Sept.

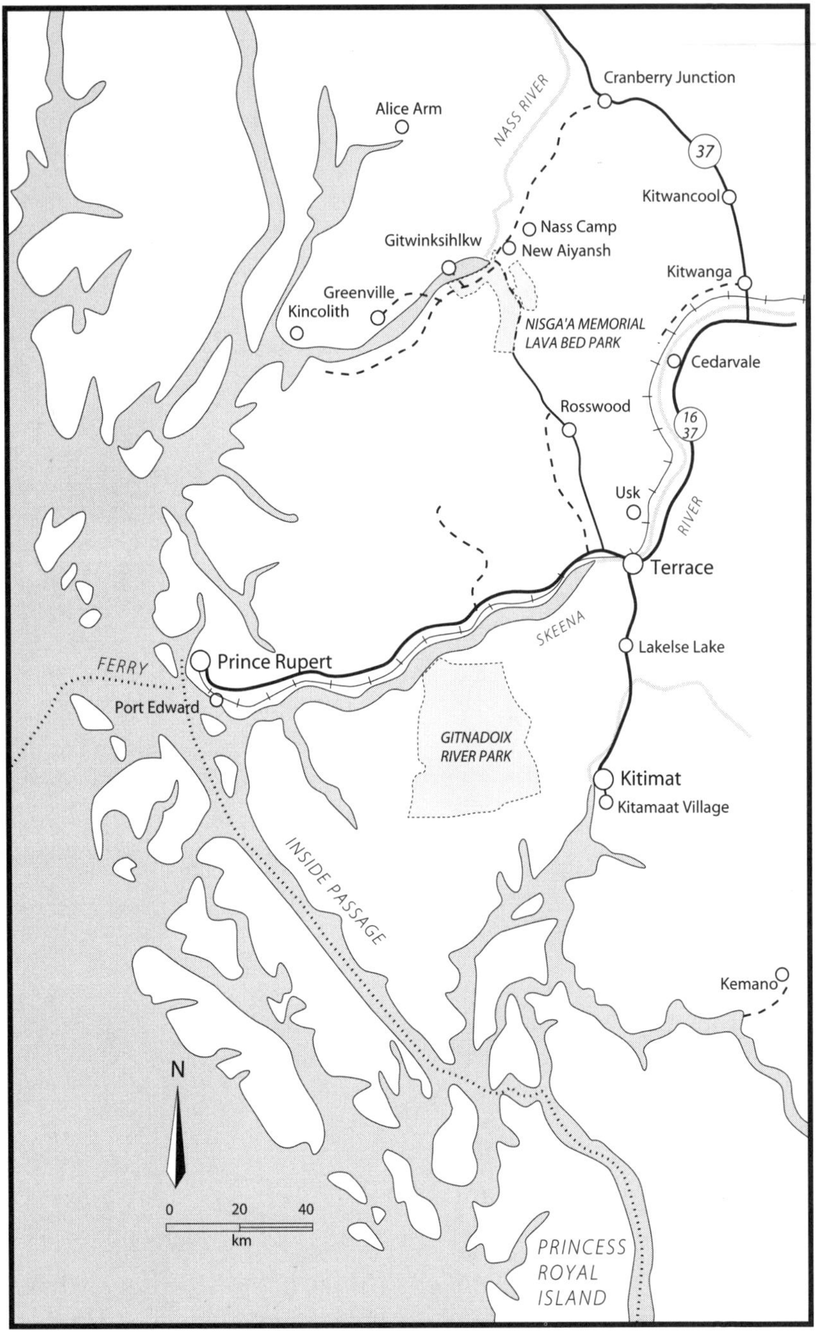

Cranberry Junction
Alice Arm
NASS RIVER
37
Kitwancool
Nass Camp
Gitwinksihlkw
New Aiyansh
Kitwanga
Greenville
Kincolith
NISGA'A MEMORIAL
LAVA BED PARK
Cedarvale
Rosswood
16
37
Usk
RIVER
Terrace
SKEENA
Lakelse Lake
FERRY
Prince Rupert
Port Edward
GITNADOIX
RIVER PARK
Kitimat
Kitamaat Village
INSIDE PASSAGE
Kemano
N
0
20
40
km
PRINCESS
ROYAL
ISLAND

7

The North Coast

British Columbia's coastline is internationally renowned for its towering stands of forest, craggy inlets, wind-swept islands, and pounding, brutal North Pacific waves. This is the province's signature land. It is immortalized in Emily Carr's paintings; celebrated in West Coast aboriginal art; and photographed, described, and memorialized in the works of dozens of British Columbian artists and writers. The northern portion of the British Columbia coast, though less travelled than the southern areas and Vancouver Island, shares all of the region's allure. An area of matchless beauty, fog-shrouded mystery, Native legends and maritime tales, the North Coast offers seemingly endless attractions for visitors and residents alike.

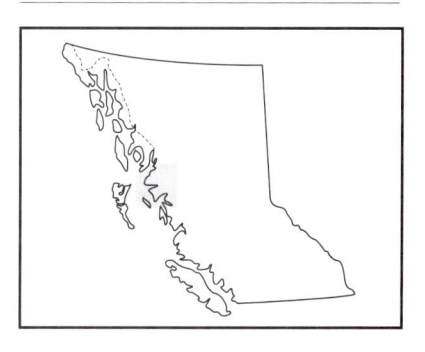

The North Coast, for our purposes, incorporates the Terrace-Kitimat-Prince Rupert triangle and the Nass River Valley. Like so much of northern British Columbia, this area offers a remarkable mix of geography and settlement: ancient Nisga'a, Haisla, and Tsimshian villages; modern industrial company towns; isolated coastal fishing communities; the bustling port of Prince Rupert; logging camps and towns; and the administrative centre of Terrace. The North Coast is dominated by the coastal islands and the rugged and seemingly impenetrable coastal mountain ranges. Mountain passes provide travellers with remarkably scenic views of the region.

A Brief History

The North Coast is a unique combination of new and old. The area's First Nations settlements date back some 8,000 to 10,000 years. At several sites, you can see totem poles and other artifacts from now-abandoned villages. The arrival of European explorers in the late eighteenth century — Juan Hernandez, Captain James Cook, and Captain George Vancouver were the first into the region — ushered in a dramatic new era. The explorers identified large supplies of highly-desirable fur-bearing animals in the region, and this information attracted the attention of English, American, and Russian traders. The resulting extremely competitive and exploitative fur trade brought major changes to aboriginal societies, including imported diseases which killed many First Nations people, new industrial age technology, and trade goods. The highly competitive trading rivalries soon decimated the fur-bearing animal populations in the area, although the coastal Natives partially offset the loss by bringing inland furs, obtained from interior trading partners, down to the coast.

The Hudson's Bay Company established a sizeable presence in the region, which was divided between themselves and the Russian American Fur Company. Trading and provisioning posts, the first substantial non-indigenous settlements in the area, were set up initially at Fort Simpson, on the Nass River, and later at Port Simpson, north of Prince Rupert. As the fur trade expanded, so did lurid tales of bacchanalian excesses. These stories drew Christian missionaries into the area — the most famous of whom was William Duncan. Duncan attracted a sizable following among the Fort Simpson Tsimshian and established an authoritarian "model" village at Metlakatla. He later ran afoul of his ecclesiastical superiors and Canadian authorities and eventually left with some of his followers to New Metlakatla in Alaska.

As the fur trade wound down, new opportunities emerged. The richness of the coastal forests was evident to all who travelled in the area, but southern timber stands remained more accessible. Salmon, the resource which had sustained the First Nations for generations, now had great commercial potential. The salmon canning operations that opened along the coast relied heavily on seasonal aboriginal labour. Over time, however, the canners squeezed many of the First Nations people out of the industry and, instead, hired Japanese or Chinese labour to work the boats and the canning lines. The salmon canneries remained an active and vital feature of the North Coast economy until the middle of the twentieth century, when jobs were lost and processing plants were closed due to the development of freezer ships and other technological advances.

As happened elsewhere in the North, the coming of the railway signalled a new era. In 1910-11, construction of the Pacific terminus of the Grand Trunk Pacific commenced in Prince Rupert, which was already the site of considerable real estate speculation and grandiose dreams of urban greatness. The town flourished, although it did not live up to its promoters' expectations; the financial difficulties of the Grand Trunk Pacific, which eventually resulted in its collapse and absorption into the government-owned Canadian National Railways stalled Prince Rupert's progress.

Terrace came into being as a consequence of the railway construction, although it remained a small regional centre for many years.

World War II brought more rapid changes. In all of Canada, the North Coast was considered to be the area most vulnerable to Japanese attack. As the United States rushed to fortify the Territory of Alaska, Canada made similar efforts on its coast, including the Terrace-Prince Rupert corridor. Actually, the American presence was more substantial, for they operated a large supply depot at Port Edward throughout the war. Canada dispatched a small contingent of troops to the region — they are, perhaps, best known for a small mutiny on the streets of Terrace — and built some defensive establishments. War-time activities also resulted in the upgrading of the road system, which provided an important transportation base for the post-war period.

The transformation of the North Coast continued in earnest after World War II. The decision of Alcan to build an aluminum smelter at Kitimat in the early 1950s was the single most important element in the industrialization of the region. Alcan sought to capitalize on the area's tremendous hydroelectric potential and secured permission to build the Kemano Hydroelectric Project — a dam on the upper reaches of the Nechako River system which diverted water using lengthy tunnels through the mountains to power stations near the coast. The power was then shipped to the aluminum plants built at the company town of Kitimat.

It is easy, given the tremendous growth and expansion of the region, to forget the importance of this initial investment. The construction of Kitimat — a well-planned settlement at the head of the scenic Douglas Channel — and the aluminum smelter provided the foundation for future development; road systems were improved and air service was expanded, and other companies had more reason to consider similar large-scale investments in the area.

The post-war period saw the continued expansion of the region's industrial capacity: sawmills at Terrace, a major pulp and paper plant at Prince Rupert (Skeena Cellulose), and additional industrial establishments at Kitimat (Eurocan and Methanax). Alcan's plans to complete the initial Kemano project (the Kemano Completion Project) initiated a series of intense debates. Logging assumed increased importance, and the industry moved into the farthest corners of the region. Signs of logging activity can now be seen along the coast and in hitherto isolated regions like the Nass River valley.

Prince Rupert enjoyed considerable growth of its port and transportation facilities after World War II. Additions to the city's grain terminal capacity and the construction of a coal terminal to support the development of northeast coal improved the community's economic stability. Prince Rupert was already a unique city, for it owned its own telephone and power services — a legacy of former Mayor and British Columbia Premier T. "Duff" Pattullo. By the 1980s, the community's diversified economy was based on fishing, logging, pulp and paper, transportation, government services, and tourism. It was, as well, the second largest city in northern British Columbia.

Terrace, a long-time rival of Prince Rupert, has likewise expanded rapidly in the past three decades. Although there has been considerable industrial growth in the city, the reasons for expansion lie in the community's emergence as a regional administrative centre, the development of the hospital, and the presence of

Northwest Community College. The annual pine mushroom harvest, which sends dozens of people into the mountains to search for the mushrooms that command high prices from Japanese purchasers, also contributes to the economy. There is a strong competition with Kitimat and Prince Rupert for available resources (such as a lengthy battle between the three communities over the location of the region's orthopedic surgeon); this rivalry is one of the hallmarks of community life in the area.

The Nass Valley, and the Nisga'a settlements of Gitwinksihlkw (Canyon City), Greenville, New Aiyansh, and Kincolith, have long existed outside the mainstream in this region. Mountain barriers, and the fact that the railway took the Smithers-Terrace route rather than running along the Nass River, isolated the valley from many of the social and economic developments of the early twentieth century.

The Nisga'a have always been fiercely independent and have been lobbying for over 100 years to have the governments of British Columbia and Canada address their land claims. They have initiated several profitable economic ventures and control their own school and health-care systems. In recent years, the construction of a road from Terrace to the Valley has improved internal travel and has drawn the Nisga'a more directly into the regional economy.

A massive volcanic eruption some 350 years ago wiped out several Nisga'a villages and left a natural mark on the land that is clearly evident to this day. The Nisga'a Memorial Lava Bed Park is designed to protect and to help interpret the remains of this important geographic event.

Getting There

The North Coast is a long way from southern British Columbia. The drive from Prince George to Prince Rupert takes eight to 10 hours, depending on the length of refueling and meal breaks — and Prince George is an additional nine to 10 hours from Vancouver. You can, of course, fly into the main centres; there is regularly scheduled service to Terrace/Kitimat (they share an airport) and Prince Rupert. Winter air travel is somewhat unreliable, for the coastal areas are subject to invasion by banks of thick cloud and fog. The Terrace airport is particularly subject to closure; when planes are unable to land, the airlines typically take passengers to Prince Rupert, which is usually open, and then bus them inland.

If you are taking your car, there are several options. The most common route is via Highway 16 from Prince George. The road is well-maintained, but caution is strongly advised when it is raining or if there is snow on the road. In mid-winter, highway closures are not uncommon, particularly on the Terrace-Prince Rupert section. If you are travelling from the North, you can reach the area by way of the Stewart-Cassiar Highway. There is a side route from this road into the Nass Valley, although it is not paved. The primary route into the Nass Valley runs from Terrace to the Nisga'a settlements of New Aiyansh and Canyon City. Except for the numerous logging trucks that run from the forests of the Nass to the sawmills of Terrace and other communities, this partially paved road (approximately half the distance is paved) is lightly travelled. Kitimat is approximately 40 kilometres (25 miles) from Terrace along a well-maintained paved highway.

Ferries represent the other transportation option. British Columbia Ferries offers service from Port Hardy on

164 / *A Traveller's Guide to Northern B.C.*

▲   B.C. Ferry's The Queen of the North *carries passengers and vehicles between Prince Rupert and Port Hardy, on Vancouver Island.*

the northern tip of Vancouver Island. The journey is remarkably scenic and quite inexpensive. The Alaska Marine Highway which also serves Prince Rupert, connects the city to points north along the Alaskan Panhandle. This northern ferry ride is stunning and highly recommended, but peak season travel can be quite expensive.

There are numerous small settlements dotted along the coast and the major rivers. Access to these villages can be quite difficult, for the coast is a major impediment to road construction. Several local airlines (mainly based in Prince Rupert) provide chartered or scheduled float-plane flights; there is also boat service to a few of these communities. Details on schedules and fares are available in Prince Rupert.

Hints for the Traveller

★

Anyone spending more than a few hours in this area will be impressed by its awe-inspiring beauty. The combination of dominating mountains, densely-forested hillsides, pulsating rivers, sharp canyons, and tumultuous North Pacific waters is enough to impress even the most cynical of travellers. This truly special land is rich in history and character, blessed with natural beauty and abundant resources, and possessed of a daring and engaging spirit. It is a land, too, of contradictions: of industrial power and aboriginal dispossession, of well-developed towns and abandoned villages, and of ancient trails and modern highways. So, given all that there is to do and see in the region, we thought it best to offer a few suggestions:

➤ Give yourself enough time to see Prince Rupert properly. Many travellers rush into town, take a quick look around, and then head onto one of the ferries. Prince Rupert is a real delight. The stores are surprisingly good for a town this size, the Museum of Northern British Columbia is well worth visiting, and a side trip to the North Pacific Cannery at Port Edward is a must. There are also some interesting hikes in the area, and the harbour offers much of interest.

➤ Check out some of the industrial establishments in the area. Tours are offered at Alcan's Kitimat Works — one of the most important manufacturing plants in the province — Methanex, Eurocan, and Skeena Cellulose. This part of northern British Columbia produces a great deal of wealth for the province and the nation.

➤ The Nass Valley does not figure prominently on most people's tour of the region. This is unfortunate; the valley offers visitors stunning scenery and an extremely interesting history. The Nisga'a are fabulous people who have a strong sense of purpose and destiny. If you want to see the future of aboriginal British Columbia, this is one of the best places to start.

▶ Don't let the views of Terrace from the main highway deter you. Like many northern towns, Terrace was built up along the railway, and the highway simply follows the railway route. At first glance, you might think that Terrace is an unattractive, gritty town, with little to offer. Look a little more closely. The surroundings, dominated by superb views of the mountains, are park-like. The river is truly impressive,

▲ *Charter trips are very popular on British Columbia's coast, which is renowned for its great fishing.* (Ray Hepting)

and the community away from the highway is actually quite attractive.

➤ Kitimat is worth an extended look — if only because company towns are becoming increasingly rare in this country. Kitimat, one of the post-war prototypes, is exceptionally popular with its residents. The people really love their town and a look at the physical setting and excellent facilities will help you understand why.

➤ There are numerous opportunities to get away from the main settlements. Charter fishing boats operate out of the main coastal settlements, and float planes provide quick access to the more isolated villages. The North Coast is sensational, particularly if you get a chance to spend some time among the islands or along one of the great fiords in the region. Don't let this opportunity pass you by; there are few places on earth that can match this scenery.

The Very Best of the North Coast

Nass Valley

To reach the Nass Valley, take the Nisga'a Highway that heads north just to the west of Terrace. It takes about an hour and a half to reach the valley from Terrace and the last half of the road can be a bit rough at times. Drive carefully as the road is quite narrow and twisty in places, and logging trucks come roaring up and down the highway.

The Nass Valley, which is home to the Nisga'a, contains four communities: Greenville, Gitwinksilkw (Canyon City), New Ainyash, and Kincolith. This is a lovely area. Mountains encircle the Tseaux Lava beds. A volcano erupted 300 or 400 years ago, and the resulting lava flow destroyed an entire Native village. The lava filled the valley floor and left a desolate moonscape: huge chunks of black lava and almost no vegetation. The 10-kilometre-long (six-mile-long), three-kilometre-wide (two-mile-wide) lava beds are considered culturally important to the Nisga'a people. The Nisga'a explanation is that God was angered by the children's treatment of spawning salmon and sent fiery lava down to punish them. The volcano's eruption also created nearby Lava Lake. At the lake's south end, original Native rock paintings can be found. The entire lava site has recently been protected as a provincial park by the British Columbia government and the local Nisga'a Tribal Council. Of recent vintage is the Victorian-era village of Old Aiyansh, located along the Nass River near New Aiyansh. Do not proceed to Old Aiyansh unless you have first received permission from the Nisga'a band office in New Aiyansh.

PLACES TO EAT
There is a small lunch counter in the general store in New Aiyansh. If you are staying at one of the beds and breakfasts, you might be able to arrange for meals to be included with your accommodations.

PLACES TO STAY
There are two beds and breakfasts in the Nass Valley, and these are the only accommodations available.

Lorene's Bed & Breakfast: *($$)* Lorene Plante is an outgoing and gracious hostess and makes you feel very welcome in her New Aiyansh home. She can tell you a lot about life in the Nass Valley, and special traditional foods are served upon request. Lorene also runs a small gift shop. Ask anyone in New Aiyansh where to find Lorene's place. *New Aiyansh, B.C. V0J 3J0 (604/633-2522).*

C.J.'s Bed & Breakfast: *($$)* Carolyn and William Martin run this very nice bed and breakfast in Greenville. *608 Cottonwood Court, Greenville, B.C. V0J 3J0 (604/621-3351).*

Terrace

Nestled in the beautiful Skeena Valley, the important forestry community of Terrace is the primary administrative centre of the northwest coast region. The community has a population of about 12,000, although when the surrounding area is included that figure rises to 17,000. Terrace and the surrounding valley is home to the Kitsumkalum and Kitselas Indian bands, and these Native cultures enhance the life of the community.

The first pioneers came to farm and mine in the Terrace area between 1889 and 1912. At this time, there were not any roads or railway connections; access was provided in the summer by steam-powered paddle wheelers that travelled up and down the Skeena River. "River Days" on the B.C. Day long weekend (first weekend in August) celebrates this history.

With the construction of the Grand Trunk Railway (1908-1914), dependence on the paddle wheelers diminished. The railway become the main method of transportation until the first road to the northwest interior of British Columbia was constructed in 1943. Before the Second World War, Terrace was a tiny community of 350 people. During the war, it served as an important military base for over 3,500 troops. When the Canadian Cellulose Company moved to Terrace after the war, and the Alcan smelter was constructed in nearby Kitimat, Terrace's prosperity was ensured.

PLACES TO EAT

Don Diegos: *($$)* Don Diegos has excellent Mexican food, fabulous daily specials, friendly service, and moderate prices. This is a fine, funky restaurant and one of the best establishments in the region. *3212 Kalum St. (604/635-2307).*

★ **Bavarian Inn:** *($$$)* The Bavarian Inn is the finest restaurant in town for continental specialties, steaks, seafood, pasta, schnitzel, and even buffalo. The décor is simple and elegant. Watch for the stuffed Kermode at the door. *4332 Lakelse Ave. (604/635-9161)*

The Lunch Box Deli: *($)* This deli serves good food at great prices. The surroundings are simple, and the service is cafeteria-style. The Lunch Box also sells cold cuts and cheeses that you can take with you to make your own lunch. *101- 4716 Lazelle (604/635-3696).*

Yip Chi Restaurant: *($)* Located at the corner of Kalum and Lazelle, this restaurant has good Chinese food at reasonable prices. *3234 Kalum (604/635-4112).*

Golden Flame: *($$)* The Golden Flame specializes in Greek food and pizza. *4606 Lazelle (604/635-7229).*

PLACES TO STAY

Coast Inn of the West: *($$$)* Terrace's Coast Inn of the West is a fine place to stay. It is located right downtown and has a White Spot restaurant attached to it. *4620 Lakelse Ave., Terrace, B.C. V8G 1R1 (1-800/549-3939 in B.C. or 1-800/663-1144 in the rest of Canada and in the U.S.).*

Mount Layton Hotsprings Resort: *($$)* This resort, located about 22 kilometres (14 miles) south of Terrace on Highway 37, is a good place to stay if you are travelling with children. There are a couple of ozone-treated mineral hot pools and some great water slides. Movies can be rented and shown in your room. *Highway 37, Box 550, Terrace, B.C. V8G 4B5 (1-800/663 3862).*

Lakelse Lake Lodge Bed & Breakfast: *($$)* The lodge is located close to Terrace and provides a bed and breakfast option for travellers. *1st Ave., S9, C39 Lakelse Lake, B.C. V8G 4V2 (604/798-9541).*

THINGS TO DO

The House of Sim-oi-ghets: Run by the Kitsumkalum Indian Band, this store has an excellent stock of authentic Native arts and crafts. Jewellery, wood carvings, moccasins, bead and leather work, and books on the First Nations of the area are all available. One can also view totem poles and a traditional log house. The House of Sim-oi-ghets is in Kitsumkalum, just west of town.

Kermode Trading Company: This unique store, located in a bright yellow house, sells local gifts and souvenirs. *4525 Keith, a short drive off Highway 16.*

Northern Light Studio: A combination art gallery and store, Northern Light Studio sells carvings, paintings, British Columbia jade, and a variety of gemstones from around the world. Behind Northern Light Studio is a beautiful Japanese garden complete with a bamboo fountain, wooden bridge, wild plants, and a Native totem pole. *4820 Halliwell Ave.*

Northern Specialty Foods: This interesting ethnic and health food store has friendly and helpful staff who would be pleased to show you around. *4621 Lazelle.*

Farmer's Market: From May until Thanksgiving, there is a farmer's market every Saturday morning in Terrace's **Little Park**. Plants, fruit, vegetables, and crafts are all sold here.

Terrace Heritage Park: The Terrace Heritage Park, operated by the Terrace Regional Museum Society, is a collection of log buildings from the pioneer days. Each building and its artifacts represent a distinct aspect of pioneer life. Guided tours are available in the summer. *4011 Sparks St. (604/635-2508).*

Red Sand Lake Demonstration Forest: If you would like to learn more about the forestry industry, the Red Sand Lake Demonstration Forest on the Kalum West logging road is worth a visit.

OUTDOOR RECREATION

Hiking: The mountains that surround Terrace are covered with hiking trails. The three-hour **Terrace Mountain** hike starts at the end of Halliwell Avenue. About half-way up the mountain, there is a small clearing with an excellent view of the city. An easy and interesting hike is the **Ferry Island Hiking Trail**. This three kilometre (two mile) trail goes through the woods and along the shoreline of the Skeena River. On your hikes, keep your eyes peeled for one of the rarest bears in the world, the Kermode bear. The Kermode is a separate and distinct member of the Black bear family. It usually weighs between 250 and 350 pounds and is recognizable by its coat which varies in colour from a light chestnut blond to a shade of steel-blue grey. The Kermodei was close to extinction and is now under provincial government protection. For information on other hikes, contact the Tourist Information Centre.

Fishing: The fishing in this area is excellent; all five species of Pacific salmon as well as steelhead, rainbow trout, and Dolly Varden can be found. The Skeena

River and its tributaries are world famous for their fishing opportunities. Local guides can be hired. Fishing trips can be made from town on a day by day basis, or you can stay in one of the excellent remote fishing lodges. Wherever you stay, make sure you read up on the latest catch restrictions, day fees, and license requirements.

Shames Mountain: Shames Mountain, approximately 22 kilometres (14 miles) west of Terrace, is known for its good skiing, relaxed family atmosphere, and abundant snowfall.

Lakelse Lake Provincial Park: Located 25 kilometres (16 miles) south of Terrace on Highway 37 and near Mount Layton Hotsprings, Lakelse Lake Provincial Park is popular for its fine swimming, canoeing, fishing, boating, and camping. There are 156 campsites, an adventure playground, picnic shelters, swimming beaches, and summer interpretive programs. There is also a self-guided nature trail through the old growth forest.

Kitimat

Named by the Haisla Indians, Kitimat, which means "people of the snow," has unique beginnings. During and after the end of the Second World War, the British Columbia government became interested in developing an electricity-intensive industry in the province. To this end, the government invited Alcan to look into the northwest area of the province, among other areas, for the possible establishment of a large aluminum smelter. When construction began in 1951, Kitimat, one of North America's first planned communities (communities whose design is carefully thought out before construction), was born. Kitimat was only accessible by boat or seaplane until the railway opened in 1954

— the year both the smelter and the hydroelectric generating station at nearby Kemano commenced operations.

Today, Kitimat is a very multicultural community of about 12,000 people. There are three major industrial operations: Alcan's Kitimat Works, Eurocan Pulp and Paper, and Methanex Corporation's ammonia and methanol plants.

PLACES TO EAT

The Chalet: *($$)* The Chalet is open for breakfast, lunch, and dinner. For lunch, a variety of soups, salads, sandwiches, and quiches are served. The dinner menu is quite extensive and features a number of international dishes. Located across from the City Centre Mall. *852 Tsimshian (604/632-4615).*

Cloverpatch: *($)* The Cloverpatch is a particularly good spot for lunch. The menu features a selection of hot and cold sandwiches, burgers, fish and chips, spaghetti, and desserts. In the evening, there is a larger menu that includes a selection of seafood dishes. *633 Dadook (604/632-2000).*

Rosario's: *($)* This restaurant is recommended for their pizza. *607 Legion (604/632-4980).*

Cor's: *($)* Cor's is a relaxed coffee shop during the day, but in the evening it is transformed into a fine dining establishment. Cor's has good food and service. *404 Enterprise (604/639-9839).*

Ol'Keg Neighbourhood Pub. *($$)* Ol'Keg is a good spot for a pub lunch or an afternoon snack. *874 Tsimshian, (604/632-692).*

PLACES TO STAY
Motels: City Centre Motel *($, 480 City Centre, Kitimat, B.C. V8C 1T6, 1-800/663-3391, 604/632-4848, fax: 604/632-5300)* and the Chalet Motel *($$, 852 Tsimshian Blvd., Kitimat, B.C. V8C 1T5, 604/632-4615, fax: 604/632-2208)* are both nice, clean, centrally-located motels.

Beds and Breakfasts: There are three beds and breakfasts in town: L & S Bed & Breakfast *($$, 63 Partridge St., Kitimat, B.C. V8C 1L6, 604/632-4388)*, Premier Bed & Breakfast *($$, 52 Finch St., Kitimat, B.C. V8C 1T2, 604/632-7137)*, and OT Bed & Breakfast *($$, 86 Kokanee St., Kitimat, B.C. V8C 2K6, 604/632-7023)*.

THINGS TO DO
Industrial Tours: Alcan, Eurocan, and Methanex all give tours of their plants. Alcan offers tours year-round, although they are more frequent in the summer months. From June 1 - August 31, tours are Monday to Friday at 10:30 a.m. and 1:30 p.m. From Sept. 1 - May 31, tours are on Tuesdays and Thursdays at 1:15 p.m. *(604/639-8259)*. Eurocan's tours are on Tuesdays and Thursdays at 10:00 a.m. and 2:00 p.m. in June, July, and August. The tour takes about one and a half hours and includes a film presentation. Children under the age of 12 are not allowed *(604/632-6111, local 409)*. Methanex only offers tours in the summer *(604/627-1212)*

Radley Park: Kitimat's Radley Park boasts one of the largest living Sitka spruce trees in British Columbia. The tree is estimated to be over 500 years old. Stop by and take a look!

Recreational Facilities: Kitimat has a good recreation centre that houses a swimming pool, squash courts, and skating rink. Hirsch Creek Golf Club has a challenging 18 hole course and a nice restaurant and outdoor patio (open only in the summer, which is no great surprise given the amount of snow this place can get in the winter). *2000 Kingfisher (604/632-4653).*

Kitimaat Village: Kitimaat Village is home to the Haisla. A tour of this community will take you along the Douglas Channel and will also you the opportunity to see the local carvers and the beautiful totem poles. Watch for the new Haisla school with its interesting architecture.

The cultures of the First Nations of the Northwest Coast figure prominently in the regional life. This is a Haisla button blanket.
(Ron Thiele)

Kitimat River Fish Hatchery: Tours of the hatchery are available in the summer. Here, you can view salmon in their different stages of growth. The Kitimat Tourist InfoCentre should be able to give you more information.

OUTDOOR RECREATION
Hiking: The city has a number of walking trails and there are also hikes on the nearby mountains. **Mount Elizabeth** is a popular hike. Check at the Kitimat Tourist InfoCentre for details.

Fishing: Fresh water and salt water fishing opportunities abound. Kitimat is located at the head of the Douglas Channel — a 140 kilometre (88 mile) fiord connecting Kitimat to the Pacific. Pick up a brochure entitled "Sport Fishing in Kitimat" from the Kitimat Travel InfoCentre. It gives lots of information on fishing in the area, including the names of all the fishing operators. The InfoCentre is located near the entrance to town at *4511 Keith St., P.O. Box 214, Kitimat, B.C. V8C 1Y3 (604/635-4689).*

Prince Rupert

Prince Rupert was founded in 1910 by Charles Hays, President of Grand Trunk Pacific Railway Company, as the westward terminus for the railway. Hays, who saw the potential of this beautiful area, had dreams of creating a large and important port, but he never realized these dreams as he lost his life in the sinking of the *RMS Titanic* in 1912. Although it took a while, Prince Rupert was designated a national harbour by Ottawa in 1972.

That Prince Rupert is on an island is not readily apparent, but it is. A short bridge connects Kaien

Island to the mainland. The community has a population of 17,500; the population of the area is 25,000.

PLACES TO EAT

The Waterfront Café: *($$)* The Waterfront, located in the Crest Motor Hotel, is a fine dining establishment with high quality food and service. The specialties are, naturally, seafood dishes. *222 1st Ave. W. (604/624-6771).*

★ **Casa Filipina Restaurant:** *($$)* This Filipino restaurant, a real find, has excellent food and friendly and attentive service. The menu is huge (96 selections), and all of the food we tried was fabulous. Particularly great was the filet of cod with black bean sauce, the chicken adobo, and the fresh spring rolls! *636 3rd Ave. (604/627-8365).*

★ **Cow Bay Café:** *($$)* This little restaurant is right on the water. The menu changes daily but always contains numerous interesting and enticing options. When fish is highlighted, you can assume that it was caught locally and is served fresh. The chef likes to use southwest flavourings in his dishes. The desserts, made on the premises, are mouth-watering. *205 Cow Bay Rd. (604/627-1212).*

Boulet's Seafood and Chowder House: *($$)* Located at Fairview Bay near the ferry terminals, this restaurant serves good seafood dishes *(604/624-9309).*

Peg Legs: *($$)* Peg Legs has tasty Mexican food. *4-101 First Ave. E. (604/624-5667).*

Rupert's Saigon Restaurant: *($$)* This restaurant serves very good Vietnamese food. *679 Second Ave. W. (604/624-9395).*

Smile's: *($$)* Smile's has been serving fish and chips to locals and tourists for years. The décor is simple, and the food is good. This is a very popular spot, so arrive early or be prepared to wait! *Smile's is located on the corner of Cow Bay Road and George Hills Way (604/624-3072).*

Lambada's Cappuccino Dessert Bar: *($)* Visit this ★ dessert bar for cappuccinos and delectable desserts. *#101-515 3rd Ave. (604/624-6464).*

Breakers Pub: *($$)* Breakers Pub is a popular spot, especially in the summer when you can sit outside on the deck. *117 George Hills Way in Cow Bay (604/624-5990).*

PLACES TO STAY

Crest Motor Hotel: *($$$)* The best hotel in Prince ★ Rupert, and probably the finest in northern British Columbia, is the Crest Motor Hotel. The Crest is located right on the harbour, and many of the rooms as well as the bar and restaurant have excellent views of the ocean. The hotel is elegant and the service excellent. *222 1st Ave. W., c/o Box 277, Prince Rupert, B.C. V8J 3P6 (1-800/663-8150, 604/624-6771, fax: 604/627-7666).*

The Best Western Highliner Inn: *($$$)* This hotel is another good place to stay. It is the tallest building in town and has a clock and temperature display on top. The rooms at the Highliner are large and modern, and many have harbour views. *815 1st Ave. W., Prince Rupert, B.C. V8J 1B3 (1-800/668-3115, 604/624-9060, fax: 604/627-7759).*

Coast Prince Rupert Hotel: *($$$)* Also recommended is the Coast Prince Rupert Hotel. The rooms have large windows to allow you to enjoy the view. On the walls of the hotel lobby, there are a number of historic photos of the city and a description of some of Prince Rupert's early history. *118 6th St., Prince Rupert, B.C. V8J 3L7 (1-800/663-1144, 604/624-6711, fax: 604/624-3288).*

Eagle Bluff Bed & Breakfast: *($$)* The Eagle Bluff Bed and Breakfast is located right (literally!) on the harbour next to the Cow Bay Wharf (see more on Cow Bay below). Single, double, and family accommodations are available. This is a lovely Bed and Breakfast with very reasonable prices. *201 Cow Bay Rd., Prince Rupert, B.C. V8J 1A2 (604/627-4955, fax: 604/627-7945).*

THINGS TO DO

★ **Cow Bay:** Cow Bay, located on the waterfront near the fish processing plants, has a number of interesting shops. Three to look out for are the **Cow Bay Gift Gallery** *(25 Cow Bay)*, the **Purple Otter** *(201 1st Ave.)* — an antique and curio shop — and **Northern Star Studios** *(1st Ave. E.).*

Local History: Various places in town sell and rent a guided heritage tour of Prince Rupert on audio-cassette. The tape discusses the architecture of the city's heritage buildings and presents the traveller with little vignettes about historic incidents and interesting people. In the summer, the **Crest Hotel** puts on Photographs and Memories, a one-person play about the life story of Prince Rupert. It features characters from the past illustrated by slides. Admission is free. *222 1st Ave. West (604/624-6771).* Just down the slope from the Crest parking lot is the **Firehall Museum.** Operated by local firefighters, and open when they are not on call and daily in the summer, the museum's exhibit includes a restored REO fire engine. Also of historic interest is **Kwinitsa Station Railway Museum** on Waterfront *(604/627-1915).*

Museum of Northern British Columbia: The Tourist Bureau and Prince Rupert's Museum of Northern British Columbia are located in the same building. (There are plans to move the museum around the corner to the long house on 2nd Avenue next to Northwest Community College.) Do stop here! This is a good museum with a collection of totem poles, Native artifacts, carvings, and relics from early settlers in the area. The museum traces the history of the Tsimshian settlers and houses a collection of carved canoes and an excellent display of carvings made from argillite — the smooth black slate that is only found on the Queen Charlotte Islands. The museum, in conjunction with the Metlakatla Development Corporation, also operates archaeological tours that examine the importance of the area's 150 archaeological sites and include stops at Metlakatla and Dodge Cove. The tours, which run daily in the summer, are free, but reservations are necessary. The museum also has a good gift shop. The museum, gift shop, and tourist bureau are open from 9:00 a.m. - 8:00 p.m. Monday to Saturday and from 9:00 a.m. - 5:00 p.m. on Sundays. *100 1st Ave. E.(604/624-3207).*

The North Pacific Cannery Village Museum: This museum at nearby Port Edward is the oldest and last remaining cannery village on the North American west coast. There are a number of historic and marine displays along the boardwalk near the actual cannery. A gift shop sells local artwork. During the Prince Rupert Seafest in June, First Nations fishermen who once worked for the cannery return for a fisherman's barbecue. The museum is open daily from 10:00 a.m. - 7:00 p.m. Rates are $5 for adults and $3 for children

▲ *Active fish canneries once dotted the northern coast. The plant and community at Port Edward have been converted into a museum.*

over six. *1889 Skeena Drive in Port Edward (604/628-3538).*

Grain Terminal: Free guided tours of the world's most technologically-advanced cleaning grain elevator include a slide presentation and a short walking tour. Phone the Travel InfoCentre for reservations *(604/624-5637).*

OUTDOOR RECREATION
Community Parks: The **sunken gardens** behind the Provincial Courthouse and **Mariner's Memorial Park** are both pleasant spots for a picnic. In the middle of Mariner's Park is a Japanese fishing boat which washed up on the shores of the Queen Charlotte Islands in 1987. Amazingly enough, the boat turned out to be from Owase, Japan - Prince Rupert's sister city! The

Prince Rupert Kinsmen's Linear Park has a nature trail system throughout the city. There are ten different trails that range in length from about one to three kilometres (one-half mile to two miles).

Ocean Activities: On the water, possibilities for adventure include whale watching, sports fishing, and relaxing nature and harbour tours. For more information on the different kinds of charters available, write to the *Department of Economic Development and Tourism, P.O. Box 669, Prince Rupert, B.C. V8J 1A6 (1-800/667-1994)*. Ask for their pamphlet entitled "Fishing Charters & Adventure Tours." If you are planning to end your trip on Vancouver Island, consider taking the Queen of the North. This fantastic ferry ride, with its breath-taking scenery, runs from Prince Rupert to Port Hardy.

★

Hiking: Mount Hays, which towers over the city, also has some excellent hiking and walking trails. Ask for maps and additional information at the Travel InfoCentre.

Selected Events Along the North Coast

All Native Basketball	Prince Rupert	February
Seafest	Prince Rupert	June
Skeena Valley Triathlon	Terrace	July
Riverboat Days	Terrace	August
Christmas Carol Sail Past	Prince Rupert	December

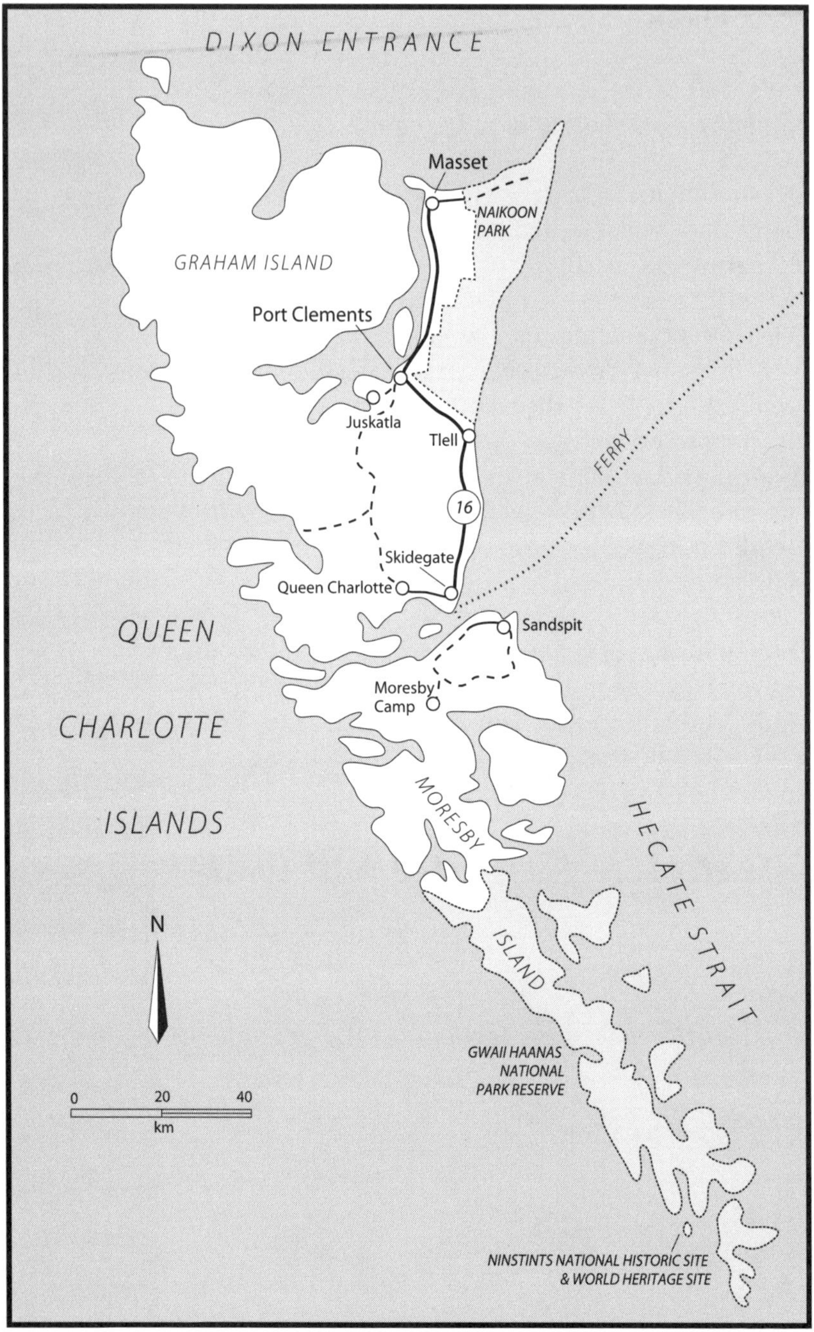
DIXON ENTRANCE
Masset
NAIKOON PARK
GRAHAM ISLAND
Port Clements
Juskatla
Tlell
FERRY
16
Skidegate
Queen Charlotte
Sandspit
QUEEN
CHARLOTTE
ISLANDS
Moresby Camp
MORESBY
ISLAND
HECATE STRAIT
N
0
20
40
km
GWAII HAANAS NATIONAL PARK RESERVE
NINSTINTS NATIONAL HISTORIC SITE & WORLD HERITAGE SITE

8
The Queen Charlotte Islands

And now for something completely different! The Queen Charlotte Islands are obviously part of northern British Columbia — the main access is by way of Prince Rupert — but they are clearly unique and unusual. The Queen Charlottes have a distinct reputation for aboriginal activism (the Haida are known around the world for their art, their outspokenness and their assertiveness), for environmental brinkmanship (particularly the battle that led to the establishment of the Gwaii Haanas National Park Reserve/Haida Heritage Site), for world-class wilderness recreation (particularly sports fishing), and for residues of the 1960s (the artistic spirit and naturalist life of the "back-to-the-landers").

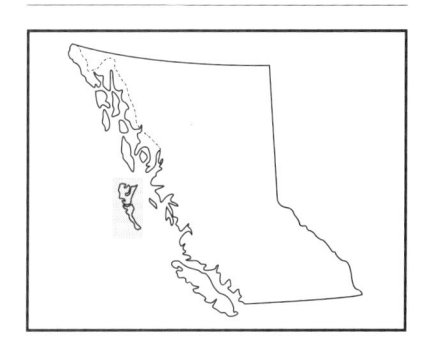

The Queen Charlotte Islands are also a fabulous tourist destination; they offer a multitude of wilderness attractions, but they are also very much a part of the contemporary development frontier. This is very much a divided land; it is a land of loggers and environmentalists, commercial fishers and artists, clearcuts and parks, military personnel and those who follow an "alternative lifestyle," and beachcombers and tourist operators. The islands, both a refuge and a destination, are marked by misty mornings, fog-shrouded beaches, sun-drenched hillsides, kilometres of driftwood-strewn waterfront, abundant wildlife, and temperamental oceans.

The Queen Charlotte Islands, which are 300 kilometres (188 miles) long, form a roughly triangular shape; they are wide across the top and taper to a point at the south end. The climate is very mild, although the islands are famous for winds, storms, and rain. In fact, the west coast of the Queen Charlottes has some of the highest rainfalls in Canada.

A Brief History

The Queen Charlotte Islands have not faced the same development pressures as other parts of northern British Columbia. The Haida, a majestic and powerful people, were dominant in the region before the first Europeans arrived in the 1780s. They quickly became active in the fur trade and coastal trading activities, although their population declined precipitously due to the introduction of European diseases. In the nineteenth century, there was a short-lived gold rush to the Charlottes, but few signs of the temporary invasion remain to be seen. At the beginning of this century, a handful of homesteaders started small ranches and farms. During World War I, Sitka Spruce was harvested from the Port Clements area for use in the construction of airplanes. The construction of the airport at Sandspit during World War II brought the first major developments to Moresby Island.

Over the past 20 years, the Queen Charlotte Islands' famous timber stands have attracted a great deal of attention. The fishing industry, although fairly small, remains active, and there has been a dramatic increase in the tourist industry (particularly in wilderness excursions). The islands' population includes a sizeable contingent of "back-to-the-lander" types who were drawn by the beauty of the place and the social freedom of the multi-cultural communities. Of particular significance was the opening, in 1972, of the Canadian high-tech military communications base in Massett—a move that vastly increased the population and changed the character of the community. Recently, the federal government announced the phased shut-down of most of the Massett military base. This decision, which has potentially fateful consequences for the town, has sparked a community-wide effort to develop an alternate plan for the area.

Change continues in the Queen Charlottes. The provision of regular ferry service between Skidegate Landing and Prince Rupert and the expansion of government services (particularly related to aboriginal and environmental matters) has given greater stability to the main settlements of Queen Charlotte and Massett. International uproar over planned logging on South Moresby, a protest skillfully organized by the Haida, resulted in the 1988 decision to set the region aside as a protected area. Gwaii Haanas is jointly managed by Parks Canada (on behalf of the Canadian government) and the Council of the Haida Nation. The establishment of the park and growing public interest in wilderness travel and aboriginal culture has spurred a marked increase in tourist travel to the region.

Of particular importance has been the cultural and political renaissance of the Haida Nation (who have large settlements at Old Massett and Skidegate). The Haida play a major role in Canadian and provincial aboriginal politics and have been negotiating land and resource rights with the provincial government for several years. The re-emergence of Haida art has captured considerable attention and has helped to increase interest in the Queen Charlotte Islands.

Getting There

Getting to the Queen Charlotte Islands may not be half the fun, but it can well be half the challenge. There are three main ways to get to the islands: by regular air service from Vancouver, by air from Prince Rupert, and by ferry from Prince Rupert. The trip can take some time; Prince Rupert is over 700 kilometres (430 miles) from Prince George, which in turn is over 700 kilometres from Vancouver, and the cost of travel can be a significant deterrent. This isolation, as locals know, is one of the prime deterrents to development and growth.

The fastest way to get to the islands is by regular jet service from Vancouver via **Canadian Airlines**. Canadian flies into Sandspit — a short drive and a 20 minute ferry ride from Queen Charlotte City. A new company, **Thunderbird Airlines** *(1-800-898-0177, 604/231-8933)*, is now offering service from Vancouver (south terminal) to Sandspit and Massett. On the islands, there are several local airlines able to take you to outlying areas. Contact **South Moresby Air Charters** *(Box 969, 3103-3rd Ave., Queen Charlotte, B.C. V0T 1S0, 604/559-4222)* or **Harbour Air** *(Sandspit Airport, 637-5350)*. If you are in Prince Rupert and wish to get across to the islands, **Waglisla Air** *(1-800/663-2875)* runs flights from Vancouver to Prince Rupert and Massett. Travel delays are not uncommon, particularly in the winter months; wind storms and heavy rains can ground planes for extended periods.

Many automobile travellers take advantage of the excellent **BC Ferries** service between Prince Rupert and Skidegate Landing *(reservations 1-800/663-7600)*. The ferry ride usually takes around eight hours, but storms on the blustery Hecate Strait can lengthen the journey considerably (a day or longer). Even when the ferry is not delayed, the crossing can be quite turbulent, and those prone to sea-sickness should take appropriate precautions. (If you don't want to take sea-sickness pills, some people swear by acupressure bracelets.) Winter travel can be problematic. The 1995 schedule listed the following Prince Rupert departures times: Sunday at 2:00 p.m., Monday at 9:00 p.m., Wednesday at 2:00 p.m., Thursday at 11:00 a.m. (July/August only), Friday at 11:00 a.m., and Saturday at 11:00 a.m. (July/August/September only). The ferry departs Skidegate Landing at the following times: Monday at 11:00 a.m., Tuesday at 11:00 a.m., Wednesday at 11:00 p.m. (July/August only), Thursday at 11:00 p.m., Friday at 11:00 p.m., and Saturday at 11:00 p.m. (July/August/September).

There is a regular ferry service between Skidegate Landing and Alliford Bay (near Sandspit on Moresby Island). The ferry leaves Skidegate at 7:30, 8:30, 10:00, and 11:00 every morning and at 1:00, 2:00, 4:00, 5:00, 6:30, 7:30, 9:30, and 10:30 every afternoon and evening. Departures from Alliford Bay are scheduled for 7:00, 8:00, 9:30, and 10:30 every morning and 12:30, 1:30, 3:40, 4:30, 5:30, 7:00, 9:00, and 10:00 every afternoon and evening.

Once you are on the islands — by plane to Sandspit or by ferry to Queen Charlotte City — you will find your options for car travel rather limited. There are a few kilometres of highway, and many more kilometres of logging roads — most of the latter busy with logging trucks. Most people travel to the outlying areas and tourist attractions, including Gwaii Haanas, the famous national park at the south end of the island chain, by float plane or boat.

As a tourist destination, the Queen Charlotte Islands are unsurpassed. You will not find chain motels or fast-food restaurants on the islands; this is a traveller's destination like they all used to be — rich in local heritage and culture, unique, and exciting. The people of the islands are an original group: the Haida, the artists, the loggers, and the government workers. This is a place of strong emotional attachments and often feverish debates about the islands' future. The Queen Charlotte Islands are a delightful place to explore, and you will quickly discover that the local facilities and hospitality are an enticing complement to the magnificent natural surroundings.

Hints for the Traveller

➤ Getting around on the islands can be a challenge. If you arrive by air at the Sandspit Airport, you can either rent a car at the airport or take the airporter into Queen Charlotte City and rent there. Car rentals are not cheap on the islands, so if money is a concern, we strongly recommend waiting until you get to Queen Charlottee City to rent. By doing this, you can save yourself a considerable amount of money on your rental and on ferry charges. Sandspit to Queen Charlotte City by airporter is $10/adult each way.

➤ The Gwaii Haanas National Park Reserve/Haida Heritage Site, with its fog-shrouded islands, is worth the effort (and the cost) of getting there. The Haida play a prominent role in the interpretation and management of this magnificent natural area. Do heed the park management's advice about areas to avoid; there are many sensitive cultural and historical sites, and the gentle but evident hand of tourist development is already being felt. Visitor information offices, open in the summer months, are located in Queen Charlotte

Gwaii Haanas (South Moresby) has been preserved as a national park. The Haida totem poles and ancient village sites are world renowned.

City and Sandspit. *(Call 559-8818, year-round, for further information.)*

► Queen Charlotte City and Skidegate have a number of interesting and fascinating places to visit. Leave plenty of time for the Queen Charlotte Museum and the local arts and crafts stores.

► Tlell is easy to miss — but don't! There are a number of small signs to off-road shops and accommodations. Plan to spend at least an afternoon in the local galleries and coffee shops. The people in Tlell are uncommonly friendly and are happy to share their knowledge of the islands and its people. And the artists are truly imaginative and creative. A number of these artists sell only direct; there are no other outlets for their art work.

➤ The Queen Charlotte Islands is one of those places where you cannot judge the book by its cover. Many of the area's businesses are in small, unimpressive structures; travellers who are accustomed to more polished surroundings might well decide not to enter certain businesses because they fail to meet southern standards. If you follow such an approach, you will be denying yourself some of the islands' best attractions. This is particularly the case in Tlell, where several nondescript buildings hold absolutely wonderful stores and services.

➤ This is one of the province's best places for ocean kayaking. Skidegate Inlet and Bearskin Bay (near Skidegate and Queen Charlotte City) are excellent places for beginners, as they are well-protected from rough seas and offer excellent wildlife viewing and wonderful scenery. The more isolated areas, particularly South Moresby, offer superb wilderness adventures and opportunities to visit several world-famous aboriginal historical sites (like Ninstints on Anthony Island).

➤ Beachcombing is an excellent, and sometimes fascinating, recreational activity. Books have been written on collecting Japanese floats, and stories abound about the weird and wonderful things pulled off the islands' shores. (The one about the shipload of Nike runners is one of the best.) Enjoy the beach, and take full advantage of the opportunity to enjoy the shells, polished rocks, interestingly-shaped driftwood (which local artists and artisans turn into pieces of art and furniture) and miscellaneous delights.

➤ Keep a close eye out for the deer when driving on the islands. Literally hundreds of these comparatively small deer can be seen along the roadway. (During a late evening drive between Massett and Tlell one April evening, we passed over 70 deer.) The situation is rather like that of the kangaroos in the Australian outback; the first dozen or so are cute and interesting, but after that they become something of a bother. Do drive carefully.

➤ There are many interesting attractions away from the main settlements and many different ways to get there. Organized overnight excursions, by boat or kayak, are becoming increasingly popular, and there are a number of seaplane operators in the area who can quickly get you to out-of-the- way locations.

➤ There are hundreds of kilometres of logging roads on the islands, and the forest companies encourage travellers to use them. Do so with care and register with the company beforehand. Most of these roads are actively used by the forest companies. Since they are narrow and not designed for regular automobile travel, they present a serious driving challenge and can easily take their toll on your vehicle (particularly on the windshield). Make sure that you get a copy of the Queen Charlotte Islands Forest District Recreation Map before you venture far afield. There are no tourist services in most back country areas, so do not travel to these areas unless you are properly prepared. On Graham Island, call **MacMillan Bloedel** at *604/559-4224 or 604/557-4212 (Juskatla)*. If you are planning to travel the logging roads on Moresby Island, call Fletcher Challenge at 604/637-5323.

➤ The Queen Charlotte Islands are laid-back — rather like the Gulf Islands and the west coast of Vancouver Island. But don't mistake the incredible friendliness and helpfulness for an absence of strong opinion; there are many serious issues at play on the islands — aboriginal land claims, control of the fishery, clear-cut logging, the future of South Moresby — and islanders have definite opinions on these issues. The residents of the Queen Charlottes are one of the region's greatest assets, and their reputation for friendliness is well-deserved. Spend some time learning about the people and the issues of this interesting part of the province.

▶ All of the communities on the Queen Charlotte Islands are small enough that you won't need directions to find your way around. Where we have listed places to stay or eat without addresses, you can rest assured that they are quite easy to find.

▶ Helicopter and airplane charters to Gwaii Haanas are available from Sandspit. There aren't any roads on this island, so you must go by boat or by air. South Moresby is beautiful; wonderful hiking and exploring

▶

The forested coastline and sheltered bays of the Queen Charlottes offer superb opportunities for wilderness kayaking.

opportunities await the visitor. Visit the sites of ancient Haida villages, soak in a hot pool on Hotspring Island, and see the totem poles at Ninstints on Anthony Island. Visiting some of the area by kayak might be a desirable option. The following companies offer kayaking tours for fairly reasonable prices: ★

Gabriola Island Cycle and Kayak Ltd. (Peter Marcus), *RR1, C-23, Gabriola, B.C. V0R 1X0 (604/247-8277).*

Butterfly Tours (Gord Pincock), *General Delivery, Tofino, B.C. V0R 2Z0 (604/725-2551).*

Moresby Explorers, *Box 109, Sandspit, B.C. V0T 1T0 (1-800/806-7633, 604/637-2215).*

Ecosummer Canadian Expeditions (based in Vancouver), *1516 Duranleau St., Vancouver, B.C. V6H 3S4 (604/669-7741, fax: 604/669-3244).*

Kwuna Point Charters, *Box 184, Sandspit, B.C. V0T 1T0 (604/637-2261 — Sandspit, 604/559-4264 — Skidegate).*

Avil Cove Charters (Keith and Barb Rowsell), *P.O. Box 454, Queen Charlotte City, B.C. V0T 1S0 (604/559-8207).*

The Very Best of the Queen Charlotte Islands

Sandspit, with a population of 700 people, is the site of the major airport on the Queen Charlottes and is a primary jumping-off point for expeditions to South Moresby and remote fishing camps. The town is

Sandspit - South Moresby

primarily a transportation centre, although there are a few stores and other services for residents and for travellers planning to head to Gwaii Haanas. All of these are within reasonable walking distance from the airport. In the summer, Parks Canada opens an information and registration office for visitors to Gwaii Haanas. Register here before visiting the wilderness reserve.

PLACES TO EAT
If you are looking for a place to eat, the **Sandspit Inn** has a nice pub and a coffee shop (see below).

PLACES TO STAY
In the Sandspit area, there only a few places to stay. Most visitors appear to continue on to Queen Charlotte City. If you do plan to stay in Sandspit, however, here are some recommendations.

Sandspit Inn: *($$$)* The Sandspit Inn is located right next to the airport and has decent rooms. *Box 469, Sandspit, B.C. V0T 1T0 (1-800/663-1144).*

The Seaport Bed & Breakfast and Guest Home: *($)* This bed and breakfast is a short walk down the main road from the airport. Located in an appealing waterfront home, Seaport offers guests separate accommodation from their hostess, full kitchen facilities, and breakfast. With its convenient location (on the beach and near Sandspit's few stores) and excellent prices, the Seaport is hard to beat. *371A Alliford Bay, Box 206, Sandspit, B.C. V0T 1T0 (604/637-5698, fax: 604/637-5697).*

Campgrounds: Gray Bay, an attractive park located 21 kilometres (13 miles) southeast of Sandspit, has a lovely and peaceful beach. The BC Forest Service and MacMillan Bloedel maintain campsites here. **Mos-**

quito Lake Park, about 44 kilometres (28 miles) southwest of Sandspit, is operated by the BC Forest Service and Western Forest Products. Mosquito Lake Park has eleven campsites.

THINGS TO DO
Fletcher Challenge: Fletcher Challenge offers forestry tours and controls the logging roads on North Moresby. Stop by the Fletcher Challenge offices on Beach Road *(604/637-5323)* before travelling on any of the logging roads.

Pallant Creek Hatchery: If you would like to visit the hatchery, which is located a couple of kilometres past Mosquito Lake park, write to them at *Box 225, Sandspit, B.C. V0T 1C0*.

OUTDOOR RECREATION
Moresby Camp: Just beyond the Pallant Creek Hatchery, this boat-launching site provides access to the Cumshewa Inlet and the South Moresby area.

Queen Charlotte City - Skidegate

The second largest settled area on the island, Queen Charlotte City has a population of close to 1,200 people. Another 500 people reside at Skidegate.

Queen Charlotte is the most interesting and complete tourist destination on the island and is worth an extended visit. Logging and fishing are the main industries, but a number of residents are employed by government agencies. Stop at the Travel InfoCentre on the way into town and get a copy of the *"Guide to the Queen Charlotte Islands"* and some advice on fishing, camping, and picnicking spots.

▲ Queen Charlotte City is an active fishing and logging community, and one of the starting points for excursions to Gwaii Haanas. *(Ken Coates)*

Skidegate is one of the main Haida communities and is a centre of Haida cultural revival. A major residential sub-division can be found in the hills behind Skidegate, and a new school and hospital are planned for the area.

PLACES TO EAT

★ **Oceana Restaurant:** *($$)* This is not only the best restaurant in Queen Charlotte City, it is also the best Chinese food restaurant in all of northern British Columbia! Newly opened, the restaurant is nicely decorated, the food is superb, and the service is warm, helpful and friendly. Ask for staff recommendations. We did and were rewarded with two wonderful dishes: a hot pot and a curry. Oceana deserves every success; it is a fabulous dining opportunity. *3119 3rd Ave. (604/559-8633).*

Summerland Pizza and Steakhouse: *($$)* Specializing in Greek and Mediterranean food, this Queen Charlotte Restaurant is another good spot for lunch or dinner. Although the furnishings are a little spartan, the food is tasty and the service friendly. The evening menu lists four or five homemade Mediterranean specials which sound tantalizing. The portions are very generous; a half serving of the ravioli or lasagna will satisfy most appetites. *223 3rd Ave. (604/559-4588).*

The Sea Raven Seafood Restaurant: *($$)* Serving a variety of fish and seafood dishes, this Queen Charlotte Restaurant is a favourite with locals and visitors. The Sea Raven is located in the motel of the same name. *3rd Ave. (604/559-4423).*

Dave's In the Village: *($)* This small trailer along the main road in Skidegate offers burgers and fries.

PLACES TO STAY

Gracie's Place: *($)* Gracie's Place offers rooms in a funky-looking wooden house along Queen Charlotte City's main street. *3113-3rd Ave., Queen Charlotte City, B.C. V0T 1S0 (604/559-4262, fax: 604/559-4622).*

Misty Island Guest House: *($$)* The Misty Island Guest House has an excellent waterfront location with superb views of the harbour. Located on the main street in Queen Charlotte toward the west end of town. *414 3rd Ave., Box 503, Queen Charlotte City, B.C. V0T 1S0 (604/559-8224).*

Premier Hotel: *($$)* Also along the main road in Queen Charlotte, this lovely spot offers historic charm and quaint accommodations. *3101-3rd Ave., Box 268,* ★

Queen Charlotte City, B.C. V0T 1S0 (604/559-8415, fax: 604/559-8198).

Sea Raven Resort Motel: *($$)* This motel will interest those looking for more standard motel rooms at reasonable rates. *3301-3rd Ave., Queen Charlotte City, B.C. V0T 1S0 (604/559-4423).*

Spruce Point Lodge: *($$)* Tucked away in a residential area in the western part of Queen Charlotte, the Spruce Point Lodge has nice rooms with balconies that overlook the ocean. *609-6th Ave., Queen Charlotte City, B.C. V0T 1S0 (604/559-8234).*

Dorothy and Mike's Guest House: *($)* Although not open while we were in Queen Charlotte (it was undergoing renovations), this bed and breakfast was strongly recommended by locals. *3125-2nd Ave., Queen Charlotte City, B.C. V0T 1S0 (604/559-8439).*

THINGS TO DO
The Long House Gift Shop: Situated at the entrance to Skidegate (just off the highway), this gift shop sells beautiful Haida art, t-shirts and books.

Joy's Island Jewellery: When you stop at the Queen Charlotte Travel InfoCentre, take a peak inside Joy's Island Jewellery. This store highlights the work of local artists. *3922 Highway 33.*

Rainbow Gallery: This interesting Queen Charlotte shop is filled with books on the area, jewellery, and a variety of crafts and artwork. *3201-3rd Ave.*

Hanging By a Fibre (Gallery, Gifts and Cappuccino Bar): Located beneath the Hummingbird Café on 3rd Ave. in Queen Charlotte, this store has some lovely art and an inviting cappuccino bar.

Observer Books: This Queen Charlotte Bookstore specializes in North Coast and nature books. *623 - 5th Ave.*

Other Shopping: Myles From Nowhere and **Bearskin Bay**, both on Wharf Street in Queen Charlotte, are two other shops that are worth a browse.

Skidegate Village: Skidegate Village is graced with the presence of many carvers. A cedar building in traditional long house style is located on the beach in front of the village. Note the nearby totem pole which was carved by the famous Canadian artist, Bill Reid.

Queen Charlotte Island Museum: Located at Second Beach in Skidegate, the Queen Charlotte Island Museum is filled with displays of Haida history and art, pioneer life, and natural history *(604/559-4643).*

Greenwood Travel Services: Jack and Sharleen Greenwood can help you make arrangements for any charters or rentals that you might need while visiting the islands. *Box 96, Queen Charlotte City (604/559-8455, fax: 604/559-8430).*

OUTDOOR RECREATION
Haida Gwaii Watchmen: This office, located beside the Queen Charlotte Island Museum in Skidegate is where you register before travelling to South Moresby *(604/ 559-8225).*

Tlell - Port Clements

In the middle of Graham Island, easily missed by travellers, are two fascinating communities. Tlell is one of the great delights in all of northern British Columbia — a vibrant artistic community in a beautiful coastal setting. This tiny village, which has a population of 150 people, does not have a community centre; it consists of a series of homes and farms spread out along the highway and several small side roads. Port Clements, with a population of about 500 people, is a small logging town that is marked by a prominent government wharf and several heritage buildings.

PLACES TO EAT
In Tlell, good dining is offered at **Tlell River House** *($$) on Beitush Rd. (604/557-4211)*. In Port Clements, the **Yakoun River Inn** *($$) on Bayview Drive at the Government Wharf (604/557-4440)* has good pub food and a nice view and the **III Cheers Restaurant** *($) on Cedar Ave. (604/557-9333)* offers travellers another place to eat.

PLACES TO STAY
Sitka Lodging: Sitka Lodging, near Tlell and quite a distance off the highway, has one deluxe cottage available for rent. *Box 460, Queen Charlotte City, B.C. V0T 1S0 (604/557-4386).*

Tlell River House: *($$)* The Tlell River House, which is on the Tlell River and not far from the ocean, has a nice restaurant. *Beltush Rd., Box 52, Tlell, B.C. V0T 1Y0 (604/557-4211).*

Hitunwa Kaitza (Feathered Headdress Star): *($)* Locally known as Cacilia's Bed & Breakfast, this is a nice place to stay. Hitunwa Kaitza is a rustic log house right on the beach near Tlell, and Cacilia is a friendly and relaxed hostess. In addition to the private rooms, there is a common area for sleeping if you have your own sleeping bag, and the charge for this or for camping on the property is $10 per person per night. *Box 3, Highway 16, Tlell, B.C. V0T 1Y0 (604/557-4664).*

Kumdis River Lodge: *($$)* Near Port Clements, this lodge is a year-round fishing retreat. For more information, write to *436 W. 2nd Ave., Vancouver, B.C. V5Y 1E2 (1-800/668-7544).*

Thelma's Bed & Breakfast: *($)* This bed and breakfast is located right in Port Clements. *3 Bayview Dr., Port Clements, B.C. (fax: 604/557-4555).*

THINGS TO DO
The Crystal Cabin Rock and Gem Shop: The Crystal Cabin (on the Richardson Road in Tlell) has a lovely selection of jewellery, polished stones, and carvings. There are some truly beautiful pieces here.

Body Currents: Body Currents, located on the Richardson Road in Tlell, is an interesting and welcoming store which sells cappuccinos, cookies, cinnamon buns, and ice cream sodas along with a great assortment of local art, ranging from t-shirts and driftwood carvings to art supplies. The owners are friendly, fun, and full of advice about what to see and do in the area. ★

Sitka Studio: Also on the Richardson Road in Tlell, this store is just across the street from the Crystal Cabin. It also sells terrific local art, including batik silk scarves, paintings, and carvings, as well as fresh-roasted coffee beans, Belgian chocolates, books, and other unique items.

Myles from Nowhere: In Port Clements, Myles from Nowhere on Tingley Street and Bayview Drive sells local art and gifts.

Port Clements Heritage Museum: Located on Bayview Drive in Port Clements, this museums focuses on pioneer life, logging, and fishing. It is open each afternoon in July and August and, during the rest of the year, weekends from 2:00 p.m. - 4:00 p.m. *(604/557-4443)*

OUTDOOR RECREATION
Hiking: A trail to the wreck of the Pesuta, a log-carrying ship which ran aground in 1928, starts from the picnic site on the west side of the Tlell River bridge. The trail is about 10 kilometres (six miles) long (one way) and winds its way through the forest and along the beach. Along the Justkatla Road (near Port Clements) watch for signs which mark the trail to the famous Golden Spruce — a giant spruce tree with golden needles. Eight kilometres further along the same road, there is a trail to an old Haida **dugout canoe.**

Fishing: Mayer Lake (in Naikoon Provincial Park) and the **Mamin and Yakoun Rivers** are all good fishing spots.

Naikoon Provincial Park: Park headquarters are just off the highway near Tlell (south of the Misty Meadows campsite). Stop here for more information about the park. Mayer Lake is a good spot for picnicking, boating, and fishing.

Masset - Old Masset

The largest settled area on the islands, its status somewhat in doubt due to the announced substantial reduction of the Masset military base, this culturally and socially divided region has a combined population of about 2,100 people. Masset is a fishing, tourist, and military community — a combination that sometimes contributes to tensions. The setting is beautiful — along Masset Sound and near the north end of Naikoon Provincial Park — and many of the residents are true fans of the place (including a number of retired service personnel who returned to Masset after leaving the forces).

The Haida settlement of Old Masset (or Haida) is an important artistic centre. Recently, a village office, new school, and several commercial outlets have been added to the community. Considerable growth has also taken place along the Tow Hill Road (from Masset to the north end of Naikoon Provincial Park), where a number of beach front residences have recently been constructed (most of these are situated on properties that were first staked by homesteaders early in the twentieth century and long before contemporary restrictions on shoreline development). Visitors to the provincial park, the most attractive feature in the region, walk kilometres of pristine beaches, clamber up Tow Hill, and marvel at the alternately beguiling and bewitching coastal forests.

PLACES TO EAT

Café Gallery: *($$)* This pleasant Masset restaurant, which serves seafood, steaks, soups, salads, and other dishes, has local art displayed on its walls. *2062 Collison (604/626-3672)*

Daddy Cool's Neighbourhood Pub: *($$)* Located at the corner of Main and Collison in Masset, this pub serves Filipino food *(604/626-3210)*.

The Path: *($)* The Path is a great spot! The only restaurant in British Columbia without electrical service, The Path advertises itself as "beyond the reach of hydro and within touch of Mother earth." Driftwood benches, kerosene lamps, vegetarian meals, interesting and friendly owners, Saturday night jam sessions, and scrumptious desserts all combine to form this unique restaurant. A definite must-see! *Located five kilome-*

tres (three miles) past the Chown River bridge on the Tow Hill Road. Open in the summer only.

PLACES TO STAY

★ **Alaska View Lodge:** *($$)* On the road to Tow Hill and across from the rain forest, the Alaska View Lodge looks directly onto a long sandy beach. Cozy rooms and complete breakfasts are available, and gourmet dinners are sometimes served upon request. This is a truly beautiful spot. *P.O. Box 227, Masset, B.C. V0T 1M0 (1-800/661-0019).*

Copper Beech House: *($$)* This is a well kept bed and breakfast overlooking Masset Harbour. *1610 Delkatla St., Masset, B.C., V0T 1M0 (604/626-5441).*

THINGS TO DO

Old Massett: Old Massett, a Haida village, is a good place to see carvers at work and to look at the variety of beautiful Haida arts and jewellery. Check in at the village office for directions and for permission to visit and/or take photographs.

Dixon Entrance Golf Course: Located along the Tow Hill Road, this golf course allows golfers to enjoy an ocean view *(604/626-3735).*

OUTDOOR RECREATION

Hiking: Driving along the Tow Hill Road, you will come to signs pointing left to the **Delkatla Wildlife Sanctuary**. There are some nice places to walk through here and, depending on the season, lots of birds to see. If you continue along the Tow Hill road, there is a small parking area at the beach from which you can stroll along for kilometres in either direction. At the end of Tow Hill Road is the parking area for the hike

★ up **Tow Hill**. (If you have a four-wheel drive vehicle, you can continue driving along the beach toward Rose

Spit.) The hike isn't too long and, although it is somewhat steep, boardwalks and steps allow climbers to avoid the slippery sections. The view from the top of Tow Hill is magnificent and well worth the energy expended in getting there. At the bottom of Tow Hill, signs point toward the **blow hole** (where the ocean surf is blown through an opening in the rocks). A short walk takes you to a rocky beach and the blow hole itself.

Lodges: If you want the full Queen Charlotte Islands treatment, you might consider the luxury resort at Naden Harbour. The **Queen Charlotte Lodge** is set up for fishing expeditions and offers superb facilities (hot tub, dining room, gift shop, etc.). All inclusive package deals (including air travel) are available from Vancouver. This is an expensive, first-class resort, but it is also a one-of-a-kind wilderness retreat. *7069 Winston St., Burnaby, B.C. V5A 3R1 (1-800/665-9980 — Canada, 1-800/688-8959 — U.S., fax: 604/420-9194).* In a similar vein, you could also try **Langara Fishing Lodge** *(436 West 2nd Ave., Vancouver, B.C. V5Y 1E2, 1-800/668-7544, fax: 604/873-5500).*

North Coast

Selected Events on the Queen Charlotte Islands

Masset Harbour Days	Masset	May
Loggers Sports	Sandspit	June
Canada Day	Port Clements	July
Tlell Fall Fair	Tlell	August
Fall Festival	Masset	September

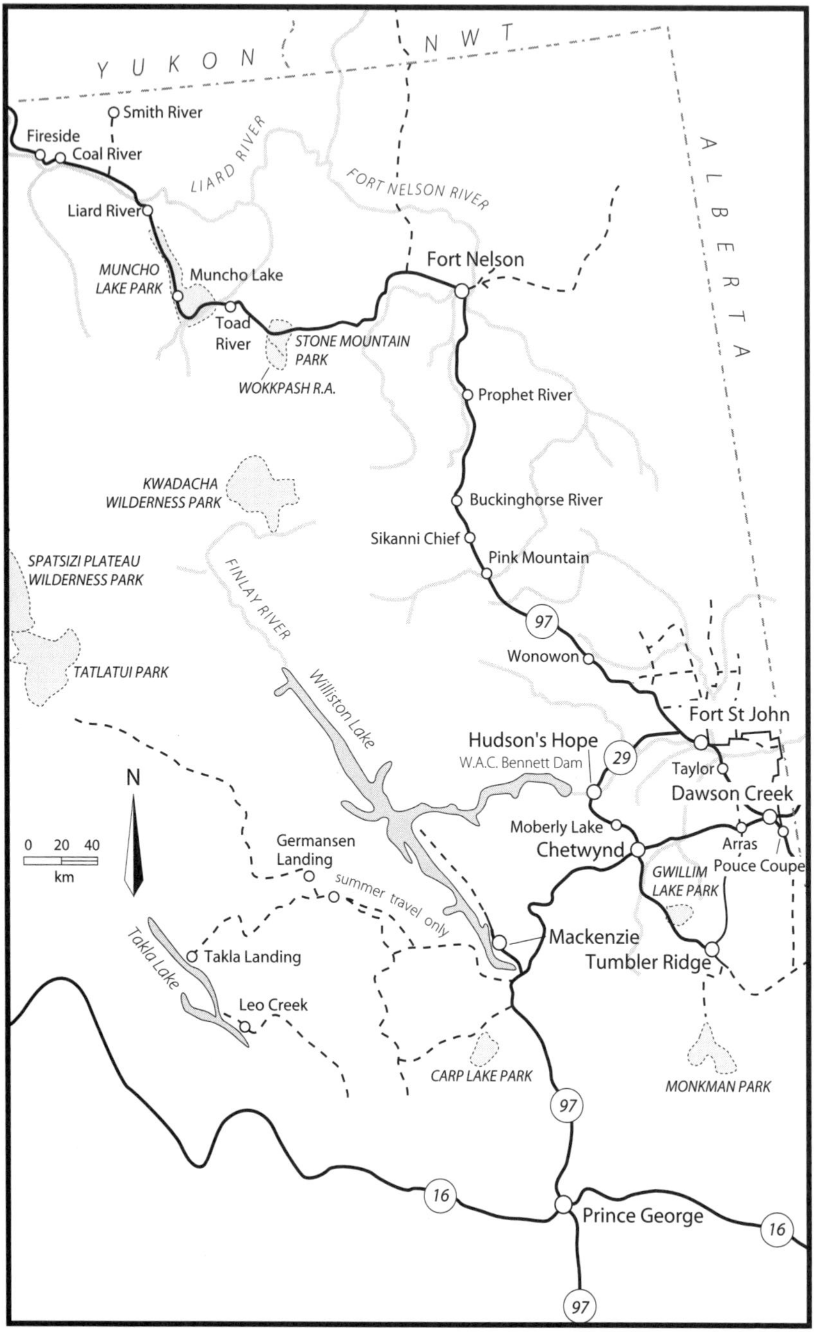

Y U K O N
N W T
A L B E R T A
Smith River
Fireside
Coal River
LIARD RIVER
FORT NELSON RIVER
Liard River
MUNCHO LAKE PARK
Muncho Lake
Toad River
Fort Nelson
STONE MOUNTAIN PARK
WOKKPASH R.A.
Prophet River
KWADACHA WILDERNESS PARK
Buckinghorse River
Sikanni Chief
Pink Mountain
SPATSIZI PLATEAU WILDERNESS PARK
FINLAY RIVER
97
TATLATUI PARK
Wonowon
Williston Lake
Fort St John
Hudson's Hope
W.A.C. Bennett Dam
29
Taylor
Dawson Creek
N
Moberly Lake
0 20 40
km
Germansen Landing
Chetwynd
Arras
Pouce Coupe
GWILLIM LAKE PARK
summer travel only
Takla Lake
Takla Landing
Mackenzie
Tumbler Ridge
Leo Creek
CARP LAKE PARK
MONKMAN PARK
97
16
Prince George
16
97

9
Peace River - Alaska Highway

One of our great friends loves to refer to the Peace River country as the "Serengetti of the North." Most of us are too swept up in his enthusiasm to ask him exactly what he means by that — the Serengetti is a great African plain that is noted for its herds of wild animals — but it is hard to avoid sharing his excitement for this vast and often forgotten land. The Peace River district is wheat country — the most northerly extension of the Great Plains — and hence is both the end of the south and the beginning of the North.

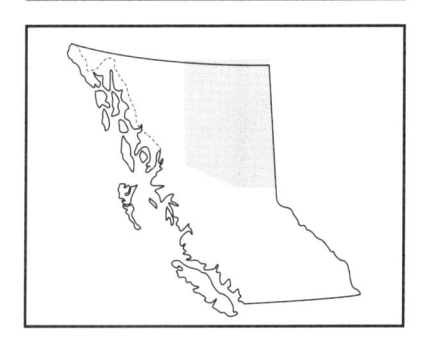

The Peace River District is a truly unique area. Closely aligned with Alberta — it is in the mountain time zone and hence is off sync with the rest of British Columbia for part of each year — the Peace shares much of that province's political and cultural outlook. Edmonton newspapers are more common on newsstands and paper boxes than those from the Lower Mainland, and many students head east, to Grande Prairie Community College or to the University of Alberta, for their post-secondary education.

This hard-working, hard-driving, politically conservative part of the province is often at odds with the rest of British Columbia and has a well-nurtured sense of grievance against the urban dwellers who live some 1,400 kilometres to the south. Area residents have been known to wonder whether the rest of the province really thinks very much about conditions in their neck of the woods. After all, it was not until after World War II that there were road and railway connections between the Peace and the rest of British Columbia.

The area is not all farmland. South of Dawson Creek is Tumbler Ridge (the central community for the Northeast Coal Development Project), the lumbering towns of Chetwynd and Mackenzie, and Hudson's Hope (a small town sustained by the work associated with the W.A.C. Bennett Dam).

The Peace River also provides access to the world's most famous highway: the Alaska Highway, which connects Dawson Creek, British Columbia, and Fairbanks, Alaska. North of Fort St. John is a vast, underdeveloped, heavily forested land that stretches for hundreds of kilometres to the Yukon boundary. There are only a handful of highway stations, a few First Nations villages, and the lumber/gas/highway town of Fort Nelson in this area. Because the distances are vast and travel times can be lengthy, the land is slow to surrender its mysteries and its diversity.

A Brief History

In the Peace River country, First Nations people pre-dated the arrival of Europeans by several thousand years. Archaeological research in the Charlie Lake caves (near Fort St. John) has revealed aboriginal habitation dating back about 10,000 years. So, when Alexander Mackenzie of the North West Company ventured into the area about 200 years ago, he entered a land with a rich and diverse human history. The establishment of a trading post near the present site of Fort St. John marked the beginning of non-indigenous settlement in the area. The other fur trade posts that followed, including Fort Nelson along the Muskwa River, formed the foundation of an industry that flourished in the area for generations.

The region attracted renewed attention in the early years of the twentieth century, when the settling of the Canadian and American prairies increased interest in the agricultural potential of the Peace River district. Farmers moved in slowly — even an attempt to settle returning World War I veterans in the area did not increase the farming population dramatically — and small settlements developed at Dawson Creek and Fort St. John. The extension of the Northern Alberta Railway to Dawson Creek in 1931 improved the viability of the northern British Columbia settlements, but not enough to spark the kind of agricultural boom that followed the development of more southerly railway lines. Still, on the vast plains above the Peace River, a viable wheat economy developed, although the farming communities were small and unremarkable.

Perhaps one of the more significant products from this area in the first half of this century was W.A.C. Bennett — later Premier of British Columbia and one of the most fervent advocates of northern development that this province has ever seen. (Bennett, after several years in the Peace, moved to the Okanagan district, where he launched his successful political career.)

No area of the province was as completely transformed by World War II as the Peace River district. When the United States government decided to build a highway to Alaska and then opted for the Edmonton-

Fairbanks route over the seemingly more obvious Prince George to Dawson City route, the fate of the Peace was sealed. Thousands of American soldiers, followed by thousands of Canadian and American civilians, flooded into Dawson Creek and Fort St. John in the spring and summer of 1942. Construction commenced a few kilometres north of Fort St. John and the Dawson Creek - Fort St. John road was upgraded. (This upgrading included a Peace River bridge, which collapsed in later years.) The Americans transformed the region; they improved the airfields of the Northwest Staging Route, built the Alaska Highway, and added to the facilities and resources of the two southern highway towns.

Further north, along the Alaska Highway, the changes were even more profound. What was, until then, a fur trading and subsistence hunting area, now faced overnight development. Highway camps opened along the route. A few, like Fort Nelson, remained after the war as sizeable communities; others were transformed into private gas stations and highway lodges. With lightning speed, as the Americans built first the military pioneer road and later a more developed civilian highway, the vast, hitherto inaccessible reaches of northeastern British Columbia gained a link to the southern world.

The Americans left at war's end, and responsibility for the highway passed to the Canadian Department of National Defence and, in 1964, to Public Works. Only in the 1960s was large-scale reconstruction undertaken, and by the next decade the condition of the Alaska Highway had improved significantly. What was, as late as the early 1970s, described as a "rough road North" had become a serviceable, dependable, mostly-paved, high-quality highway.

The mystique of the Alaska Highway remains a powerful force in this region. The fiftieth anniversary of the highway brought thousands of visitors into the area and encouraged the tourist industry and communities to reconsider the importance of the highway to their lives. Many towns have attractions featuring highway themes — Mile Zero in Dawson Creek is the most famous — and there is a great deal more awareness about the highway's historical and contemporary role. Each year, the chance to drive the highway and visit Alaska and the Yukon draws thousands of tourists into the Peace River district and forms the backbone of a vibrant tourist industry.

The construction of the W.A.C. Bennett Dam brought hundreds of workers into the area in the 1960s; only a handful remained behind to maintain this massive plant. The Bennett Dam, initially presented as the centre-piece for a vast scheme of northern development, was intended (like Kemano to the southwest) to bring new communities and industries into existence. Little of that occurred; most of the electricity flows south to the Lower Mainland.

Anxious to promote further development in the area, the government decided in the 1980s to promote the exploitation of the vast northeast coal deposits. Long-term deals (subject to renegotiation if market conditions warrant) were signed with several Japanese companies. The provincial government helped out by making major investments in regional infrastructure (including an upgrading of the BC Rail line), regional road construction, and the development of a coal port in Prince Rupert. The mining companies built a company town at Tumbler Ridge and two mines — Quintette and Bullmoose — went into production. The coal operations continue, although the viability of the enterprise has been threatened from time to time by declining world prices and Japanese insistence on renegotiations.

There is far more to the Peace River - Alaska Highway district than the fur trade, agriculture, and the Alaska Highway. Dawson Creek remains an agricultural centre (supported by the summer tourist trade), although several years of drought have added to the historical difficulties of the wheat economy. The area has a boom and bust oil and gas industry (it is currently booming) and hundreds of millions of dollars in oil and gas are taken out of the region each year. Fort St. John is the centre of this industry, but the Fort Nelson area also has important oil and gas reserves. Chetwynd — known locally for its logging and across the continent for a bizarre item in "Ann Landers" about the alleged shortage of marriageable women in the community and the alleged surplus of well-off, marriable men — is an important forestry centre. Mackenzie, to the south and west, is a company town that serves several major pulp mills.

Getting There

Access to this part of northern British Columbia is fairly simple. If you are travelling by plane, you can fly AirBC to Dawson Creek and Central Mountain Airlines or Canadian Airlines to Fort St. John. The AirBC flights connect Prince George and Dawson Creek in British Columbia to Grande Prairie and Edmonton in Alberta. Most people drive the John Hart Highway (Highway 97) from Prince George or along Highways 2 and 49 from Edmonton and Grande Prairie. The Alaska Highway which runs through the district like an arrow, bisects this largely unsettled and underdeveloped land. There are only a handful of smaller roads. You can reach Tumbler Ridge via a paved road from Chetwynd or over a gravel road from the highway heading south from Dawson Creek. There is also a cut-off at Chetwynd for Fort St. John.

There are a few things to keep in mind when travelling by car in this area. The Alaska Highway is in a lot better shape than mythology would have it. Except for a few hundred kilometres of well-sealed gravel road, the entire distance from Dawson Creek to Fairbanks is paved. Services, however, are quite dispersed, and you are well-advised to take a few basic precautions, particularly if you are travelling in the winter. Distances are considerable, and there are often sizeable gaps between gasoline stations, so keep an eye on your fuel gauge. Winter driving can be treacherous, particularly through the Pine Pass (between Prince George and Chetwynd). Do not travel unprepared.

Hints for the Traveller

Plan for some long driving, for this is a land of vast distances. With the exception of Dawson Creek, this is also an area of new towns that are oriented toward highways and industrial operations; there is comparatively little thought given to travellers. Historically, tourists have moved quickly through this area. Regional tourist organizations have increased their efforts to keep travellers in the area, but this is a difficult challenge given that so many tourists are fixated on Alaska and the Yukon and rarely leave time for more southerly diversions. This is unfortunate as there is a great deal to do and see in the Peace River - Alaska Highway Region. Here are a few suggestions on how to make the most of your time in the area.

➤ If you are travelling along the Alaska Highway, leave at least half a day for the Liard Hotsprings. It is rare to find such an interesting site that has not been fully commercialized. Enjoy yourself, but be sure to obey bear warnings.

▶ Muncho Lake is a truly beautiful spot. Don't just rush through; give yourself time to look around this wonderful, deep, cold lake and its surrounding barren mountainsides. There are often sheep in the area, so keep an eye out for them.

▶ Monkman Park, only recently opened as a park site, is quite spectacular. The Kinuseo Falls, within the park, are remarkable and well worth the short side trip.

▶ Visiting a power dam hardly seems like an exciting holiday adventure, but we think you will be surprised. The W.A.C. Bennett Dam is one of the largest in North America, and the tour of the dam's inner workings is very worthwhile.

▶ Area museums are quite good and are worth visiting. These communities have long and varied histories, and local historical societies have done a very good job of memorializing the past.

▶ After a long, dry day on the road, you might want to pull into the wave pool in Chetwynd. It's a real treat, particularly in a small town, and provides a welcome break from driving.

▶ Most people driving along the Alaska Highway only slow long enough to refill gas tanks and stomachs. There are many scenic viewpoints and interesting sites along the Alaska Highway and the occasional stop actually makes the long drive (remember that it is over 1,440 kilometres (900 miles) from Dawson Creek to Whitehorse) much more palatable.

➤ This region is rich in wildlife and other natural resources. Travel early in the morning or at dusk (which comes very late in the summer months) if you expect to see animals along the road. Fishing is great in area lakes, and there are excellent opportunities for photography and hiking.

➤ If you intend to travel on the Alaska Highway, it will be worth your while to pick up an *"Alaska Highway Historic Milepost Mile By Mile Guide"* at the Tourist Information Centre in Fort St. John. This guidebook describes all the points of historic interest along the Alaska Highway.

Liard Hotsprings, one of the north's many natural wonders, offers a warm, soothing respite for the weary traveller. *(Don Pettit)*

The Very Best of the Peace River - Alaska Highway Region

Mackenzie Mackenzie lies about 200 kilometres (125 miles) north of Prince George along the southern end of Williston Lake (the lake created by the WAC Bennett Dam). To reach Mackenzie, head north on Highway 97, and then turn onto Highway 39. Mackenzie is at the end of Highway 39 (about a thirty minute drive from the junction of Highways 97 and 39). The community has a population of approximately 5,800 people and most of these are employed in the forest sector. The world's largest tree-crusher, which was used to clear timber from the land that would be flooded by the construction of the WAC Bennett Dam, is found in Mackenzie.

PLACES TO EAT
The restaurant in the **Alexander Mackenzie Hotel** *($$)* (see entry below) has the best food in town. In general, because Mackenzie is primarily oriented toward the wood products industry, tourist facilities are limited.

PLACES TO STAY
Alexander Mackenzie Hotel: *($$)* There are a couple of motels in Mackenzie, but the nicest place to stay is the Alexander Mackenzie Hotel. The hotel has executive suites, licensed dining, and a whirlpool and sauna. *c/o Box 40, Mackenzie, B.C. V0J 2C0 (1-800/663-2964, 604/997-3266).*

OUTDOOR RECREATION
Golfing, hiking, and camping are all popular summer sports in the Mackenzie area. Nearby **Morfee Lake** is

a very pretty area with good swimming and boating. There is a free municipal campground here.

Skiing: The little-known but high-quality **Powder King Ski Village** is a 45-minute drive from Mackenzie and offers some of the best skiing in the province *(604/997-6323)*. Closer to Mackenzie, the **Little Mac Ski Hill**, is a fine place to take children skiing. In addition, there are 42 kilometres (26 miles) of cross-country ski trails in the area.

★

Chetwynd

Chetwynd (known as "Little Prairie" when the first white settlers arrived in 1912) is located in the foothills of the Rocky Mountains about 300 kilometres (188 miles) north of Prince George. It has a population of about 3,000 people and is primarily a forestry community.

PLACES TO EAT
Swiss Inn Restaurant: *($$)* The Swiss Inn, which serves a variety of European and Canadian dishes, including schnitzels and pasta, is the best place to eat in Chetwynd. Portions are generous and the food is very tasty. The pizza, in particular, is excellent. *Located on Highway 97 just east of the turn-off to Fort St. John (604/788-2566).*

PLACES TO STAY
Chetwynd's three hotels are all along the main highway. There is also a free municipal campground.

THINGS TO DO
Keep an eye out for the world-famous **chain-saw sculptures** of animals and birds that were hand-crafted by British Columbian artists and are displayed throughout the community. Chetwynd has a lovely new **leisure**

wave pool (off Highway 97 and north of the Swiss Inn) which is an enticing place to stop if you have been on the road for a while. During the summer, the **Little Prairie Heritage Museum,** the **Railway Museum,** and an authentic old **Trapper's Cabin** are all open to visitors. The Little Prairie Heritage Museum is on the hill two kilometres (one mile) west of town, and the Railway Museum and the Trapper's Cabin are next to the InfoCentre. **Moberly Lake Provincial Campground,** north of Chetwynd, has a marina and a golf course.

OUTDOOR RECREATION
Powder King Ski Village is only 100 kilometres (63 miles) away, and there is good hunting, fishing, boating and hiking in this area. If you have some time to explore, ask for details at the information centre *(604/788-3345).* There is a nature walk along the hiking trails on **Mount Old Baldy.**

Hudson's Hope

This small community, which has long historical roots, grew quickly during the construction of the W.A.C. Bennett Dam. It now has a population of 1,000 people.

PLACES TO EAT
J.J. Substop: *($)* This restaurant, which is located, on the main street in Hudson Hope, is worth a try *(604/783-9425).*

PLACES TO STAY
Hotels: There are two places to stay in Hudson's Hope: the **Peace Glen Hotel** *($, Dudley Dr., c/o Box 248 Hudson's Hope, B.C. V0C 1V0, 604/783-9966)* or the **Sportsman's Inn** *($, 10501 Carter Ave., c/o Box 237, Hudson's Hope, B.C. V0C 1V0, 604/783-5523, fax: 604/783-5511).*

Campgrounds: Cameron Lake *(Highway 29, c/o Box 330, Hudson's Hope, B.C. V0C 1V0, 604/783-9901)*, Dinosaur Lake *(Peace Canyon Dam Rd. W., c/o Box 330, Hudson's Hope, B.C. V0C 1V0, 604/783-9901)*, and Alwin Holland Park *(Alwin Holland Rd. E., c/o Box 330, Hudson's Hope, B.C. V0C 1V0, 604/783-9901)* campgrounds are all beautiful spots to camp for a few days. The fishing is excellent in all three places.

THINGS TO DO

It is worth a stop in Hudson's Hope to look around a little; this is a pretty community.

Heritage Park: Beside the highway near the dam access road, there is a heritage park with a number of historic buildings. **The Hudson's Hope Museum** in the old Hudson's Bay company store displays trapping, farming, and coal-mining artifacts along with a fabulous fossil collection *(604/783-5735)*. Beside the museum is St. Peter's Church — a log church built in 1938.

W.A.C. Bennett Dam: The dam and the Gordon Shrum Generating Station are a few kilometres west of Hudson's Hope. Tours of the dam are available weekdays year-round by appointment and weekends from Victoria Day to Thanksgiving between 9:30 a.m. and 4:30 p.m. *(604/783-5211)*. A small information centre provides visitors with facts about the dam, shows a film about the dam's opening, and has a number of hands-on displays about electricity. You pick up your tickets for the tour here. The tour is free but, as part of it is by bus, you are required to pick up a ticket so that they can keep track of numbers. The visit to the dam is very interesting and informative. Williston Lake, the dam reservoir, flooded three rivers and stretches 362 kilometres (226 miles). Very little of this area was even logged prior to the flooding, so boating in Williston Lake can be dangerous. It is interesting to contemplate that this large scale flooding took place with almost no protest from environmental groups.

Peace Canyon Dam: The visitor's centre at the Peace Canyon Dam presents visitors with two life-sized dinosaurs, excellent photo displays and exhibits of the area's natural and pioneer history, and documentation of the building of the Peace Canyon Project. Open daily from 8:00 a.m. - 4:00 p.m.

Tumbler Ridge

Tumbler Ridge, a modern company town of 4,500 people, was built in the 1980s to service the two mines of the Northeast Coal Project: Bullmoose and Quintette.

PLACES TO EAT
The Ridge House *($$, 101-215 Main, 603/242-3433)* is Tumbler's Ridge's fine dining establishment. There are also fast food, pizza, and Chinese restaurants in town.

PLACES TO STAY
Hotels: Hotel accommodations are available at the **Tumbler Ridge Inn** *($$, 275 Southgate Tumbler Ridge, B.C. V0C 2W0, 1-800/663-3898, 604/242-4277)*.

Campgrounds: There are a couple of campgrounds in or near Tumbler Ridge: **Monkman Way R.V. Park** *(1 Monkman Way, c/o Box 100, Tumbler Ridge, B.C. V0C 2W0, 604/242-5717)* and **Lions Flatbed Creek Campground** *(c/o Box 100, Tumbler Ridge, B.C. V0C 2W0, 604/242-4242)*, which is two kilometres (one mile) from Tumbler Ridge on Highway 29.

THINGS TO DO
Tours: Tours of the Quintette and Bullmoose mines are available in the summer. Free tickets are available

from the Tourist Information Centre, *Southgate Rd., Box 606, Tumbler Ridge, B.C. V0C 2W0 (604/242-4702).*

Recreational Facilities: Tumbler Ridge has a recreation centre and a nine-hole golf course.

OUTDOOR RECREATION
Hiking: There are hiking trails near the **Flatbed Creek Campground,** including one to **Flatbed Falls. Kinuseo Falls,** at the northern end of **Monkman Wilderness Park,** is a popular day trip from Tumbler Ridge. The falls, which are 60 metres (200 feet) high, are taller than Niagara Falls (although they are not as wide). The provincial park campsite is a short walk away from the

Kinuseo Falls, in Monkman Provincial Park, is one of the province's most majestic waterfalls.
(Earl Brown)

lookout point at the falls. For the adventurous, there are marked hiking trails into the wilderness area. This a good place for spotting wildlife; black bears, grizzly bears, moose, deer, elk, caribou, sheep and mountain goats all live in this area. To reach Kinuseo Falls, follow Highway 29 south to the Quintette Mine sign and turn right. Continue along this road until you reach the falls. You will pass the mine property (where the road becomes gravel), go through two tunnels, and drive over a small bridge. The trip takes about an hour and a half, and the road will be relatively rough in places.

Snowmobiling: Snowmobiling is very popular in the Tumbler Ridge area. If you are interested, pick up a "District of Tumbler Ridge Snowmobiling Guide" from the tourist information centre. This brochure gives you information on the best snowmobiling in the area. **Babcock Mountain** is one of the more popular spots.

Dawson Creek

Dawson Creek was established when the Northern Alberta Railway Line was extended to the area in 1931. In 1942, when American soldiers and engineers arrived to build the Alaska Highway, Dawson Creek flourished as a supply town. Today, Dawson Creek has a population of approximately 12,000 people and is the supply town for the Peace River farmers.

PLACES TO EAT
Mile Zero Café: *($$)* The Mile Zero Café, a classic small-town eatery, serves a few breakfast items, burgers, sandwiches, soups and salads. Good food at reasonable prices. *1901 Alaska Highway (604/782-1456).*

Finnigan's Pub: *($$)* The walls in Finnigan's Pub, which is situated in a big alpine-style house, are adorned with books and hunting trophies. The pub serves great food - the usual pub fare of sandwiches, chicken fingers, fries, burgers, soups, etc. - and is a fun place to eat. *12121 8th St.(604/782-6462).*

Alaska Café: *($$)* The Alaska Café, which has good food and interesting surroundings, is worth a visit. The menu is filled with a great number of selections for both lunch and dinner. Steaks, seafood, sandwiches, burgers, quiches, schnitzels, soups, and European tortes and other desserts fill the menu. The Alaska Café is part of a hotel complex that was originally known as the Dew Drop Inn. The owners of the Alaska Café also own the hotel, and they are refurbishing it to reflect the time span from the gay nineties of the last century to the present decade. *10209 10th St. (604/782-7040).*

Rosie's Steak and Seafood House: *($$)* Rosie's is one of the most interesting restaurants in the Peace district. Specializing in steak and seafood, the restaurant also offers good salads, and pizza. *800-102nd Ave. (604-782-8419).*

PLACES TO STAY

The George Dawson Inn: *($$)* This is the best hotel in Dawson Creek. *11705 8th St., Dawson Creek, B.C. V1G 4N9 (1-800/663-2745, 604/782-9151).*

Dawson Creek Bed & Breakfast Inns: *($)* There are nice rooms available here. *933-111th Ave., Dawson Creek, B.C. V1G 2X4 (604/782-4319).*

Red Roof Bed & Breakfast: *($$)* For a farm setting, try the Red Roof Bed and Breakfast, which is located about 20 minutes from Dawson Creek. *Box 524, Pouce Coupe, B.C. V0C 2C0 (604/786-5581).*

THINGS TO DO

Northern Alberta Railway Park: The Northern Alberta Railway Park, a good first place to stop in Dawson Creek, is home to the original Dawson Creek NAR station (built in 1931). Inside this building is the **Tourist InfoCentre** *(604/782-9528)* and the **Dawson Creek Station Museum.** The museum provides visitors with information on the construction of the Alaska Highway and the history of the Peace region. There are also some archaeological displays. Next door, a restored grain elevator (circa 1949) houses an art gallery. On the southeast corner of the Northern Alberta Railway Park is a stone cairn marking the beginning of the Alaska Highway. *900 Alaska Ave.*

Mile Zero Post: A three-metre-high marker noting Mile Zero of the Alaska Highway stands at the centre of 102nd Ave. and 10th St. Many tourists get their photos taken by this Mile Zero Post.

Mile Zero Rotary Park: Located just west of Dawson Creek along the Alaska Highway, this park is based on a 1940s theme; visitors are transported back to the time when troops arrived in Dawson Creek to begin construction of the Alaska Highway. Within the park is the **Walter Wright Pioneer Village**, where a number of historical buildings — a tea house, a photography studio, a corner store, a printing press — can be found. The Pioneer Village is open daily from Victoria Day to Labour Day *(604/782-9595)*. Mile Zero Rotary Park also contains an outdoor man-made lake, picnic facilities, a playground, and a BMX track. **Sudeten Hall**, a heritage building that is also located in the park, hosts dinner theatre productions in the summer *(604/782-7144)*.

The Centre for Agricultural Diversification Mile Zero Farm of Northern Lights College: An interesting spot for a visit, this centre does research and development on the bison and reindeer industries. Plains and wood bison roam the property, but reindeer research is carried out on local reindeer farms. If you would like to visit the farm and see the buffalo, you are welcome to do so, but you must phone ahead. Currently, there is no charge for a visit although this might change. To reach the Mile Zero Farm from the Mile Zero traffic circle head east on Highway 49 for three kilometres/ two miles *(604/784-7502).*

Fort St. John

Fort St. John is one of the oldest non-Native settlements in British Columbia. Archaeological evidence that Paleo Indians lived here over 10,000 years ago suggests that it is also one of the oldest Native settlement areas. The original Fort St. John post was moved several times to locations on the Peace and other nearby rivers. The founder of the first post was Alexander Mackenzie, and a monument to this famous fur trader/explorer can be found in Centennial Park beside the museum. The construction of the Alaska Highway precipitated tremendous growth for Fort St. John, and this growth was augmented by later developments in rail and air transportation links to the south and in forestry and agriculture. Gas and oil were discovered in 1952, and today Fort St. John boasts of being the energy capital of British Columbia. The community has a population of 14,000 people.

PLACES TO EAT
Northern Lights Restaurant: *($$)* This is a popular spot with a large and varied menu. Steak, seafood, Greek and Italian dishes, pizza, and a salad bar are all available. *9823 100th St. (604/787-9085).*

Anna's Deli: *($)* Delicious sandwiches made up of fresh delicatessen products make this an appealing lunch spot. *Located in the Totem Mall, 9600 93rd Ave. (604/785-9741).*

The Forty-Niner Restaurant: *($$)* This restaurant, which is highly recommended by Fort St. John residents, specializes in Greek and Italian dishes and donairs. *10120 100th St. (604/787-2273).*

Other Possibilities: Micci's Pub *($, 10419 Alaska Rd. on the highway north of town, 604/785-6464)*, **Casey's Pub** *($, 8163 100th Ave. toward the airport, 604/787-1661)*, and **Sneaker's Sports Lounge** *($)* in the Mackenzie Inn *(9223 100th St. , 604/785-8364)* all serve tasty food.

PLACES TO STAY

The Pioneer Inn: *($$$)* This very good hotel, located in downtown Fort St. John, has clean and attractive rooms, an indoor pool, a sauna and weight room, and a nice coffee shop and dining room. *9830 - 100th Ave., Fort St. John, B.C. V1J 1Y5 (1-800/663-8312, 604/787-0521).*

Alexander Mackenzie Inn: *($$)* This hotel also has an indoor pool. *9223 - 100th St., Fort St. John, B.C. V1J 3X3 (1-800/663-8313, 604/785-8364).*

THINGS TO DO:

Shopping: For local products, try the **K & D Smoke and Gift Shop** in the Totem Mall or the **Village Shop** at *10143 100th St.* **Homesteader Health Foods** at *9941-101st Ave.* is a good health food store.

The North Peace Museum Complex: The North Peace Museum Complex has on display over 6,000 artifacts from the area, a reconstructed schoolhouse, a trapper's cabin, and a one-room hospital. The museum also has a good gift shop that sells books by local authors about the Peace region and local crafts and artwork *(604/ 787-0430).* Outside the museum complex, the **Chapel of the Holy Cross** was built in 1934 by Monica Storrs — an Anglican missionary who lived in the region from 1929 to 1950. Also outside the museum, the 41-metre-high (136-foot-high) oil derrick is a testament to the discovery of oil and gas in the Fort St. John area. The base of this derrick is often used as a stage for entertainers in the summer. Locals call these performances "Doin's at the Derrick." The museum is open daily from 8:00 a.m. - 8:00 p.m. in the summer and from 11:00 a.m. - 4:00 p.m. Monday to Saturday in the winter months. *9323 100th St. (604/787-0430).*

Cultural Centre Theatre and the Peace Gallery North: Various entertainers perform at the Cultural Centre Theatre. The Peace Gallery North, which hosts an exciting variety of exhibitions, also has a good gift store. The gallery and theatre are both located at *10015 100th Ave. (604/785-1992).*

Troy's Family Amusement Park: This amusement park, with its go-carts, mini-golf, batting cages, and driving range is a fun place to take the kids. *South of Fort St. John — Mile 45 on the Alaska Highway (604/785-8655).*

Lorcon Rainbow Trout Farm: Along with the fishing, this family attraction offers picnic areas, horse shoe pits, a ball diamond, volleyball, and basketball. *Located 13 kilometres (eight miles) north of the city. Procced along 101 Road and then turn left on 250 Road (604/787-0130).*

Lakepoint Golf and Country Club: This 18-hole course is located on the shores of Charlie Lake. *Head north* *along the Alaska Highway to Mile 54 and watch for the Golf Course Road (604/785-5566).*

Fish Creek Community Forest: Located beside Northern Lights College, this community forest has a number of interpretive forest walks. A local nature club also schedules outings in the area. For information, ask at the Travel InfoCentre.

Scenic Viewpoints: There are numerous scenic viewpoints that are accessible by car: views of the Kiskatinaw River from both the new bridge on the Alaska Highway or from the wooden bridge on the old highway, all the marked viewpoints along Highway 29 (between Hudson's Hope and Fort St. John), a fantastic view of the Peace River at the far south end of 100th Street, and the view of the flats and the Peace River as you come down the hill toward Taylor from Dawson Creek.

North on the Alaska Highway

If you are heading north to Alaska (or to the Yukon), you will do so along the world-famous Alaska Highway. This highway was constructed during World War II and reconstructed over the past thirty years by the Canadian government. The road is generally in very good shape; most of it is even paved. There can be problems when the heavy summer rains hit — particularly in the Muncho Lake area (massive rainfalls in 1974 and 1975 resulted in lengthy road closures).

The Alaska Highway is a special experience; it crosses hundreds of kilometres of sparsely-settled territory. Facilities are few and far between, so keep a close eye on your gas gauge, and make sure you have the standard extra equipment. There are intermittent roadside stations that offer gas, lodgings, food, and car repairs, but they are not set up for fancy holiday excursions. Most travellers will find the facilities adequate, but basic. The real attractions of the route are the friendly, knowledgeable people who work along the highway; these people have a unique history and culture of their own.

The next few pages will discuss some of the major attractions and facilities along the Alaska Highway. There are, of course, other roadside stations along this route that offer good, solid food, friendly hospitality and the services necessary to keep your vehicle on the road. The major stops, going from Dawson Creek to the Yukon border (and leaving out the larger centres), are Wonowon, Pink Mountain, Sikanni Chief, Steamboat, Summit, Toad River, Muncho Lake, Liard River, and Fireside. When the Alaska Highway was still a

First Nations handicrafts are available in stores throughout northern British Columbia. (Earl Brown)

gravel road, these road-side stations were the very foundation of life and travel in the region. Now, with improved vehicles, better gas mileage and a much better highway, they are not quite as prominent. You will soon discover, however, as you make your way along the "kilometres and kilometres of kilometres and kilometres" of the Alaska Highway, that these roadside stations are still invaluable to and appreciated by travellers.

Large's Ranch: Horse riding, hiking, and wagon rides are all offered. *Turn-off at Mile 68 (604/785-6414).*

Shepherd's Inn: *($$)* This small hotel, restaurant, and gas station is a good place to stop on your journey. The food, which includes burgers, sandwiches, soups, and salads, is excellent. On Friday evenings, there is often live music. *Mile 71 (604/827-3676).*

Don's Hobbies: Don's Hobbies offers a collection of hand-built miniatures depicting pioneer life, logging, and farming. There is also a superb collection of antiques and artifacts. Call first for an appointment. *To get there, turn right at Mile 73 onto 151 Road and continue driving for 29 kilometres/18 miles (604/630-2440).*

Crystal Springs Ranch: This working ranch offers trail rides, river tours, canoeing, kayaking, fishing, snowshoeing, cross-country skiing and dog-sledding. Crystal Springs, which is located on *Road 117, is 52 kilometres (33 miles) off the Alaska Highway. Turn-off at Mile 95 (604/787-3960).*

Pink Mountain: The **Pink Mountain Campsite** has groceries, a liquor store, showers, a laundry, a post office, hunting and fishing licenses, gas, propane, diesel, and an RV Park and sani-dump. The **Pink**

Mountain Motor Hotel *($$)* has a restaurant and a lounge and also has gas, propane, and diesel for sale *Mile 143 (604/774-3234).*

Mae's Kitchen and Ed's Garage: *($)* Mae's Kitchen serves homemade breads, pies, and soups. Sleeping units are available here. *Mile 147 (604/772-3215).*

Fort Nelson

Fort Nelson, with a population of 3,800 people and an area population of 5,000 people, is located at Mile 300 of the Alaska Highway. Its relatively diversified economy is based on North America's largest gas processing plant, a large plywood plant, and the world's largest chopstick plant. The Japanese-owned Canadian Chopstick Manufacturing Company Ltd. produces nine million pairs of chopsticks daily!

PLACES TO EAT
Coachouse Inn Restaurant: *($$)* This restaurant serves good meals in comfortable surroundings (see details below).

Northern Lights Deli. *($)* Try this delicatessen if you are looking for a quick lunch. *Downtown in the Landmark Plaza (604/774-3311).*

PLACES TO STAY
Coachhouse Inn: *($$)* The best hotel in Fort Nelson, the Coachouse Inn has a licensed dining room, a sauna, and a whirlpool. *4711 - 50th Ave. S., c/o Box 27, Fort Nelson, B.C. V0C 1R0 (604/774-3911).*

Beds and Breakfasts: Fort Nelson Bed & Breakfast *($$)* has several rooms available *(Box 58, Fort Nelson, B.C. V0C 1R0, 604/774-6050).* You can also try

Home on the Hill Bed & Breakfast *($$, Box 1689, Fort Nelson, B.C. V0C 1R0, 604/774-3000)*.

THINGS TO DO
Fort Nelson Heritage Museum: Located next to the Visitors Information Centre, this museum is run by a non-profit society. Its collection includes a display on the Alaska Highway construction, pioneer artifacts, and a spruce bark canoe. A small admission fee is charged *(604/774-3536)*.

OUTDOOR RECREATION
The Fort Nelson region has some spectacular scenery. The possibilities for hiking, canoeing, cross-country skiing, kayaking, and other outdoor activities are endless. Fly-in fishing and big game hunting are popular activities for visitors. There are eight provincial parks in this area, including **Stone Mountain Provincial Park, Muncho Lake Provincial Park,** and **Liard River Provincial Park.**

Muncho Lake ★

Muncho Lake is spectacular. The deep, clear waters of the lake are surrounded by high, rocky mountains. There is abundant wildlife in the area, including a herd of sheep that routinely crosses the highway.

PLACES TO STAY
Highland Glen Lodge Motel and Dining Room: *($$)* The lodge operators show bush pilot films each night and will organize charter flights into the surrounding wilderness. *Mile 462, Alaska Highway, Muncho Lake, B.C. V0C 1Z0 (604/776-3481, off season: 604/774-2909, fax: 604/774-2908)*.

Liard River, at Mile 497 of the Alaska Highway, is home to the fabulous **Liard Hotsprings**. Facilities are fairly rustic — the place has not been commercialized yet — but the hotsprings are quite wonderful. One important piece of advice: if there are warning signs about bears, heed them!!

Liard River ★

PLACES TO STAY
Lodges: **Trapper Ray's Liard Hotsprings Lodge** *($$)* is a European-style log lodge with 12 units. There are also cabins and campsites for rent. Attached to the lodge is a café with home cooking and baking *(Mile 497, Alaska Highway, B.C. V1G 4J8, 604/776-7349, fax: 604/776-7349)*. Close by is the **Liard River Lodge** *($$, Mile 496, Alaska Highway, B.C. V1G 4J8, 604/776-7341, fax: 604/776-7340)*.

Selected Events in the Peace River - Alaska Highway Region

Winter Carnival	Mackenzie	February
Hudson's Hope Rodeo	Hudson's Hope	June
Great Peace Raft Run	Taylor	July
Fort St. John Rodeo	Fort St. John	July
Bluegrass Festival	Mackenzie	August
Grizzly Valley Days	Tumbler Ridge	August
Fall Fair and Rodeo	Dawson Creek	August
Fort Nelson Rodeo	Fort Nelson	September
Dinosaur Paddlers Raft Race	Hudson's Hope	August
North Peace Fall Fair	Fort St. John	August
N.R.A. Rodeo Finals	Chetwynd	September
Fort Nelson Fall Fair	Fort Nelson	September

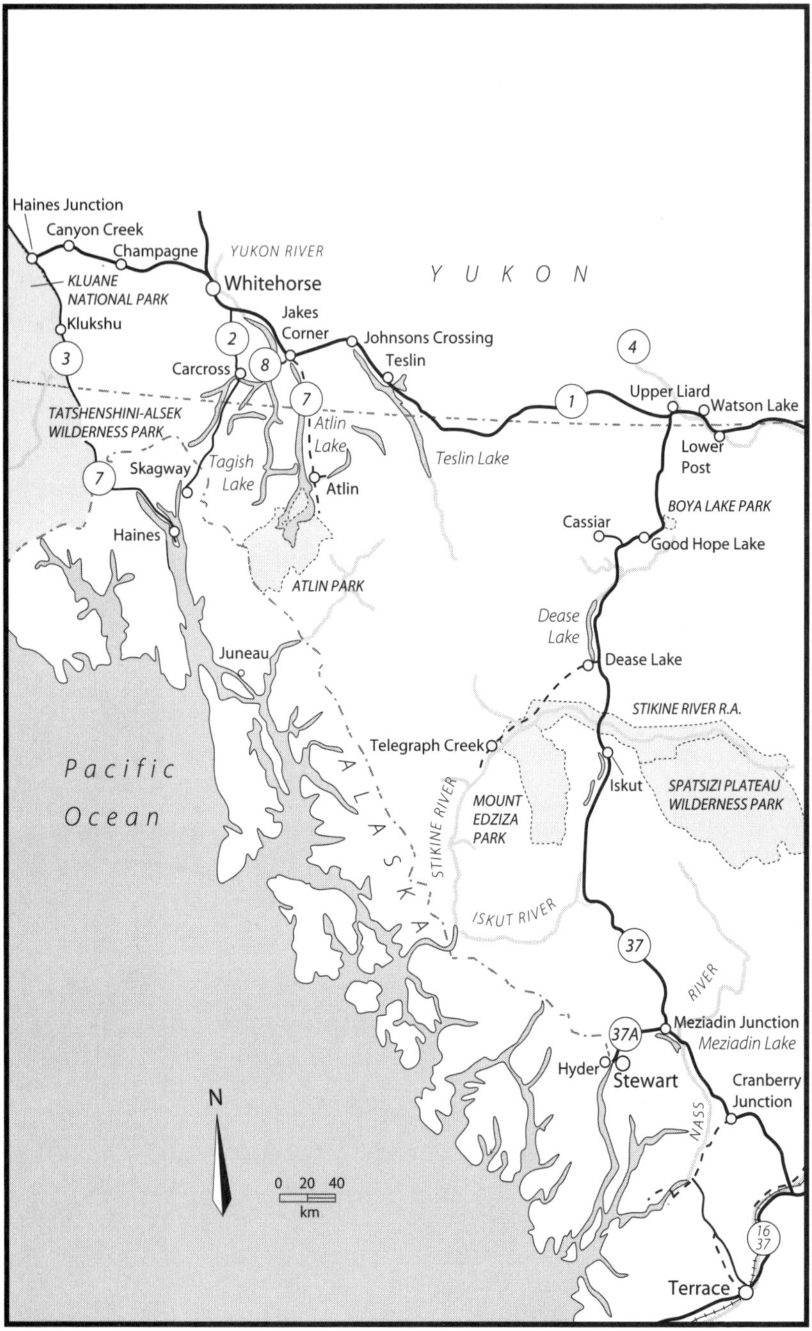
Haines Junction
Canyon Creek
Champagne
YUKON RIVER
KLUANE NATIONAL PARK
Whitehorse
Y U K O N
Klukshu
2
3
Jakes Corner
Johnsons Crossing
Teslin
4
8
Carcross
7
1
Upper Liard
Watson Lake
TATSHENSHINI-ALSEK WILDERNESS PARK
Atlin Lake
Lower Post
Teslin Lake
Tagish Lake
Skagway
7
Atlin
BOYA LAKE PARK
Haines
Cassiar
Good Hope Lake
ATLIN PARK
Dease Lake
Juneau
Dease Lake
STIKINE RIVER R.A.
Telegraph Creek
Pacific Ocean
ALASKA
Iskut
SPATSIZI PLATEAU WILDERNESS PARK
STIKINE RIVER
MOUNT EDZIZA PARK
ISKUT RIVER
37
RIVER
37A
Meziadin Junction
Meziadin Lake
Hyder
Stewart
Cranberry Junction
N
NASS
0 20 40
km
16
37
Terrace

10

The Stikine and the Far Northwest

British Columbia is, as you will know from an even casual glance at the map, a massive province. But when you realize that the half-way point of the province, measured from north to south, runs approximately through Prince George and Terrace and that the extreme northwest corner of the province is several hundred kilometres west of Vancouver, you start to get a better perspective on the place. Vast distances, less than perfect roads, and small, scattered settlements often deter travellers from exploring the far corners of British Columbia.

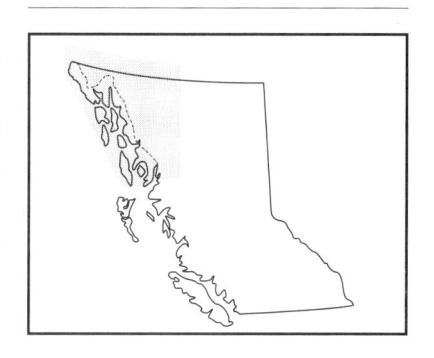

Don't let yourself be stopped. There are precious few places you can still go in this world where the hand of industry and development has not already transformed the land. Even many of the most famous "wilderness" attractions on the globe — Niagara Falls, Banff and Jasper National Parks, Kakadu and Uhlaru (Ayres Rock) National Parks in Australia, Denali National Park in Alaska — are heavily developed, sanitized, and controlled. These are places where one goes to be herded, collected, and directed toward scenic sites and unusual wildlife.

Northern British Columbia's far northwest corner — the area bordered on the east by the Stewart-Cassiar Highway, on the north by the Yukon boundary, and on the west by the Alaska Panhandle — is different. It has world-class scenery — the views at the southern end of Atlin Lake rival any mountain spot in the world — thousands of square kilometres of undeveloped land, a tiny population, and very little tourist traffic. The fishing and hunting are superb, there are wilderness experiences galore awaiting you, and there are enough tourist services — although you should plan ahead — to look after human comforts.

You won't find many people following in your footsteps. Although the popularity of the place increases each year, few people know much about British Columbia's Far Northwest. Most people travelling through the area are headed for Dawson City in the Yukon or for Alaska and scarcely slow down for gasoline and a bite to eat. But if you love the outdoors, want to get away from the crowds, are willing to put up with more rustic accommodations, and are anxious to see beautiful scenery and fascinating people, plan your expedition to include the Far Northwest.

A Brief History

The Far Northwest, with the exception of Stewart and Atlin, has generally existed outside the provincial mainstream. The aboriginal people remained active trappers until the collapse of the fur market in the late 1940s, and many continued to live off the land long after that time. Several small gold rushes, most notably the Cassiar rush of the 1870s, brought hundreds of gold miners into the area, but all to little avail. The pockets of gold-bearing ground bore no resemblance to the rich fields of central British Columbia or the

Yukon's Klondike, and the mini-stampedes soon stopped.

Stewart, founded in 1903, enjoyed a great boom at the turn of the century, when gold, silver, and copper mines drew thousands into the area. Like all of the great northern booms, this one faded, although mines remained active in the area. Over time, Stewart's population declined steadily to its present 1,000 residents. There is still a great deal of active prospecting in the region, and several mines have opened in recent years. The trend toward fly-in mining camps, thus avoiding the cost and commitments of the company town, has limited the regional impact of these new businesses.

Miners ventured into other parts of the North. A rush along the Stikine River (the Cassiar rush) and the planned construction of a transcontinental telegraph line to Russia and Europe resulted in the creation of the small village of Telegraph Creek. Dease Lake, along the Stewart-Cassiar highway, was the supply-centre for a spate of mining exploration and development in the 1960s and 1970s. Cassiar, for some thirty years one of the most stable company towns in Canada, was the site of a major asbestos mine that opened in the late 1950s and finally closed, after numerous efforts to save the mine and the town, in 1992. Virtually the entire town site, including the school, company buildings, and homes, has been removed; in its place is a ghost town that doesn't even have houses for the ghosts.

Atlin began as one of the many "echo-booms" that occurred during and after the great Klondike Gold Rush. When the strike was announced, several hundred men working on the construction of the White Pass and Yukon Route railway threw down their tools and raced to the site of the newest "bonanza." Atlin never rivalled Dawson City, but the creeks produced a sizeable number of paying claims. The town flourished for a time and then, inevitably, experienced the decline that accompanies the exhaustion of gold fields. The area attracted additional attention in the 1920s and 1930s, when wealthy tourists plied the waters of the Tagish-Atlin area aboard luxury vessels.

The Far Northwest of British Columbia has, in many ways, been a by-way — a land passage for a number of the great events of northern history. Klondike stampeders, making their way to the gold fields, passed through the province via the famous Chilkoot Pass and White Pass; a much smaller number entered by way of the Stikine and Dalton Trails — the latter a precursor of the Haines Road. The White Pass and Yukon Route Railway, the famous narrow-gauge railway built during the gold rush, runs for part of its length through northern British Columbia. (The railway, incidentally, shut down in the early 1980s but is running again from Skagway to the British Columbia border as a tourist attraction.)

During World War II, the Far Northwest faced another human stampede as American and Canadian construction workers, including thousands of American soldiers arrived to construct the Alaska Highway, the Haines Road, the Northwest Staging Route, the CANOL pipeline and refinery project, and other northwest defence projects. Today, travellers can still see signs of this important construction era that reshaped the Far Northwest.

The region remains an active mining area that is served by the regional supply centres of Atlin and Stewart. There have been few major discoveries, although you would never know it from the much-ballyhooed announcements of the stock and mining promoters who hold properties in the area. First Nations people play a prominent role in the region; their claims to the land and the resources remain unresolved and the subject of negotiations with the federal and provincial governments.

Getting There

The far northwest corner of the province is a long way from major population centres. If you are driving from the Vancouver area, count on a two-day drive to get to the southern fringe of this area. And, because road conditions are not quite as good as in more heavily-travelled areas, make sure you budget a little more time to go between towns. It is because the region is hard to reach that so few people travel here each year.

The primary access route into the Far Northwest, particularly into the Stewart district, is off Highway 16 at Kitwanga. Turning north off Highway 16, travellers take the Stewart-Cassiar Highway (Highway 37), which runs some 700 kilometres (438 miles) north to join the Alaska Highway just west of Watson Lake. A side road, leading to the small coastal community of Stewart, leaves the main highway at Meziadin Junction. Tourists travelling this road will see magnificent scenery, including glaciers that plunge close to the highway, but, because the area receives very heavy snowfalls, winter driving can be quite a challenge.

The main Stewart-Cassiar highway continues on from Meziadin Junction, through Dease Lake and past the former mining town of Cassiar, and on to the Yukon. This road is not of the same standard as the other main highways in British Columbia. While certain sections have been upgraded, widened, and paved, much of the highway retains its gravel surface and can be quite rough and twisty in sections.

A large number of people entering the Far Northwest do so via the Alaska Highway (see Chapter 9, which covers the British Columbia section of the Alaska Highway). After you cross the Yukon border south of Watson Lake, (a small traveller's stop and supply centre in south-central Yukon), the Alaska Highway continues west along the British Columbia - Yukon boundary (it actually dips back into British Columbia near Swift River), swings north to the Yukon capital of Whitehorse, and then heads west to Alaska.

➤

The lakes and rivers of the far northwest offer excellent fishing. A young fisher tries his hand in Meziadin Lake, on the Stewart - Cassiar Road.
(Ron Thiele)

From the Alaska Highway, three roads lead back into northwestern British Columbia. At Jake's Corner, some 100 kilometres (63 miles) south of Whitehorse, you can take the Atlin Road 100 kilometres south to Atlin, British Columbia. There are few amenities on this scenic, winding road — several Yukon campgrounds and small lodges — and it's a dead-end trip. (There has been talk of continuing the road through to Juneau, Alaska, but there has been no construction on this route to date.) From Atlin, you can travel a short distance south (to some warm springs at the southern end of Atlin Lake) and a few kilometres to the east.

The second route into northwestern British Columbia turns off from the Alaska Highway about 30 kilometres (19 miles) south of Whitehorse. The Carcross-Skagway Road, some 100 kilometres (63 miles) long, begins in the small settlement of Carcross, Yukon — situated in a beautiful setting at the head of Bennett Lake of Klondike fame, and home to a fine ice cream and gift shop — and continues along the shores of Tagish and Tutchi Lakes — the latter in British Columbia. There are no settlements here, save for a small customs and highway maintenance yard at Log Cabin on the British Columbia - Alaska boundary. The highway continues across a fascinating, moonscape-like landscape and then plunges down the White Pass to tidewater at Skagway — once the centre-point for the rush to the Klondike and now a major seasonal tourist centre. (Note that you can get to the Carcross Road from Atlin. Shortly before rejoining the Alaska Highway at Jake's Corner, the Atlin Road meets the Tagish Road. Travel west along the Tagish Road for about 55 kilometres (34 miles), and you will reach the Carcross-Skagway Road.)

The third access route to northern British Columbia from the Alaska Highway begins at the Yukon community of Haines Junction (the headquarters for Kluane National Park). The Haines Road, hastily constructed during World War II to provide an alternate route from tidewater to the Alaska Highway (the only other access was via the White Pass and Yukon Route railway), was recently upgraded and is now a fine, reliable, smooth highway. This road is, incidentally, one of the finest and most scenic pieces of highway in the world; it runs along the eastern side of Kluane National Park, and the entire stretch is framed by the majesty of the St. Elias Mountains. The road runs for a few kilometres through northern British Columbia before it reaches the Alaska boundary. There are no sizeable settlements along the highway — a maintenance camp on the Yukon side and a small customs station at the border — but there is a tremendous amount to see. Look out for signs to Million Dollar Falls — one of the most spectacular waterfalls anywhere.

The Stewart - Cassiar Road

The Stewart-Cassiar Road is generally in good condition, although it is not paved along its entire length. Do watch for logging trucks on the lower half of the highway. Services are few and far between along the road, so make sure that you proceed with due caution. Gas, food, and repair services are available at the following locations:

Kitwanga: at the junction of Highways 16 and 37
Nass River Bridge: 140 kilometres (88 miles) north of Kitwanga
Meziadin Junction: 150 kilometres (94 miles) north of Kitwanga

Stewart: turn west at Meziadin Junction and proceed approximately 65 kilometres (41 miles) to the end of Highway 37A

Bell II: 96 kilometres (60 miles) north of Meziadin Junction

Eastman Creek: approximately 200 kilometres (125 miles) north of Meziadin (limited facilities)

Iskut: 75 kilometres (47 miles) north of Eastman Creek

Dease Lake: an old gold-mining town and regional service centre at the junction of the road to Telegraph Creek

Telegraph Creek: 120 kilometres (95 miles) west of Dease Lake on a rough but beautiful road (Drive with caution, and do not try to pull a trailer into Telegraph Creek. Arrangements can be made in Dease Lake to store your trailer.)

Cassiar: no services (an abandoned and long-prosperous mining community a short distance off the main highway)

Good Hope Lake: just north of the Cassiar turn-off

Upper Liard/Watson Lake: along the Alaska Highway near the turn-off from the Stewart-Cassiar road (Watson Lake, a large highway and service community, is about 20 kilometres/13 miles further east.)

The Very Best of the Stikine and Far Northwest

The far northwest corner of British Columbia has much to offer outdoor enthusiasts, particularly those drawn by dramatic mountain ranges, crystal clear rivers and lakes, clear skies, and abundant wildlife. History buffs will find the communities of Atlin,

Stewart, and Telegraph Creek to be particular interest. Fishers and hunters will discover some of British Columbia's finest wilderness opportunities. This, clearly, is a land very much worth seeing as part of your excursion into northern British Columbia.

The Yukon - Alaska - Northern British Columbia Triangle

There is one remarkable trip, involving two different parts of northern British Columbia that we wanted to single out for special attention. The journey is very simple. Begin in Whitehorse and head south on the Carcross-Skagway Road. Stop for an ice-cream cone in Carcross, and then continue on the highway to Skagway. Leave a few hours to visit Skagway (or stay overnight), for there is usually a lot to do here during the summer. You then depart Skagway aboard the Alaska Marine Highway ferry that runs regularly between Skagway and Haines — a short cruise away. (You must phone ahead for reservations, as the ferry is very busy in the summer months.)

Take time to look around Haines — a lively fishing and forestry town that is set amidst mountains and ocean. Leave Haines by way of the improved and scenic Haines Road. The highway begins near sea level, rises dramatically once you cross the British Columbia border at Pleasant Valley, and then runs through high mountain passes and into the Shakwak Valley. Make sure you stop at Million Dollars Falls and Klukshu — a Native fishing village just inside the Yukon Territory. Turn in at Kathleen Lake. This lake is within the Kluane National Park and is one of the most beautiful lakes anywhere in the world. There is also great fishing, particularly for kokanee (land-locked salmon).

Haines Junction, where the Haines Road meets the Alaska Highway, is worth a short visit. The Kluane

National Park Visitors' Information Centre shows a superb audio-visual presentation on the park. You now turn east on the Alaska Highway to travel back to Whitehorse. The full expedition can be completed in as little as two days (or a single day, if you hit the right ferry and you don't mind capitalizing on being in the "land of the midnight sun").

Stewart

Stewart (and its eccentric neighbour, Hyder, Alaska — population 85) is not your average tourist destination. The attraction here is the town and its spectacular setting — not a set of tourist facilities. Stewart sits at the end of a long side road and the difficulty of access ensures that comparatively few travellers make their way into the district. There are numerous remnants of Stewart's glory days — during the turn of the century mining stampede — and enough signs of vitality to convince you of the town's determination to survive. The drive is worth the effort; Stewart and Hyder are an added bonus. The people here are exceptionally friendly and have a well-deserved reputation for treating visitors extremely well.

PLACES TO STAY

In Stewart, try the **Portland Bed & Breakfast** *($$, Box 234, Stewart, B.C. V0T 1W0, 604/636-9133, fax: 604/636-9131)* and the **King Edward Motel/Hotel** *($$)* at 5th and Columbia *(Box 86, Stewart, B.C. V0T 1W0, 604/636-2244)*. In Hyder, options include the **Sealaska Inn** *($$)* on Premier and Nevada Aves., Hyder, Alaska *(P.O. Box 214, Stewart, B.C. V0T 1W0, 604/636-2486, fax: 604/636-9003)* and the **Grand View Inn** *($$, Box 49, Hyder, Alaska 99923, 604/636-9174)*. There is a nice campground in Stewart **Stewart Lions Campground and RV Park,***($, Box 431,*

Stewart B.C., V0T 1W0, 604/636-2537, fax: 604/636-2668).

THINGS TO DO

★ On the drive to Stewart, stop at the **Bear Glacier**. This spectacular glacier is easily seen from the road. Closer to Stewart is the magnificent **Salmon Glacier**. In town, the museum, located in the Fire Hall Heritage Building, is worth checking out. **Seaport Limousine** *(P.O. Box 217, Stewart, B.C. V0T 1W0, 604/636-2622, fax: 604/636-2633)* offers an excellent guided tour of the area.

Iskut

Iskut, with a population of 300 people, is the primary jumping-off spot for Mount Edziza and Spatsizi Plateau Provincial Parks. Local services include trail rides and river tours.

PLACES TO STAY

★ **Guest Ranches:** There are several excellent wilderness ranches in the area, including the **Bear Paw Ranch** *($$, Box 69, Iskut, B.C. V0J 1K0, Radio Telephone 2M3 858, Whitehorse Operator, Meehaus Channel)*. Located in magnificent surroundings a short distance north of Iskut, this ranch offers wonderful hospitality in comfortable surroundings and comes highly recommended by several of its many repeat customers. You can also visit the **Mountain Shadow Guest Ranch and Campground** *($$, Iskut, B.C. V0J 1K0, 604/234-3333)*.

Other Possibilities: Other places to stay include the **Red Goat Lodge and Bed & Breakfast** *($$$, Hwy. 37, Box 101 Iskut, B.C. V0J 1K0, 604/234-3261, fax: 604/234-3261)*, the **Tatogga Lake Resort** *($$, Iskut, B.C., V0J 1K0, 604/234-3526)*, and the **Black Sheep**

Motel and Restaurant *($$, Box 120, Iskut, B.C. V0J 1K0, 604/234-3141)*.

THINGS TO DO
For information on recreational opportunities in the area, try contacting the **Iskutine Lodge** *(Box 39, Iskut, B.C., V0J 1K0, 604/234-3456)*. For further information on the Iskut area, write to the **Northern Wilderness Travel Association** *(Iskut, B.C. V0J 1K0)*.

Provincial Parks: Both **Mount Edziza** and **Spatsizi Plateau** are wilderness parks; no facilities are provided. You should check with the BC Parks office in Smithers or Dease Lake before heading in. The parks, incidentally, are extremely beautiful; Spatsizi is particularly well-known for its abundant wildlife.

Dease Lake

Dease Lake is a service and supply centre for the region's population and for the mining industry.

PLACES TO STAY
Northway Motor Inn and Restaurant: *($$)* This motor inn offers clean rooms and good food. *Box 158, Dease Lake, B.C. V0C 1L0 (604/771-5341, fax 604/771-5342)*.

Telegraph Creek

Telegraph Creek is a fascinating place to visit; many of the gold-rush era buildings still stand. It is now a predominantly Native settlement and has a population of 300 people.

PLACES TO STAY
Stikine River Song Lodge: *($)* An excellent base for your stay in Telegraph Creek is Stikine River Song

The white tailed ptarmigan is common in alpine areas. Its feathers are all white during the winter months.
(Ron Thiele)

Lodge. The lodge includes accommodations, a café, and a store and can provide boat trips on the Stikine River. *The Stikine River Song Lodge, c/o General Delivery, Telegraph Creek, B.C. V0J 2W0 (604/235-3196).*

Atlin Atlin, with a population of 500 people, is an interesting and historic old town situated in one of the most stunningly beautiful places on earth. Tall mountains rise up majestically from Atlin Lake — the largest natural lake in British Columbia. Untouched wilderness stretches in all directions as far as the eye can see. Atlin is only accessible from the Yukon (Highway 7 south from the Alaska Highway). It is situated on the boundary of Atlin Provincial Park. This area (like the Tatshenshini Wilderness Reserve along the Haines Road) offers unparalleled exploring. The park contains no services whatsoever and should only be visited by experienced wilderness campers.

PLACES TO EAT

Atlin does not have many restaurants. The **Atlin Inn Café** *($)* in the Atlin Inn on Lake Street *(604/651-7546)* and the **Pine Tree Café** *($)* on Discovery Ave. *(604/651-7636)* are easy to find. In the summer, the **Mountains of Fudge Ice Cream Parlor** at First and Pearl is also open. There is a grocery store where you can buy your own supplies.

PLACES TO STAY

Noland House: *($$$)* This luxury bed and breakfast, operated by Bob and Lyn Coutts, is located in a remodelled historic cabin in downtown Atlin. Complimentary wine and hors d'oeuvres are served, but a full breakfast is extra. *Box 135, Atlin, B.C. V0B 1A0 (604/651-7585).*

The Fireweed Inn: *($$)* This nice-looking bed and breakfast is located downtown on Second Street. *Box 316, Atlin, B.C. V0W 1A0 (604/651-7729, fax: 604/351-7719).*

Atlin Inn and Kirkwood Cottages: *($$$)* The cottages, located on the lake (on aptly named Lake Street), are particularly attractive and rustic. *Lake St., Box 39, Atlin, B.C. V0W 1A0 (604/651-7546, fax: 604/651-7500).*

★ **Sidka Tour's Glacier View Cabins:** *($)* Our favourite spot to stay in Atlin is Sidka Tour's Glacier View Cabins. These are located about fifteen minutes from town on Warm Bay Road. Perched on a hill, the cabins provide a stunning view of the Llewellyn Glacier and the mountains of Atlin Provincial Park. The cabins, which are small and basic, have wood stoves and no electricity. You can arrange for a cheese fondue dinner in your cabin and, as Atlin does not have a large number of restaurants to choose from, this is a good option. Bring candles, a bottle of wine, and some food for breakfast, and you are set for a wonderful stay. Sidka Tours also offers a number of guided motorcycle, canoe, or dog sled tours, so inquire if you are interested. *Box 368, Atlin, B.C. V0W 1A0. (radio phone number is JR3-6430 on the White Mountain Channel; fax: 604/651-7500).*

Campgrounds: There is one campground that accommodates recreational vehicles — the **Norseman Adventures RV Park** on Mill Street. The Norseman has electrical hook-ups and water and charges $10 per day (c/o P.O. Box 184, Atlin, B.C. V0W 1A0, 604/651-7535). There are six other campgrounds in the area. Look for maps in the Atlin Claim community newspaper.

THINGS TO DO

Atlin is a wonderful community for walking, and it is such a small town that it is very easy to find things. Check out the interesting pyramid-shaped building in the centre of town. The structure began as part of a holistic healing centre. It now appears to be used as an apartment building. Atlin has a thriving artistic community and there are a number of shops that sell jewellery, pottery, watercolours, sculptures, and Tlingit Native art.

Historic Sites: Atlin is filled with historic buildings, and most of them have signs posted which describe their history. A few of the most interesting historic sites include the old schoolhouse on 3rd Street, which now houses the **Atlin Historical Museum** *(604/651-7522)*; the **pioneer cemetery**, where weathered grave markers tell the story of Atlin's pioneer past; a **courthouse**; a **theatre**; **St. Joseph's Catholic Church**; and **St. Mark's Anglican Church**. If you feel like doing a self-guided walking tour, a book entitled "Historic Walking Tour of Atlin" is available from the museum, the Fireweed Inn, or the Atlin Inn. Occasionally, guides from the museum also give tours.

M.V. Tarahne: The recently restored M.V. Tarahne is well worth visiting. This 23-metre (78-foot) cargo and passenger lake boat was built in Atlin over the winter of 1916-1917. She transported miners and offered elegant tours of Atlin Lake for wealthy tourists. In 1936, her last season, the Tarahne carried 6,029 passengers. Until a few years ago, the Tarahne was listing severely and falling into disrepair. Community fund raising and support enabled the restoration project to begin. In 1991, she opened for regular tours. The **Tarahne Tea** is held the first weekend of July. Hosts dress in period costume and serve a delicious tea after boat tours.

Summit Air Charters Ltd.: For a closer look at some of the scenery, Summit Air Charters Ltd. runs charter flights over beautiful Atlin Lake and the breathtaking Llewellyn Glacier. They will also fly you to Juneau for $125 *(604/651-7600, fax: 604/651-7537)*.

OUTDOOR RECREATION
Along with its history, Atlin's biggest attraction is its spectacular location. There is lots of hiking, snow

▲ The M.V. Tarahne, *which once carried tourists and miners on Atlin Lake, has been recently restored.* (Peter Steele)

shoeing, and cross-country skiing all around Atlin. Check with locals for advice on where to go.

Norseman Adventures Ltd.: This company rents houseboats from June through September for a day, a couple of days, or a week. Prices depend on the size of the boat but range from $995 to $1395 for seven days and from $550 to $845 for a three day weekend or four mid-week days *(604/651-7535 from May through October or 604/826-2559 during the rest of the year).*

Whitehorse (Yukon)

As Atlin is only accessible via the Yukon, we thought we would include a brief section on the territory and its capital city. Whitehorse was born during the early days of the Klondike Gold Rush when its location at the end of the infamous White Horse Rapids made it a natural stopping place for riverboats plying the mighty Yukon River. The same condition made it the logical terminus for the White Pass and Yukon Route Railway. The town remained a small, seasonal shipping centre until World War II.

The establishment of Whitehorse as the headquarters for the Northwest Defence Projects, and the arrival of tens of thousands of soldiers and construction workers in the spring of 1942, transformed the settlement into the Yukon's largest town. The federal government acknowledged Whitehorse's ascendancy in the early 1950s when it named Whitehorse the capital of the Yukon. This move stripped Dawson City of its prestige and much of its remaining population. The mining boom of the 1960s and the expansion of the regional civil service in the 1970s and 1980s added to Whitehorse's size and status. The city now has close to 22,000 people — about 75 percent of the Yukon total — and completely dominates the territory.

Whitehorse, an unusual and fascinating city, is a mixture of pioneering mineral exploration, laissez-faire economics, massive government spending, and generally successful Native-non-Native interaction. Many Whitehorse residents have moved north to experience the outdoors and the pristine environment of the Yukon. The town, consequently, has an exceptionally active outdoors life and excellent recreational facilities for a community of its size.

As a result of some fundamental and fascinating transitions, the Yukon has developed into a remarkably engaged, dynamic, and politically- and culturally-aware society. The Yukon First Nations have, after more than 20 years at the bargaining table, signed a land claims settlement. The territory, long administered as a colony of the federal government, achieved partial responsible government only in the late 1970s and is still in the process of assuming control of its share of regional administrative operations. There are, as well, long-standing debates between developers (primarily in the mining sector, which provides the bulk of the region's private enterprise) and environmentalists (who wish to preserve the unique ecology of the Canadian sub-Arctic).

Whitehorse is a place that is not to be missed — and not to be dismissed simply because the town looks a little dusty and unkempt. You'll find an excellent bookstore, many fine restaurants, a number of excellent stores, and some great places to stay — a town far better, we guess, than you expected. Give Whitehorse a shot, and do not simply dash through along the Alaska Highway. We're sure that the stopover will bring great dividends.

PLACES TO EAT

Chocolate Claim: *($$)* The Chocolate Claim sells cappuccinos, soups, quiches, sandwiches, and tasty desserts. *305 Strickland St. (403/667-2202).*

No Pop Sandwich Shop: *($$)* No Pop opens early and serves up sandwiches, burgers, crêpes, and interesting daily specials. For Sunday brunch, there are a good variety of tasty dishes to choose from. *Corner of 4th Ave. and Steele St. — one block north of Main St. (403/668-3227).*

Sam & Andy's: *($$)* This casual restaurant serves good-quality, Mexican food. *506 Main St. (403/668-6994).*

Panda's: *($$$)* Panda's is a European fine-dining establishment. *212 Main St. (403/667-2632).*

Cellar Dining Room: *($$$)* For prime rib, steaks or fish, try the Cellar Dining Room in the Edgewater Hotel. *101 Main St. (403/667-2572).*

Angelo's: *($$)* Angelo's serves Greek food. *Upstairs at 202 Strickland Ave. (403/668-6266).*

Gilligan's: *($$$)* This quaint and interesting restaurant offers a number of delicious pasta, seafood, and chicken dishes. *Corner of 3rd and Wood St.(403/667-4455).*

PLACES TO STAY

Hotels: Whitehorse has a number of hotels downtown — the fanciest and most expensive being the two Westmark-owned hotels: the **Westmark Klondike Inn** *($$$, 2288 Second Ave., Whitehorse, Yukon, Y1A 1C8, 403/668-4747)* and the **Westmark Whitehorse** *($$$)* at Second and Wood Street *(Box 4250, Whitehorse, Yukon Y1A 3T3, 403/668-4700). For both hotels, call toll-free at 1-800/999-2570.* The **High Country Inn** *($$, 4051 4th Ave., 1-800/554-4471)* is a converted YWCA located next to the city's swimming pool and offers clean and comfortable rooms at excellent prices. Some rooms come with complete kitchen facilities and/or Jacuzzi bathtubs. Other possibilities are **The Edgewater** *($$, 101 Main St., Whitehorse, Yukon Y1A 2A7, 403/667-2572)* and the **Gold Rush Inn** *($$, 411 Main St., Whitehorse, Yukon Y1A 2B6, 403/668-4500).*

Hawkins House Bed & Breakfast: *($$$)* This bed and breakfast is located on a quiet residential street in downtown Whitehorse. The house has been specifically designed as a bed and breakfast and has four beautiful rooms. Each room is designed and decorated in a specific theme to represent important parts of Yukon heritage. There is the French Canadian room, the First Nations room, the Yukon Past room, and the

Yukon Today room. Artwork and furnishings all reflect the theme, and a little booklet in your room gives details about the designs and the artists. A delicious hearty breakfast features a number of Yukon delicacies like moose sausage and wild berries. *303 Hawkins St., Whitehorse, Yukon Y1A 1X5 (403/668-7638, fax: 403/668-7632).*

Highland Home: *($$)* This bed and breakfast features an outdoor hot tub! The friendly hosts, Dorothy and Richard Martin, are both extremely knowledgeable about the Yukon Territory. *#1-11th Ave., Whitehorse, Yukon Y1A 4H5 (403/633-5804, fax: 403/668-5705).*

THINGS TO DO

Murdock's Gem Shop: This store sells Yukon gold nugget earrings and pendants and other kinds of jewellery. *207 Main St.*

Mac's Fireweed Bookstore: This bookstore stocks an excellent selection of books on the Yukon along with a wide variety of books on other subjects. The specialty bookstore in the basement is a real gem and is worth an extended visit to stock up on holiday reading. *203 Main St.*

Yukon Gallery: The Yukon Gallery has a large selection of northern original art, limited edition prints, posters, moose hair tuftings, and sculptures by local artists. *2093 2nd Ave.*

Yukon Native Products: Yukon Native Products is an Indian arts and crafts co-operative. They make and sell authentic northern Native parkas, anoraks, fleece jackets, and blanket coats. They also sell a wide variety of other Native artwork. *4230 4th Ave.*

Historic Sites: There are many interesting historical sites in Whitehorse, including the **Old Log Church**, the **S.S. Klondike** (a National Historic Site), and the **McBride Museum**. There is also an excellent self-guided walking tour of the town available.

Selected Events in the Stikine and the Far Northwest

Sourdough Rendezvous	Whitehorse	February
International Days	Stewart/Hyder	July
Northern Storytelling Festival	Whitehorse	June
Whitehorse Rodeo	Whitehorse	July
'98 Klondike Road Relay	Skagway-Whitehorse	September

Provincial Parks of Northern British Columbia

British Columbia is blessed with an excellent set of provincial parks. Most of these are well-patrolled and have well-maintained campsites and excellent recreational facilities. The parks range from magnificent wilderness reserves, like Spatsizi and Tweedsmuir, to family-oriented campgrounds like West Lake (near Prince George) and Moberly Lake (near Hudson's Hope).

BC Parks provides excellent information packages for travellers, including regional maps and brochures on each park. Rather than reproduce the superb information contained in the BC Parks publications, we invite you to write to BC Parks, 430-1011 Fourth Ave., Prince George, B.C. V2L 3H9 or phone them at 604/565-6135. The parks publications can be picked up — free of charge — in any of the BC Travel InfoCentres scattered throughout the province.

As a guide to your planning, we have identified the major parks in the northern part of the province. Please note that this is only a partial list; there are many smaller parks, with excellent facilities, near the towns and major lakes.

Wilderness Parks

Atlin Park (near Atlin)
Bowron Lake Park (near Barkerville)
Gwaii Haanas (South Moresby) **National Park Reserve** (at the southern end of the Queen Charlotte Islands)
Mount Edziza Park (off Highway 37, near Iskut
Mount Robson Park (on Highway 16, near Jasper and Valemount)
Muncho Lake Park (on the Alaska Highway, north of Fort Nelson)
Spatsizi Plateau Wilderness Park (off Highway 37, but accessible by air from Smithers)
Tatshenshini Park (off the Haines Road)
Tweedsmuir Park (southern entrance by way of Highway 20 linking Williams Lake and Bella Coola; northern entrance from Ootsa Lake, south of Burns Lake)
Wells Gray Park (north of Kamloops on the way to Valemount)

Campgrounds / Recreational Parks

Barkerville Park (near Barkerville)
Charlie Lake Park (near Fort St. John, along the Alaska Highway)
Crooked River Park (north of Prince George on Highway 97)
Kinaskan Lake Park (on Highway 37, near Iskut)
Lakelse Lake Park (near Terrace)
Liard Hotsprings Park (on the Alaska Highway)
Moberly Lake Park (between Chetwynd and Hudson's Hope)
Monkman Park (near Tumbler Ridge)

Mount Robson Park (on Highway 16, near Jasper and Valemount)
Naikoon Park (on the northeast tip of Graham Island, Queen Charlotte Islands)
Paarens Beach Park (near Fort St. James)
Purden Lake Park (between McBride and Prince George on Highway 16)
Red Bluff Park (on Babine Lake)
Ten Mile Lake Park (north of Quesnel on Highway 16)
West Lake Park (near Prince George)

If you plan to get off the main roads and are interested in back-country hiking, camping, and fishing opportunities, the BC Ministry of Forests publishes an indispensable series of Forest Recreation maps. These very detailed maps mark all of the campsites and roads (most of them developed for logging and many still in use for that purpose) in a given district. The maps can be collected through the Forest District offices in major communities or, more readily, from BC Travel InfoCentres.

Tourist and Travel Information

For additional information (maps, brochures, accommodation guides, etc.) on a particular region within northern British Columbia, contact the appropriate regional or local tourist information centre.

Alaska Marine Highway, P.O. Box R, Juneau, Alaska 99811 (1-800/642-0066 — U.S., 1-800/665-6414 — Canada).
Barkerville Historic Town, Box 19, Barkerville, B.C. V0K 1B0 (604/994-3332).
BC Ferries, 1112 Fort St., Victoria, B.C. V8V 4V2 (604/656-0757).
BC Rail Passenger Services, Dept. 112, Box 8770, Vancouver, B.C. V6B 4X6 (604/631-3500, fax: 604/984-5505).
Burns Lake & District Chamber of Commerce, P.O. Box 339, Burns Lake, B.C. V0J 1E0 (604/692-3773, fax 604/692-3493).
Cariboo Tourist Association, 190 Yorston Ave., Box 4900, Williams Lake, B.C. V2G 2V8 (604/392-2226, fax 604/392-2838).
Chetwynd Chamber of Commerce, Box 1000, Chetwynd, B.C. V0C 1J0 (604/788-3345, fax: 604/788-7843).
District of Stewart, Box 460, Stewart, B.C. V0T 1W0 (604/636-2251).
Fort Nelson-Liard Regional District, Bay Service 399, Fort Nelson, B.C. V0C 1R0 (604/774-2541).

Fort St. James Chamber of Commerce, P.O. Box 1164, 115 Douglas Ave., Fort St. James, B.C. V0J 1P0 (604/996-7023, fax: 604/996-7047).

Fraser Lake, Box 430, Fraser Lake, B.C. V0J 1S0 (604/699-6257).

Granisle Travel Information Centre, Box 128, Granisle, B.C. V0J 1W0 (604/697-2428, fax 604/697-2568).

Gwaii Haanas National Park Reserve/Haida Heritage Site (South Moresby) Box 37, Queen Charlotte, B.C. V0T 1S0 (604/559-8818).

The Hazelton Area InfoCentre, P.O. Box 340, New Hazelton, B.C. V0J 2J0 (604/842-6071, fax: 604/842-6271).

Houston and District Chamber of Commerce, P.O. Box 396, Houston, B.C. V0J 1Z0 (604/845-7640, fax 604/845-3682).

Kitimat, 270 City Centre, Kitimat, B.C. V8C 2H7 (604/632-2161, fax: 604/632-4995).

Mackenzie Chamber of Commerce, P.O. Box 880, Mackenzie, B.C. V0J 2C0 (604/997-5459, fax: 604/997-6117).

McBride and District Chamber of Commerce, Box 2, McBride, B.C. V0J 2E0 (fax: 604/569-3394).

Mount Robson Park, Box 579, Valemount, B.C. V0E 2Z0 (604/566-4325).

North by Northwest Tourism Association, 11-3167 Tatlow, Box 1030, Smithers, B.C. V0J 2N0 (604/847-5227, fax: 604/847-7585).

Peace River Alaska Highway Tourist Association, 9908-106th Ave., Box 6850, Fort St. John, B.C. V1J 4J3 (1-800/663-6000, 604/785-2544, fax: 604/785-4424).

Prince George Tourism, 1198 Victoria St., Prince George, B.C. V2L 2L2 (1-800/668-7646, 604/562-3700).

Prince Rupert, P.O. Box 669, Prince Rupert, B.C. V8J 3S1 (1-800/667-1994).

Queen Charlotte Islands Chamber of Commerce, Box 38, Massett, B.C. V0T 1M0 (604/559-4742, fax 604/559-8188) Don't be discouraged if you reach a jewellery store; you have reached the right place.

Quesnel Chamber of Commerce, Stn. B., 703 Carson Ave., Quesnel, B.C. V2J 2B6 (604/992-8716, fax: 604/992-9606).

Smithers District Chamber of Commerce, Box 2379, Smithers, B.C. V0J 2N0 (604/847-9854).

South Cariboo Chamber of Commerce, Box 2312, 100 Mile House, B.C. V0K 2E0 (604/395-5353).

Stewart-Hyder Chamber of Commerce, Box 306, Stewart, B.C. V0T 1W0 (604/636-9224, fax: 636-2199).

Terrace Tourism and Economic Development, 3215 Eby St., Terrace, B.C. V8G 2X8 (604/635-6311, fax: 604/638-4777).

Tourism B.C., Parliament Buildings, Victoria, B.C. V8V 1X4 (1-800/663-6000).

Tourism Bella Coola Travel InfoCentre, Box 670, Bella Coola, B.C. V0T 1C0 (604/799-5919).

Tumbler Ridge, P.O. Box 100, Tumbler Ridge, B.C. V0C 2W0 (604/242-4242).

Valemount Tourism, P.O. Box 168, Valemount, B.C. V0E 2Z0 (604/566-4846, fax: 604/566-4249).

Williams Lake and District Chamber of Commerce, 1148 S. Broadway, Williams Lake, B.C. V2G 1A2 (604/392-5025).

Yukon Tourism, Box 2703, Whitehorse, Yukon Y1A 2C6 (403-667-5340, fax: 403-667-2634).

Accomodation Assistance

There are various services available to assist you with your accommodation arrangements. Some of the services do not provide information on the accommodation; they will simply take bookings.

Discover B.C. — province-wide accommodation booking service (1-800/663-6000, 663-6000 in Greater Vancouver).
Prince George Bed & Breakfast Association (604/651-2337, fax: 604/562-6699).
Northern Network of Bed & Breakfasts (403/993-5644, fax: 403/933-5648).
British Columbia Bed & Breakfast Association, 810 West Broadway Ave., Box 593, Vancouver, B.C. V5Z 4E2 (604/298-8815, fax: 604/298-5917).
British Columbia Fishing Resorts and Outfitters Association, Box 3301, Kamloops, B.C. V2C 6B9 (604/374-6836, fax 604/374-6640).
British Columbia Guest Ranchers' Association, c/o Box 489, Ashcroft, B.C. V0K 1A0 (604/459-2255).
Guide-Outfitters Association of British Columbia, Box 759, 100 Mile House, V0K 2E0 (604/395-2438).
Hostelling International, Canada - B.C. Region, 402-134 Abbott St., Vancouver, B.C. V6B 2K4 (1-800/661-0020, fax: 604/684-7181).

★

The Very Best of Northern British Columbia

If you've read through this book from beginning to end, you will know that we have clear favourites. There are some remarkable restaurants, wonderful resorts, excellent camp grounds, amazing scenic spots, and unique attractions throughout northern British Columbia. Now we want you to know about the places that we think are the very best. The following lists are highly personal; they reflect our experiences and, obviously, our preferences. But we are pretty confident in encouraging people to try these choice spots.

The Best Restaurants

Rainbow Retreat, Tête Jaune Cache *(p. 149)*
Tachick Lodge, south of Vanderhoof *(p. 123)*
Da Moreno, Prince George *(p.90)*
Casa Filipina, Prince Rupert *(p. 178)*
Trattoria, Williams Lake *(p. 73)*
Bavarian Inn, Terrace *(p. 170)*
The Taj, Prince George *(p. 90)*
Vaughan House, Quesnel *(p. 78)*
Little Onion, Smithers *(p. 130)*
Cow Bay Café, Prince Rupert *(p. 178)*
The Log House, Prince George *(p. 91)*
Oceana, Queen Charlotte City *(p. 198)*
Rosel's, Prince George *(p. 92)*
Winston's, Prince George *(p. 92)*

Stellako Lodge, near Fraser Lake *(p. 126)*
Richard's Bistro, Williams Lake *(p. 74)*

Great Spots for Cappuccino and/or Dessert

Bagel Street Café, Prince George *(p. 95)*
Body Currents, Tlell, Queen Charlotte Islands *(p. 203)*
Earl's, Prince George *(p. 93)*
Granville's Coffee House, Quesnel *(p. 79)*
Java's, Smithers *(p. 130)*
Lambada's Cappuccino and Dessert Bar, Prince Rupert *(p. 179)*
Other Art Cafe, Prince George *(p. 91)*
The Path, near Masset, Queen Charlotte Islands *(p. 205)*
Sandy's Cappuccino, Fort St. James *(p. 123)*
Schloss Café, 100 Mile House *(p. 68)*

Our Ten Favourite Places to Stay

Alaska View Lodge, Masset *(p. 206)*
Bear Paw Resort, Iskut *(p. 248)*
Cambridge Bed & Breakfast, Prince George *(p. 98)*
Crest Motor Hotel, Prince Rupert *(p. 179)*
Glacier View Cabins, Atlin *(p. 252)*
Log House, 108 Mile House *(p. 71)*
Rainbow Retreat, Tête Jaune Cache *(p. 149)*
Terracana Ranch & Resort, McBride *(p. 148)*
The Premier Hotel, Queen Charlotte City *(p. 199)*
Wildeman Lodge, near McBride *(p. 146)*

Beautiful Scenic Spots

Bear Glacier, on the road to Stewart *(p. 248)*
Chilko Lake, west of Williams Lake *(p. 56)*

Highway 16, Terrace to Prince Rupert *(p. 165)*
Kinuseo Falls, near Tumbler Ridge *(p. 223)*
Mount Robson *(p. 150)*
Mount Tweedsmuir Provincial Park *(pp. 56, 129)*
Muncho Lake *(p. 234)*
Peace River Valley, near Hudson's Hope *(p. 18)*
Prince Rupert Harbour *(p. 183)*
Tatshenshini Wilderness area *(p. 35)*
Tow Hill, near Masset *(p. 205)*

Great Things to Do

Art and jewellery shopping on the Queen Charlotte Islands *(p. 203)*
Barkerville, east of Quesnel *(p. 82)*
Canoeing the Bowron Lakes *(p. 82)*
Concerts at Other Art Cafe, Prince George *(p. 91)*
Cow Bay, Prince Rupert *(p. 180)*
Cross-country skiing at 100 Mile House/108 Mile House *(pp. 69-70)*
Heli-skiing in the Robson Valley *(p. 154)*
Horseback riding in the Chilcotin *(p. 69)*
K'san National Historic Site, Hazelton *(p. 136)*
Kayaking in the South Moresby area (Gwaii Haanas) *(p. 195)*
Liard Hotsprings, along the Alaska Highway *(p. 235)*
Skiing at Powder King, near Mackenzie, or Ski Smithers *(pp. 219, 133)*
Suswaka White Water Rafting (near Smithers) *(p. 134)*
Williams Lake Stampede *(p. 77)*

And camping, hiking, fishing, boating, etc. almost everywhere in Northern British Columbia

Index

100 Mile House 16, 25, 56, 59-61, 67-70, 83, 265, 268-269
108 Mile House 25, 67, 70-72, 268-269
150 Mile House 25, 65, 72

Aboriginal people, see First Nations
Air BC 41, 89, 214
Air travel 41-42; see also Canadian Airlines, Central Mountain Air, Harbour Air, South Moresby Air Charters, Summit Air Charters, Thunderbird Airlines, Waglisla Air
Aiyansh, see New Aiyansh; Old Aiyansh
Alaska 19, 27-28, 37, 40, 48, 113, 159-160, 164, 208-235, 238, 240-247, 251, 261, 263- 264, 269
Alaska Highway 27-28, 40, 48, 208-235, 240-247, 251, 261, 264, 269
Alaska Marine Highway 164, 246, 263
Alberta 12, 55, 88, 154, 209, 214
Alcan 28, 36, 38, 118, 160-161, 165, 169, 173-174, 175
Alliford Bay 189
Aluminum, see Alcan
Americans 24, 27-28, 35, 37, 38, 158, 160, 211-212, 224, 240
Anahim Lake 56, 61-62
Anglicans 120, 229
Anthony Island 192
Archaeology 23, 181, 210, 227
Asbestos, see Cassiar
Asians 24 (China), 27, 32, 159 (Chinese)
Atlin 13, 19, 27, 238-240, 243, 245, 250-254, 261, 268
Atlin Lake 19, 238, 243, 250, 253
Atlin Provincial Park 251-252, 261
Aurora Borealis 14
Automobiles, see Car travel

Babine Forest Products 127
Babine Lake 20, 113,

117, 120, 131-132, 262
Babine River 134
Backhouse, John 85
Badlands (Alta.) 12
Banff National Park 12, 97, 139, 141, 144, 237
Barker, Billy 25, 82
Barkerville 25, 27, 48, 56-58, 66-67, 82-83, 261, 263, 269
Barkerville Park 261
BC Ferries 163-164, 188-189, 263
BC Forest Service 196-197, 262
BC Parks 249, 260
BC Rail 42-43, 60, 88, 213, 263
Bear Glacier 248, 268
Bears 21, 48-50, 172, 216, 224, 235
Bearskin Bay 192
Beaver (natives) 23
Beds and breakfasts 51-53; associations 266; see also references throughout
Begbie, William 78
Bell II: 245
Bella Coola 13, 55-56, 59-60, 65, 77-78, 83, 261, 265
Bennett, W.A.C. 211
Bennett, W.A.C. (dam) 29, 210, 213, 216, 218, 220-222
Bennett Lake 243
Bering Strait 23
Bighorn sheep, see Mountain sheep
Bison 227
Black bears, see Bears
Blackwater River 61
Boats, see Hazelton, Japanese boat, Klondike, Pesuta, Queen of the North, River Days, Tarahne, Titanic
Bowron Lakes 16, 56, 61, 81, 269
Bowron Lakes Provincial Park 82-83, 261
Bridge Creek House 67
Bridge Lake 61, 63
British traders 24, 158
Bulkley River 19
Bulkley Valley 13, 19-20, 27, 32, 112-136
Bullmoose Mine 213, 222
Burns Lake 20, 32, 114, 116-117, 119, 127-129, 137, 261, 263
Bus travel 43-44

Cache Creek 60
Calgary 26, 88-89
California 24
Cameron Lake 221
Canada. Dept. of Indian Affairs 33
Canada. Dept. of National Defence 212
Canada. Dept. of Public Works 212
Canada. Parks Canada 22, 187, 196
Canadian Airlines 41,

Index / 273

89, 188, 214
Canadian Cellulose Co., see Skeena Cellulose
Canadian Chopstick Manufacturing Co. 233
Canadian Forest Products 86, 108
Canadian National Railway (CN) 26, 87-88, 114, 143, 159
Canfor, see Canadian Forest Products
Canim Lake 61, 64
Canneries, see Port Edward
Canoe Mountain 142, 152
Canoeing, 16, 56, 82-83, 135, 154, 232, 269
CANOL pipeline project 28, 240
Canyon City (Gitwinksihlkw) 162-163, 167
Car travel 45-48; see also Highways
Carcross (Yukon) 243, 246
Cariboo-Chilcotin 15-16, 54-83, 269
Cariboo Mountains 17, 140, 148, 152
Cariboo Tourist Association 263
Cariboo Trail (Wagon Road) 25, 57, 67, 72, 82
Cariboo Wagon Road, see Cariboo Trail
Caribou 224
Carr, Emily 157
Carrier (natives) 23, 34, 125-126
Cassiar 25, 29, 31, 39-40, 45, 113, 163, 238-239, 241, 244-245
CBC radio 48
Cedar trees 21
Cedarvale 120
Central Interior 16-17
Central Mountain Air 41, 89, 214
Charlie Lake 210, 229
Charlie Lake Park 261
Cheslatta (natives) 36
Chetwynd 18, 29, 32, 210, 214-216, 219-220, 235, 261, 263
Chilcotin region, see Cariboo-Chilcotin
Chilcotin River 16
Chilcotin War 58-59
Chilko Lake 56, 61, 63-64, 268
Chilkoot Pass 240
China 24
Chinese 159; Asians, 27, 32
Chopstick factory 233
Chown River 206
Clayoquot Sound 37
Clearwater 16
Clinton 63
CN, see Canadian National Railway
Coal, Northeast 29, 38, 161, 210, 213-214, 222-224

Coastal Interior 20
Coastal Range Mountains 13, 15, 19, 21
College of New Caledonia 98-99, 125
Colleges, see College of New Caledonia, Grande Prairie, Northwest, Northern Lights
Confederation 25-26
Cook, James 24, 158
Copper 35, 239
Coquihalla Highway 144
Cottonwood House 81
Cow Bay 178-180, 267, 269
Crescent Spur 142
Crooked River Park 261
Croyden 147
Cumshewa Inlet 197

Dalton Trail 240
Dams, see Bennett, Kenney, Peace Canyon
Dawson City (Yukon) 212, 238, 240, 255
Dawson Creek 27-28, 32, 210-216, 224-227, 230, 235
Dease Lake 13, 19, 239, 241, 245, 249
Deck Lake 129
Decker Lake Forest Products 127
Deer 22, 48, 193, 224
Delgamuukw case 35
Delkatla Wildlife Sanctuary 206

Dinosaur Lake 221
Dodge Cove 181
Dolly Varden (fish) 172
Dome Creek 142
Douglas Channel 28, 160, 176-177
Douglas fir 21
Driftwood Provincial Park 132
Duncan, William 159
Dunster 142, 147

East Indians 32
Edmonton 88-89, 141, 209, 211, 214
Education, schools 29, 33, 72, 176; see also College; University
Edziza, see Mount Edziza
Elk 50, 224
Endako 29, 118, 126-127
English, see British
Eskers Provincial Park 111
Eurocan 161, 165, 174, 175
Europeans 23-24, 27, 56, 158, 186, 210, 239

Fairbanks (Alaska) 27-28, 210, 212, 215
Ferries, see Alaska Marine Highway, BC Ferries, Queen Charlotte Islands
First Nations (natives) 20, 22-24, 27, 30-36, 56, 58-59, 86,

103, 116-117, 119-122, 125-126, 134-136, 157-159, 162-163, 165-179, 171, 173, 176, 181, 185, 187, 191-195, 201, 204, 207, 210-211, 227, 238, 240-241, 246, 252, 255-256, 258, 268-269
Fish Creek Community Forest 230
Fishing 36; fish hatcheries 177, 197; see also references throughout
Flatbed Creek 223
Flatbed Falls 223
Fletcher Challenge 193, 197
Forests 37-38; demonstration forests 110, 172, 230; mills 29, 38, 58, 86-87, 126, 163, 214; mill tours 77, 108, 197; roads 46-47, 193
Forests for the World 110
Fort Fraser 126-127
Fort George 86
Fort George Canyon 111
Fort Nelson 28, 210-212, 214, 233-235, 261, 263
Fort St. James 31, 47, 117, 120-121, 122-126, 137, 263-264, 268
Fort St. John 28, 32, 42, 89, 210-212, 214-215, 217, 227-230, 235, 261
Fort Simpson 158-159
Fox, Terry 150-152
Foxes 49
Francois Lake 20, 113, 119, 127, 136-137
Fraser, Simon 117
Fraser Canyon 25, 86
Fraser Lake 20, 113-114, 116-119, 126-127, 137, 264, 268
Fraser Lake Sawmills 126
Fraser River 17, 25-26, 37, 55, 57-58, 69-70, 78, 86, 111, 141, 147-148, 155
Fraser Valley 14
Fur trade 24, 56, 117-118, 143, 158-159, 186, 211-212, 214, 238

Gang Ranch 55, 70
Geography, northern B.C. 15-22
George Hicks Park 152
Germans 32
Germanson Landing 47, 117, 124
Gibraltar 29, 58
Gitksan (native group) 34-35, 119-120
Gitwangak 120
Gitwinksihlkw, see Canyon City
Glaciers 13, 133-134, 241, 248, 252, 268
Goats, see Mountain

goats
Gold rush 24-25, 57-58, 67, 77-78, 82, 86, 117, 143, 186, 238-240, 243, 245, 247, 254-255
Golf 69, 80, 88, 107, 125, 127, 129, 175-176, 206, 218, 220, 223, 229-230
Good Hope Lake 245
Gore, Al 35
Gotchen Lake 62
Graham Island 193, 201, 262
Grand Trunk Pacific Railway 26, 114, 117, 143, 148, 159, 169, 177
Grande Prairie (Alta.) 89, 214
Grande Prairie Community College 209
Granisle 29, 39, 113, 118-119, 128, 136, 264
Gray Bay 196
Great Cariboo Trail Ride 55, 69-70
Green Lake 61
Greenville 162, 167, 169
Greyhound 145; see also Bus travel
Grizzly, see Bears
Gulf Islands 193
Gwaii Haanas National Park 22, 185, 187, 189-191, 194, 196, 261, 264, 269

Haida (natives) 22-23, 34, 185-187, 190-191, 195, 198, 204-206, 263; see also Gwaii Haanas
Haida Gwaii, see Queen Charlotte Islands
Haines Road 28, 240, 246, 251, 261
Haines Junction 244, 246
Haisla (natives) 34, 157, 173, 176
Harbour Air 188
Hart, John see Highway 97
Hart Highway, see Highway 97
Hays, Charles 177; see also Mount Hays
Hazelton, boat 136
Hazelton (New, Old) 114, 116-117, 119-121, 134-137, 264, 269
Hecate Strait 22, 189
Hernandez, Juan 158
Highway 1: 60
Highway 2: 214
Highway 5: 56, 60, 142, 144, 151-152
Highway 7: 251
Highway 16 (Yellowhead) 45, 48, 88-89, 110, 113-114, 116-118, 126, 128, 142, 144-145, 147-148, 151, 163, 241, 244, 261-262, 268
Highway 20: 56, 59-60,

261
Highway 26: 48, 80
Highway 27: 121
Highway 29: 224, 230
Highway 37 (Stewart-Cassiar): 45, 113, 120, 163, 170, 238-239, 241, 244-245, 261
Highway 37A: 245
Highway 39: 218
Highway 49: 214
Highway 97 (Hart): 14, 29, 32, 45, 48, 56, 60, 70, 88-89, 214, 218, 261
Highways, see also Alaska, Cariboo Trail, Coqhihalla, Forest roads, Haines, Nisga'a, Trans-Canada
History, northern B.C. 22-32; see also references throughout
Hixon 83
Hockey 86
Hope 14
Horsefly 83
Horsefly Lake 61
Hotsprings 170-171, 173, 195, 215, 261, 269
Hotsprings Island 195
Houston 32, 114, 118-119, 127-129, 137, 264
Huble Farm 105
Hudson Bay Glacier 133-134

Hudson Bay Mountain 115, 117, 120, 130, 133
Hudson's Bay Co. 24, 31, 86, 117, 121, 125, 158, 221
Hudson's Hope 29, 210, 220-221, 230, 235, 260-261, 269
Hyder (Alaska) 247, 259, 265
Hydro, see Dams

Indian Affairs, see Canada. Dept. of Indian Affairs
Indians, see First Nations
Iskut 245, 248-249, 261, 268

Jake's Corner 243
Japanese 27, 38, 159-160, 162, 182 (boat), 192, 213-214, 233
Jasper National Park (Alta.) 12, 42, 88, 97, 139, 141-142, 144, 237, 261-262
Juneau (Alaska) 243

K'san National Historic Site 31, 119, 121, 136, 269
Kaien Island 177-178
Kamloops 14, 24, 26, 42, 60, 89, 141-142, 144, 261
Kathleen Lake 246
Kayaking 22, 192-195,

232, 269
Kelowna 42, 89
Kemano 28, 36-37, 161, 174, 213
Kenney Dam 118
Kermodei, see Bears
Kinaskan Lake Park 261
Kincolith 162, 167
Kinuseo Falls 216, 223-224, 268
Kiskatinaw River 230
Kispiox 120, 135, 137
Kitimaat village 176
Kitimat 28-29, 31-32, 36, 38, 47, 118, 157, 160-163, 165, 167, 169, 173-177, 264
Kitimat River 177
Kitlope watershed 21
Kitseguecla 120
Kitselas (natives) 169
Kitsumkalum (natives) 169, 171
Kitwancool 120
Kitwanga 113, 120, 241, 244
Kleena Kleene 64
Klondike, S.S. (boat) 259
Klondike gold rush 25, 239-240, 243, 254
Kluane National Park 19, 244, 246-247
Klukshu 246
Knewstub Lake 125
Kokanee (salmon) 246

Lheit- Lit'en (natives) 86
Lac La Hache 65-66, 83
Lake Kathlyn 131

Lakelse Lake and Park 171, 173, 261
Lakes, see individual names of lakes
Land claims 33, 35, 187, 194, 240, 255-256
Lava Lake 168
Layton, see Mount Layton
Liard 245, 263
Liard Hotsprings 215-217, 234-235 (park), 261, 269
Liard River 19, 235
Lillooet 25, 43, 67
Llewellyn Glacier 252-253
Logging, see Forests
Lower Mainland 14, 32, 209, 213; see also Vancouver; Fraser Valley

Mackenzie 29, 210, 214, 235, 264, 269
Mackenzie, Alexander 24, 56, 210, 218-219, 227
MacMillan Bloedel 193, 196
Mahood Lake 61
Mamin River 204
Manson Creek 117
Maps xi, 54-55, 84-85, 112-113, 138-139, 156-157, 184-185, 208-209, 236-237; forest maps 45-46, 61, 193, 262; parks 260

Masset 39, 187-188, 193, 204-207, 268-269
Mayer Lake 204
McBride 26, 88, 139-143, 145-148, 155, 262, 264, 268
McBride, Richard 143
McLeese Lake 66
Methanex Corp. 161, 165, 174-175
Metlakatla 159, 181
Meziadin 241-242, 244-245
Million Dollar Falls 244, 246
Mills, see Forests
Mines, see Alcan, Asbestos, Cassiar, Coal, Copper, Endako, Gibraltar, Gold, Granisle
Missionaries, see Morice; Duncan
Miworth 110
Moberly Lake 220, 260
Moberly Park 261
Monashee Mountains 15, 17, 140, 152
Monkman Park 216, 223, 261
Moose 48-49, 224
Moresby Island (North, South) 22, 186-187, 189, 192-197, 201, 261, 269
Morfee Lake 218
Morice, A.G. 120
Moricetown 120, 134
Mosquito Lake Park 196-197

Mount Edziza Provincial Park 248, 261
Mount Elizabeth 177
Mount Hays 183
Mount Layton Hotsprings 170-171, 173
Mount Old Baldy 220
Mount Pope 125
Mount Resplendent 64
Mount Robson 48, 50, 139-143, 146, 148, 151, 155, 269
Mount Robson Provincial Park 50, 139, 143, 150, 155, 261-262, 264
Mount Terry Fox 150-152
Mount Tweedsmuir, see Tweedsmuir
Mountain goats 224
Mountain sheep 48-49, 216, 224, 234
Muncho Lake and Park 19, 48, 216, 230, 234, 261, 269
Museums 31, 72, 77, 81, 104-105, 121-122, 125, 133, 136, 165, 172, 180-182, 191, 201, 203-204, 216, 220-221, 226-229, 234, 248, 253-254, 259
Mushrooms, Pine 162
Muskwa River 211

Naden Harbour 207
Naikoon Provincial Park 204-205, 262

Nass River 20, 158, 162, 168, 244
Nass River Valley 20, 157, 161-163, 165, 167-168
Natives, see First Nations
Nechako River 19, 28, 36, 86, 116, 118, 122, 160
Nechako River Valley 112-136
Nemaiah Valley 63, 83
Ness Lake 109, 111
New Aiyansh 162-163, 167-168
New Hazelton, see Hazelton
New Westminster 26
Nimpo Lake 61-62
Ninstints 192, 195
Nisga'a (natives) 20, 23, 33-35, 157, 162-163, 166-168
Nisga'a Highway 167
Nisga'a Memorial Lava Bed Park 162
North By Northwest Tourism Association 264
North Moresby, see Moresby
North Pacific Cannery, see Port Edward
North Vancouver 42
Northern Alberta Railway 211, 224, 226
Northern Lights, see Aurora Borealis
Northern Lights College 226-227, 230
Northwest Community College 33, 162, 181
Northwest Company 24, 117, 210
Northwest Staging Route 28, 212, 240
Northwood Pulp and Paper 38, 86, 108
Nuxalk (natives) 59

Oil and gas 28, 214, 227, 229, 233, 240
Okanagan Lake 12
Okanagan region 12, 14, 144, 211
Old Aiyansh 168
Old Baldy, see Mount Old Baldy
Old Hazelton, see Hazelton
Old Masset, see Masset
Omineca gold rush 117
Ootsa Lake 119, 261
Oregon 24-25

Paarens Beach Provincial Park 124, 262
Pacific Coast 20-21
Pacific Great Eastern Railway 58
Pacific Ocean 13, 21, 56, 157, 165, 177, 183
Paddlewheelers, see Boats
Paleo (natives) 227
Pallant Creek Fish Hatchery 197
Paper mills, see Forests

Parks 260-262; see also Atlin, Banff, Barkerville, Bowron, Charlie Lake, Crooked River, Driftwood, Eskers, George Hicks, Gwaii Haanas, Jasper, Kinaskan Lake, Kluane, Lakelse, Liard, Monkman, Mosquito Lake, Mount Edziza, Mount Robson, Muncho Lake, Naikoon, Nisga'a, Paarens Beach, Purden, Red Bluff, Sowchea Bay, Spatsizi, Stone Mountain, Tatshenshini, Ten Mile Lake, Tweedsmuir, Wells Gray, Wilkins

Parks Canada, see Canada. Parks Canada

Pattullo, T. "Duff" 161

Peace Canyon Dam 222

Peace River 18, 56

Peace River region 13, 15, 17-18, 27-29, 32, 47, 208-235, 264, 269

Pemberton 43

Petroleum, see Oil and gas

Pesuta (ship) 204

Pine trees 16-17

Pine mushrooms 162

Pine Pass 17, 47, 215

Pink Mountain 232-233

Pipelines, see Oil and gas

Planes, see Air travel

Pleasant Valley 246

Plywood plant 233

Potlatch 24, 136

Port Clements 186, 201-204, 207

Port Edward 31, 160, 165, 181-182

Port Hardy 163-164

Port Simpson 158

Powder King Ski Village 219-220, 269

Prince George 15, 17, 19-20, 24, 26-27, 29, 31-32, 38-39, 42-43, 45, 47-48, 58, 60, 83, 84-111, 113, 122, 126, 141-142, 144-146, 148, 163, 188, 212, 214-215, 218-219, 237, 260-262, 264, 266-269

Prince Rupert 26-27, 29, 31-32, 42, 47, 88, 113, 157-165, 177-183, 185, 187-189, 213, 264, 267-269

Pulp mills, see Forests

Puntzi Lake 61

Purden Lake Provincial Park 146, 262

Queen Charlotte City 187-192, 196-200,

267-268
Queen Charlotte Islands 13, 22, 39, 48, 181-182, 184-207, 261-262, 265, 268-269
Queen of the North (ferry) 183
Quesnel 25, 29, 32, 39, 48, 56-58, 60-61, 65, 78-80, 83, 88, 262, 265, 267-269
Quesnel Lake 16, 61-62
Quesnellemouth 78
Quintette Mine 213, 222, 224

Rafting, whitewater 36, 134-135, 269
Railways 26-29, 31, 42-43, 58, 60, 87, 104-105, 114, 117-118, 143, 148, 159-160, 162, 166, 169, 173, 177, 181, 210-211, 213, 220, 226, 239-240, 244
Rearguard Falls 150
Red Bluff Park 262
Red Sand Lake Demonstration Forest 172
Reid, Bill 201
Reindeer 227
River Days (Riverboat Days) 169, 183
Rivers see Babine, Blackwater, Bulkley, Chilcotin, Crooked, Fraser, Kiskatinaw, Kitimat, Liard, Mamin, Muskwa, Nass, Nechako, Peace, Skeena, Stellako, Stikine, Stuart, Swift, Yakoun
Roads, see Highways
Robson, see Mount Robson
Robson Valley 17, 138-155, 269
Rock paintings 168
Rocky Mountains 12-13, 16-18, 26, 139-141, 148, 150, 152, 219
Royal Engineers 25
Russians 24, 158, 239
Ruth Lake 65

Salmon 37, 60, 121, 152, 155, 159, 168, 172, 177, 246
Salmon Glacier 248
San Juan Islands 51
Sandspit 186, 188-191, 194-197, 207
Sawmills, see Forests
Schools, see Education
Sebastian, Ron 135
Sekani (natives) 23, 34
Selkirk Mountains 15
Seven Sisters Mountain Range 115
Shakwak Valley 246
Shames Mountain 173
Sheep, see Mountain sheep
Sheridan Lake 61
Ships, see Boats
Shuswap Lake 12
Sikh, see East Indians
Silver 239

Sitka spruce, see Spruce
Skagway 240, 243, 246, 259
Skeena Cellulose 161, 165, 169 (Canadian Cellulose)
Skeena River 20, 37, 169, 172-173
Skeena Train 42
Skeena Valley 169
Skidegate Inlet 192
Skidegate Landing 187-189, 191-192, 197-201
Skidegate Village 201
Skiing 269; see also references throughout
Smelters, see Alcan
Smithers 15, 26, 32, 41-42, 47, 89, 113-120, 129-134, 137, 162, 249, 261, 265, 267-269
Soda Creek 78
South Hazelton, see Hazeltons
South Moresby, see Moresby
South Moresby Air Charters 188
Sowchea Bay Provincial Park 124
Spatsizi Plateau Provincial Park 248, 260-261
Spruce trees 16-17, 175, 186, 204
St. Elias Mountains 19, 244
St. John Ambulance 48

Stampede, Williams Lake 55, 77, 269
Steamboats, see Boats
Steelhead fish 135, 172
Stellako River 126-127, 268
Stewart 40, 45, 113, 163, 238-241, 244-248, 259, 263, 265, 268
Stewart-Cassiar Road, see Highway 37
Stikine region 236-259
Stikine River 239, 249-250
Stikine trail 240
Stone Mountain Provincial Park 234
Storrs, Monica 229
Stuart Lake 20, 113, 117, 119, 122, 124-125, 136
Stuart River 19
Summit Air Charters 253
Swans 126
Swift Creek 152
Swift River 242

Tabor Lake 91
Tachick Lake 124, 267
Tagish Lake 19, 240, 243
Takla Lake 119
Tarahne, M.V. (ferry) 253-254
Taseko Lake 63
Tatla Lake 61, 64
Tatogga Lake 248
Tatshenshini Wilderness Area 35, 251, 261,

269
Taylor 230, 235
Tchesinkut Lake 129
Telegraph Creek 239, 245-246, 249-250
Telkwa 117, 120, 129-134, 137
Ten Mile Lake Park 262
Terrace 15, 27, 29, 32, 41, 47, 89, 137, 157-158, 160-163, 166-167, 169-173, 183, 237, 261, 265, 267-268
Terrace Mountain 172
Tete Jaune Cache 26, 142-143, 147-148, 267-268
Thunderbird Airlines 188
Tlell 191-193, 201-204, 207, 268
Tlingit (natives) 252
Titanic, R.M.S. (ship) 177
Topley Landing 129
Totem poles 22-23, 120, 136, 158, 171, 176, 181, 191, 195, 201
Trails, see Dalton Trail, Great Cariboo Trail Ride, Stikine trail, West Coast Trail, and hiking references throughout
Train travel, see Railways
Trans-Canada Highway 14, 59
Trees, see Cedar, Douglas fir, Pine, Spruce
Trout fishing 55, 60, 100, 172, 229
Tseaux lava beds, see Volcanoes
Tsimshian (natives) 23, 157, 159, 181
Tukii Lake 132
Tumbler Ridge 29, 38-39, 210, 213-214, 222-224, 235, 261, 265, 268
Tutchi Lake 243
Tutshi Lake 19
Tweedsmuir Park 56, 64, 119, 129, 136, 260-261, 269
Tyee Lake 120

UNBC, see University of Northern B.C.
United States, see American
University of Alberta 209
University of Northern B.C. (UNBC) v, 33, 85, 87-88, 98-99, 107-108
Upper Liard, see Liard

Valemount 139-143, 146, 148, 151-155, 261-262, 265
Vancouver 12, 14, 18, 26, 42, 58, 60, 88-89, 120, 141, 163, 188, 207, 237, 241
Vancouver, George 158
Vancouver Island 14, 25, 37, 56, 157,

164, 193
Vanderhoof 39, 88, 113-117, 121, 122-126, 137, 267
VIA Rail 42
Victoria 12, 25, 32, 42, 86
Volcanoes 20, 162, 167-168

Waglisla Air 41, 188
War, World War: 27, 58, 114, 118, 143, 160-161, 169, 173, 186, 210-212, 240, 244, 255
Washington (State) 25, 140
Waterfalls, see Flatbed, Kinuseo, Million Dollar, Rearguard
Watson Lake (Yukon) 28, 241-242, 245
Wells 58, 81-82
Wells Gray Provincial Park 141, 144, 261
West Coast Trail 12
West Lake 98, 109-111, 260, 262
Western Forest Products 197
Wet'suwet'en (natives) 35, 119
Whistler Mountain 12, 43, 63, 97, 141
White Horse Rapids 255
White Pass 239-240, 243-244, 255
Whitehorse (Yukon) 28, 216, 242-243, 246-247, 254-259
Whitewater rafting, see Rafting
Wildlife 48-50, 217; Scout Island Nature Centre 76; Wildlife Sanctuary 206; see also Bears, Bison, Deer, Elk, Moose, Mountain goats, Mountain sheep, Reindeer
Wilkins Park 110
Williams Creek 82
Williams Lake 16, 29, 32, 55-56, 58-61, 63, 65, 72-77, 83, 261, 265, 267-269
Williston Lake 218, 221
Windy Craggy 35
Winter driving, see Car travel
World War, see War

Yakoun River 204
Yellowhead Highway, see Highway 16
Yinka Dene Language Institute 125
Yukon 14, 19, 28, 35, 45, 113, 210, 213, 215, 230, 238-239, 241-244, 246, 251, 254-259, 265

*A Traveller's Guide
to Northern British Columbia*

Response Form

Based on my personal experience, I wish to nominate / confirm / disapprove (of) the following listing.

_____

_____

_____

_____

These are my responses, based on the following: food, service, style, comfort, value, date of visit, other.

_____

_____

_____

_____

_____

I am not concerned, directly or indirectly, with the management or ownership of any establishment mentioned.

Name: _____

Address: _____

_____

Tel: _____ Date: _____

Send to: *A Traveller's Guide to Northern British Columbia*
c/o The Caitlin Press, P.O. Box 2387, Station B, Prince George B.C. V2N 2S6